Corporate and White Collar Crime

Selected Statutes, Guidelines,
and Documents

Corporate and White Collar Crime

Selected Statutes, Guidelines, and Documents

Fifth Edition 2011-2012

Kathleen F. Brickey

James Carr Professor of Criminal Jurisprudence
Washington University

Wolters Kluwer
Law & Business

Published by Wolters Kluwer Law & Business in New York.

Wolters Kluwer Law & Business serves customers worldwide with CCH, Aspen Publishers, and Kluwer Law International products. (www.wolterskluwerlb.com)

To contact Customer Service, e-mail customer.service@wolterskluwer.com, call 1-800-234-1660, fax 1-800-901-9075, or mail correspondence to:

Wolters Kluwer Law & Business
Attn: Order Department
PO Box 990
Frederick, MD 21705

Printed in the United States of America.

3 4 5 6 7 8 9 0

ISBN 978-0-7355-0744-9

ISSN 1538-3113

Summary of Contents

Contents

PART I FEDERAL STATUTES, REGULATIONS, AND SENTENCING GUIDELINES

PART II DOCUMENTS

I

Federal Statutes, Regulations, and Sentencing Guidelines

United States Code

TITLE 15
COMMERCE AND TRADE

15 U.S.C. § 77q. FRAUDULENT INTERSTATE TRANSACTIONS

(a) Use of interstate commerce for purpose of fraud or deceit

It shall be unlawful for any person in the offer or sale of any securities (including security-based swaps) or any security-based swap agreement (as defined in section 78c(a)(78) of this title) by the use of any means or instruments of transportation or communication in interstate commerce or by the use of the mails, directly or indirectly—

(1) to employ any device, scheme, or artifice to defraud, or

(2) to obtain money or property by means of any untrue statement of a material fact or any omission to state a material fact necessary in order to make the statements made, in the light of the circumstances under which they were made, not misleading; or

(3) to engage in any transaction, practice, or course of business which operates or would operate as a fraud or deceit upon the purchaser.

(b) Use of interstate commerce for purposes of offering for sale

It shall be unlawful for any person, by the use of any means or instruments of transportation or communication in interstate commerce or by the use of the mails, to publish, give publicity to, or circulate any notice, circular, advertisement, newspaper, article, letter, investment service, or communication which, though not purporting to offer a security for sale, describes such security for a consideration received or to be received, directly or indirectly, from an issuer, underwriter, or dealer, without fully disclosing the receipt, whether past or prospective, of such consideration and the amount thereof.

(c) Exemptions of section 77c not applicable to this section

The exemptions provided in section 77c of this title shall not apply to the provisions of this section.

(d) Limitation

The authority of the Commission under this section with respect to security-based swap agreements (as defined in section 78c(a)(78) of this title) shall be subject to the restrictions and limitations of section 77b-1(b) of this title.

15 U.S.C. § 78ff. PENALTIES

(a) Willful violations; false and misleading statements. Any person who willfully violates any provision of this chapter (other than section 78dd-1 of this title), or any rule or regulation thereunder the violation of which is made unlawful or the observance of which is required under the terms of this chapter, or any person who willfully and knowingly makes, or causes to be made, any statement in any application, report, or document required to be filed under this chapter or any rule or regulation thereunder or any undertaking contained in a registration statement as provided in subsection (d) of section 78(*o*) of this title, or by any self-regulatory organization in connection with an application for membership or participation therein or to become associated with a member thereof, which statement was false or misleading with respect to any material fact, shall upon conviction be fined not more than $5,000,000, or imprisoned not more than 20 years, or both, except that when such person is a person other than a natural person, a fine not exceeding $25,000,000 may be imposed; but no person shall be subject to imprisonment under this section for the violation of any rule or regulation if he proves that he had no knowledge of such rule or regulation. . . .

TITLE 18
CRIMES AND CRIMINAL PROCEDURE

18 U.S.C. § 2. PRINCIPALS

(a) Whoever commits an offense against the United States or aids, abets, counsels, commands, induces or procures its commission, is punishable as a principal.

(b) Whoever willfully causes an act to be done which if directly performed by him or another would be an offense against the United States, is punishable as a principal.

18 U.S.C. § 201. BRIBERY OF PUBLIC OFFICIALS AND WITNESSES

(a) For the purpose of this section—

(1) the term "public official" means Member of Congress, Delegate, or Resident Commissioner, either before or after such official has qualified, or an officer or employee or person acting for or on behalf of the United States, or any department, agency or branch of Government thereof, including the District of Columbia, in any official function, under or by authority of any such department, agency, or branch of Government, or a juror;

(2) the term "person who has been selected to be a public official" means any person who has been nominated or appointed to be a public official, or has been officially informed that such person will be so nominated or appointed; and

(3) the term "official act" means any decision or action on any question, matter, cause, suit, proceeding or controversy, which may at any time be pending, or which may by law be brought before any public official, in such official's official capacity, or in such official's place of trust or profit.

(b) Whoever—

(1) directly or indirectly, corruptly gives, offers or promises anything of value to any public official or person who has been selected to be a public official, or offers or promises any public official or any person who has been selected to be a public official

to give anything of value to any other person or entity, with intent—

    (A) to influence any official act; or

    (B) to influence such public official or person who has been selected to be a public official to commit or aid in committing, or collude in, or allow, any fraud, or make opportunity for the commission of any fraud, on the United States; or

    (C) to induce such public official or such person who has been selected to be a public official to do or omit to do any act in violation of the lawful duty of such official or person;

(2) being a public official or person selected to be a public official, directly or indirectly, corruptly demands, seeks, receives, accepts, or agrees to receive or accept anything of value personally or for any other person or entity, in return for:

    (A) being influenced in the performance of any official act;

    (B) being influenced to commit or aid in committing, or to collude in, or allow, any fraud, or make opportunity for the commission of any fraud, on the United States; or

    (C) being induced to do or omit to do any act in violation of the official duty of such official or person;

(3) directly or indirectly, corruptly gives, offers, or promises anything of value to any person, or offers or promises such person to give anything of value to any other person or entity, with intent to influence the testimony under oath or affirmation of such first-mentioned person as a witness upon a trial, hearing, or other proceeding, before any court, any committee of either House or both Houses of Congress, or any agency, commission, or officer authorized by the laws of the United States to hear evidence or take testimony, or with intent to influence such person to absent himself therefrom;

(4) directly or indirectly, corruptly demands, seeks, receives, accepts, or agrees to receive or accept anything of value personally or for any other person or entity in return for being influenced in testimony under oath or affirmation as a witness

upon any such trial, hearing, or other proceeding, or in return for absenting himself therefrom;

shall be fined under this title or not more than three times the monetary equivalent of the thing of value, whichever is greater, or imprisoned for not more than fifteen years, or both, and may be disqualified from holding any office of honor, trust, or profit under the United States.

(c) Whoever—

(1) otherwise than as provided by law for the proper discharge of official duty—

(A) directly or indirectly gives, offers, or promises anything of value to any public official, former public official, or person selected to be a public official, for or because of any official act performed or to be performed by such public official, former public official, or person selected to be a public official; or

(B) being a public official, former public official, or person selected to be a public official, otherwise than as provided by law for the proper discharge of official duty, directly or indirectly demands, seeks, receives, accepts, or agrees to receive or accept anything of value personally for or because of any official act performed or to be performed by such official or person;

(2) directly or indirectly, gives, offers, or promises anything of value to any person, for or because of the testimony under oath or affirmation given or to be given by such person as a witness upon a trial, hearing, or other proceeding, before any court, any committee of either House or both Houses of Congress, or any agency, commission, or officer authorized by the laws of the United States to hear evidence or take testimony, or for or because of such person's absence therefrom;

(3) directly or indirectly, demands, seeks, receives, accepts, or agrees to receive or accept anything of value personally for or because of the testimony under oath or affirmation given or to be given by such person as a witness upon any such trial, hearing, or

other proceeding, or for or because of such person's absence
therefrom;
shall be fined under this title or imprisoned for not more than two
years, or both.

(d) Paragraphs (3) and (4) of subsection (b) and paragraphs (2)
and (3) of subsection (c) shall not be construed to prohibit the
payment or receipt of witness fees provided by law, or the payment,
by the party upon whose behalf a witness is called and receipt by a
witness, of the reasonable cost of travel and subsistence incurred and
the reasonable value of time lost in attendance at any such trial,
hearing, or proceeding, or in the case of expert witnesses, a
reasonable fee for time spent in the preparation of such opinion, and
in appearing and testifying.

(e) The offenses and penalties prescribed in this section are
separate from and in addition to those prescribed in sections 1503,
1504, and 1505 of this title.

18 U.S.C. § 287. FALSE, FICTITIOUS OR FRAUDULENT CLAIMS

Whoever makes or presents to any person or officer in the civil,
military, or naval service of the United States, or to any department
or agency thereof, any claim upon or against the United States, or any
department or agency thereof, knowing such claim to be false,
fictitious, or fraudulent, shall be imprisoned not more than five years
and shall be subject to a fine in the amount provided in this title.

18 U.S.C. § 371. CONSPIRACY TO COMMIT OFFENSE OR TO DEFRAUD UNITED STATES

If two or more persons conspire either to commit any offense
against the United States, or to defraud the United States, or any
agency thereof in any manner or for any purpose, and one or more of
such persons do any act to effect the object of the conspiracy, each
shall be fined under this title or imprisoned not more than five years,
or both.

If, however, the offense, the commission of which is the object of
the conspiracy, is a misdemeanor only, the punishment for such

conspiracy shall not exceed the maximum punishment provided for such misdemeanor.

18 U.S.C. § 666. THEFT OR BRIBERY CONCERNING PROGRAMS RECEIVING FEDERAL FUNDS

(a) Whoever, if the circumstance described in subsection (b) of this section exists—

(1) being an agent of an organization, or of a State, local, or Indian tribal government, or any agency thereof—

(A) embezzles, steals, obtains by fraud, or otherwise without authority knowingly converts to the use of any person other than the rightful owner or intentionally misapplies, property that—

(i) is valued at $5,000 or more, and

(ii) is owned by, or is under the care, custody, or control of such organization, government, or agency; or

(B) corruptly solicits or demands for the benefit of any person, or accepts or agrees to accept, anything of value from any person, intending to be influenced or rewarded in connection with any business, transaction, or series of transactions of such organization, government, or agency involving any thing of value of $5,000 or more; or

(2) corruptly gives, offers, or agrees to give anything of value to any person, with intent to influence or reward an agent of an organization or of a State, local or Indian tribal government, or any agency thereof, in connection with any business, transaction, or series of transactions of such organization, government, or agency involving anything of value of $5,000 or more;

shall be fined under this title, imprisoned not more than 10 years, or both.

(b) The circumstance referred to in subsection (a) of this section is that the organization, government, or agency receives, in any one year period, benefits in excess of $10,000 under a Federal program involving a grant, contract, subsidy, loan, guarantee, insurance, or other form of Federal assistance.

(c) This section does not apply to bona fide salary, wages, fees, or other compensation paid, or expenses paid or reimbursed, in the usual course of business.

(d) As used in this section—

(1) the term "agent" means a person authorized to act on behalf of another person or a government and, in the case of an organization or government, includes a servant or employee, and a partner, director, officer, manager, and representative;

(2) the term "government agency" means a subdivision of the executive, legislative, judicial, or other branch of government, including a department, independent establishment, commission, administration, authority, board, and bureau, and a corporation or other legal entity established, and subject to control, by a government or governments for the execution of a governmental or intergovernmental program;

(3) the term "local" means of or pertaining to a political subdivision within a State;

(4) the term "State" includes a State of the United States, the District of Columbia, and any commonwealth, territory, or possession of the United States; and

(5) the term "in any one-year period" means a continuous period that commences no earlier than twelve months before the commission of the offense or that ends no later than twelve months after the commission of the offense. Such period may include time both before and after the commission of the offense.

18 U.S.C. § 1001. STATEMENTS OR ENTRIES GENERALLY

(a) Except as otherwise provided in this section, whoever, in any matter within the jurisdiction of the executive, legislative, or judicial branch of the Government of the United States, knowingly and willfully—

(1) falsifies, conceals, or covers up by any trick, scheme, or device a material fact;

(2) makes any materially false, fictitious, or fraudulent statement or representation; or

(3) makes or uses any false writing or document knowing the same to contain any materially false, fictitious, or fraudulent statement or entry;

shall be fined under this title, imprisoned not more than 5 years or, if the offense involves international or domestic terrorism (as defined in section 2331), imprisoned not more than 8 years, or both. If the matter relates to an offense under chapter 109A, 109B, 110, or 117, or section 1591, then the term of imprisonment imposed under this section shall be not more than 8 years.

(b) Subsection (a) does not apply to a party to a judicial proceeding, or that party's counsel, for statements, representations, writings or documents submitted by such party or counsel to a judge or magistrate in that proceeding.

(c) With respect to any matter within the jurisdiction of the legislative branch, subsection (a) shall apply only to —

(1) administrative matters, including a claim for payment, a matter related to the procurement of property or services, personnel or employment practices, or support services, or a document required by law, rule, or regulation to be submitted to the Congress or any office or officers within the legislative branch; or

(2) any investigation or review, conducted pursuant to the authority of any committee, subcommittee, commission or office of the Congress, consistent with applicable rules of the House or Senate.

18 U.S.C. § 1030. FRAUD AND RELATED ACTIVITY IN CONNECTION WITH COMPUTERS

(a) Whoever—

(1) having knowingly accessed a computer without authorization or exceeding authorized access, and by means of such conduct having obtained information that has been determined by the United States Government pursuant to an Executive order or statute to require protection against unauthorized disclosure for reasons of national defense or foreign relations, or any restricted data, as defined in paragraph [(y)] of

section 11 of the Atomic Energy Act of 1954, with reason to believe that such information so obtained could be used to the injury of the United States, or to the advantage of any foreign nation willfully communicates, delivers, transmits, or causes to be communicated, delivered, or transmitted, or attempts to communicate, deliver, transmit or cause to be communicated, delivered, or transmitted the same to any person not entitled to receive it, or willfully retains the same and fails to deliver it to the officer or employee of the United States entitled to receive it;

(2) intentionally accesses a computer without authorization or exceeds authorized access, and thereby obtains—

(A) information contained in a financial record of a financial institution, or of a card issuer as defined in section 1602(n) of title 15, or contained in a file of a consumer reporting agency on a consumer, as such terms are defined in the Fair Credit Reporting Act (15 U.S.C. § 1681 et seq.);

(B) information from any department or agency of the United States; or

(C) information from any protected computer;

(3) intentionally, without authorization to access any nonpublic computer of a department or agency of the United States, accesses such a computer of that department or agency that is exclusively for the use of the Government of the United States or, in the case of a computer not exclusively for such use, is used by or for the Government of the United States and such conduct affects that use by or for the Government of the United States;

(4) knowingly and with intent to defraud, accesses a protected computer without authorization, or exceeds authorized access, and by means of such conduct furthers the intended fraud and obtains anything of value, unless the object of the fraud and the thing obtained consists only of the use of the computer and the value of such use is not more than $5,000 in any 1-year period;

(5)(A) knowingly causes the transmission of a program, information, code, or command, and as a result of such conduct, intentionally causes damage without authorization, to a protected computer;

(B) intentionally accesses a protected computer without authorization, and as a result of such conduct, recklessly causes damage; or

(C) intentionally accesses a protected computer without authorization, and as a result of such conduct, causes damage and loss.

(6) knowingly and with intent to defraud traffics (as defined in section 1029) in any password or similar information through which a computer may be accessed without authorization, if—

(A) such trafficking affects interstate or foreign commerce; or

(B) such computer is used by or for the Government of the United States;

(7) with intent to extort from any person any money or other thing of value, transmits in interstate or foreign commerce any communication containing any—

(A) threat to cause damage to a protected computer;

(B) threat to obtain information from a protected computer without authorization or in excess of authorization or to impair the confidentiality of information obtained from a protected computer without authorization or by exceeding authorized access; or

(C) demand or request for money or other thing of value in relation to damage to a protected computer, where such damage was caused to facilitate the extortion;

shall be punished as provided in subsection (c) of this section.

(b) Whoever attempts to commit an offense under subsection (a) of this section shall be punished as provided in subsection (c) of this section.

(c) The punishment for an offense under subsection (a) or (b) of this section is—

(1)(A) a fine under this title or imprisonment for not more than ten years, or both, in the case of an offense under subsection (a)(1) of this section which does not occur after a conviction for another offense under this section, or an attempt to commit an offense punishable under this subparagraph; and

(B) a fine under this title or imprisonment for not more than twenty years, or both, in the case of an offense under subsection (a)(1) of this section which occurs after a conviction for another offense under this section, or an attempt to commit an offense punishable under this subparagraph;

(2)(A) except as provided in subparagraph (B), a fine under this title or imprisonment for not more than one year, or both, in the case of an offense under subsection (a)(2), (a)(3), or (a)(6) of this section which does not occur after a conviction for another offense under this section, or an attempt to commit an offense punishable under this subparagraph;

(B) a fine under this title or imprisonment for not more than 5 years, or both, in the case of an offense under subsection (a)(2), or an attempt to commit an offense punishable under this subparagraph, if—

(i) the offense was committed for purposes of commercial advantage or private financial gain;

(ii) the offense was committed in furtherance of any criminal or tortious act in violation of the Constitution or laws of the United States or of any State; or

(iii) the value of the information obtained exceeds $5,000; and

(C) a fine under this title or imprisonment for not more than ten years, or both, in the case of an offense under subsection (a)(2), (a)(3) or (a)(6) of this section which occurs after a conviction for another offense under this section, or an attempt to commit an offense punishable under this subparagraph; and

(3)(A) a fine under this title or imprisonment for not more than five years, or both, in the case of an offense under subsection (a)(4) or (a)(7) of this section which does not occur after a conviction for another offense under this section, or an attempt to commit an offense punishable under this subparagraph; and

(B) a fine under this title or imprisonment for not more than ten years or both, in the case of an offense under subsection (a)(4), or (a)(7) of this section which occurs after a conviction for another offense under this section, or an attempt to commit an offense punishable under this subparagraph;

(d)(1) The United States Secret Service shall, in addition to any other agency having such authority, have the authority to investigate offenses under this section.

(2) The Federal Bureau of Investigation shall have primary authority to investigate offenses under subsection (a)(1) for any cases involving espionage, foreign counterintelligence, information protected against unauthorized disclosure for reasons of national defense or foreign relations, or Restricted Data (as that term is defined in section 11y of the Atomic Energy Act of 1954 (42 U.S.C. 2014(y)), except for offenses affecting the duties of the United States Secret Service pursuant to section 3056(a) of this title.

(3) Such authority shall be exercised in accordance with an agreement which shall be entered into by the Secretary of the Treasury and the Attorney General.

(e) As used in this section—

(1) the term "computer" means an electronic, magnetic, optical, electrochemical, or other high speed data processing device performing logical, arithmetic, or storage functions, and includes any data storage facility or communications facility directly related to or operating in conjunction with such device, but such term does not include an automated typewriter or typesetter, a portable hand held calculator, or other similar device;

(2) the term "protected computer" means a computer—

(A) exclusively for the use of a financial institution or the United States Government, or, in the case of a computer not exclusively for such use, used by or for a financial institution or the United States Government and the conduct constituting the offense affects that use by or for the financial institution or the Government; or

(B) which is used in or affecting interstate or foreign commerce or communication, including a computer located outside the United States that is used in a manner that affects interstate or foreign commerce or communication of the United States;

(3) the term "State" includes the District of Columbia, the Commonwealth of Puerto Rico, and any other commonwealth, possession or territory of the United States;

(4) the term "financial institution" means—

(A) an institution, with deposits insured by the Federal Deposit Insurance Corporation;

(B) the Federal Reserve or a member of the Federal Reserve including any Federal Reserve Bank;

(C) a credit union with accounts insured by the National Credit Union Administration;

(D) a member of the Federal home loan bank system and any home loan bank;

(E) any institution of the Farm Credit System under the Farm Credit Act of 1971;

(F) a broker-dealer registered with the Securities and Exchange Commission pursuant to section 15 of the Securities Exchange Act of 1934;

(G) the Securities Investor Protection Corporation;

(H) a branch or agency of a foreign bank (as such terms are defined in paragraphs (1) and (3) of section 1(b) of the International Banking Act of 1978); and

(I) an organization operating under section 25 or section 25(a) of the Federal Reserve Act.

(5) the term "financial record" means information derived from any record held by a financial institution pertaining to a customer's relationship with the financial institution;

(6) the term "exceeds authorized access" means to access a computer with authorization and to use such access to obtain or alter information in the computer that the accesser is not entitled so to obtain or alter;

(7) the term "department of the United States" means the legislative or judicial branch of the Government or one of the executive departments enumerated in section 101 of title 5;

(8) the term "damage" means any impairment to the integrity or availability of data, a program, a system, or information;

(9) the term "government entity" includes the Government of the United States, any State or political subdivision of the United States, any foreign country, and any state, province, municipality, or other political subdivision of a foreign country;

(10) the term "conviction" shall include a conviction under the law of any State for a crime punishable by imprisonment for more than 1 year, an element of which is unauthorized access, or exceeding authorized access, to a computer;

(11) the term "loss" means any reasonable cost to any victim, including the cost of responding to an offense, conducting a damage assessment, and restoring the data, program, system, or information to its condition prior to the offense, and any revenue lost, cost incurred, or other consequential damages incurred because of interruption of service; and

(12) the term "person" means any individual, firm, corporation, educational institution, financial institution, governmental entity, or legal or other entity.

(f) This section does not prohibit any lawfully authorized investigative, protective, or intelligence activity of a law enforcement agency of the United States, a State, or a political subdivision of a State, or of an intelligence agency of the United States.

(g) Any person who suffers damage or loss by reason of a violation of this section may maintain a civil action against the violator to obtain compensatory damages and injunctive relief or other equitable relief. A civil action for a violation of this section may be brought only if the conduct involves 1 of the factors set forth in subclauses (I), (II), (III), (IV), or (V) of subsection (c)(4)(A)(i). Damages for a violation involving only conduct described in subsection (c)(4)(A)(i)(I) are limited to economic damages. No action may be brought under this subsection unless such action is begun within 2 years of the date of the act complained of or the date of the discovery of the damage.

(h) The Attorney General and the Secretary of the Treasury shall report to the Congress annually, during the first 3 years following the date of the enactment of this subsection, concerning investigations and prosecutions under subsection (a)(5).

18 U.S.C. § 1031. MAJOR FRAUD AGAINST THE UNITED STATES

(a) Whoever knowingly executes, or attempts to execute, any scheme or artifice with the intent—

(1) to defraud the United States; or

(2) to obtain money or property by means of false or fraudulent pretenses, representations, or promises,

in any grant, contract, subcontract, subsidy, loan, guarantee, insurance, or other form of Federal assistance, including through the Troubled Asset Relief Program, an economic stimulus, recovery or rescue plan provided by the Government, or the Government's purchase of any troubled asset as defined in the Emergency Economic Stabilization Act of 2008, or in any procurement of property or services as a prime contractor with the United States or as a subcontractor or supplier on a contract in which there is a prime contract with the United States, if the value of such grant, contract, subcontract, subsidy, loan, guarantee, insurance, or other form of Federal assistance, or any constituent part thereof, is $1,000,000 or more shall, subject to the applicability of subsection (c) of this section, be fined not more than $1,000,000, or imprisoned not more than 10 years, or both.

(b) The fine imposed for an offense under this section may exceed the maximum otherwise provided by law, if such fine does not exceed $5,000,000 and—

(1) the gross loss to the Government or the gross gain to a defendant is $500,000 or greater; or

(2) the offense involves a conscious or reckless risk of serious personal injury.

(c) The maximum fine imposed upon a defendant for a prosecution including a prosecution with multiple counts under this section shall not exceed $10,000,000.

(d) Nothing in this section shall preclude a court from imposing any other sentences available under this title, including without limitation a fine up to twice the amount of the gross loss or gross gain involved in the offense pursuant to 18 U.S.C. § 3571(d).

(e) In determining the amount of the fine, the court shall consider the factors set forth in 18 U.S.C. §§ 3553 and 3572, and the factors set forth in the guidelines and policy statements of the United States Sentencing Commission, including—

(1) the need to reflect the seriousness of the offense, including the harm or loss to the victim and the gain to the defendant;

(2) whether the defendant previously has been fined for a similar offense; and

(3) any other pertinent equitable considerations.

(f) A prosecution of an offense under this section may be commenced any time not later than 7 years after the offense is committed, plus any additional time otherwise allowed by law.

(g)(1) In special circumstances and in his or her sole discretion, the Attorney General is authorized to make payments from funds appropriated to the Department of Justice to persons who furnish information relating to a possible prosecution under this section. The amount of such payment shall not exceed $250,000. Upon application by the Attorney General, the court may order that the Department shall be reimbursed for a payment from a criminal fine imposed under this section.

(2) An individual is not eligible for such a payment if—

(A) that individual is an officer or employee of a Government agency who furnishes information or renders service in the performance of official duties;

(B) that individual failed to furnish the information to the individual's employer prior to furnishing it to law enforcement authorities, unless the court determines the individual has justifiable reasons for that failure;

(C) the furnished information is based upon public disclosure of allegations or transactions in a criminal, civil, or administrative hearing, in a congressional, administrative, or GAO report, hearing, audit or investigation, or from the news media unless the person is the original source of the information. For the purposes of this subsection, "original source" means an individual who has direct and independent knowledge of the information on which the allegations are based and has voluntarily provided the information to the Government; or

(D) that individual participated in the violation of this section with respect to which such payment would be made.

(3) The failure of the Attorney General to authorize a payment shall not be subject to judicial review.

(h) Any individual who—

(1) is discharged, demoted, suspended, threatened, harassed, or in any other manner discriminated against in the terms and conditions of employment by an employer because of lawful acts done by the employee on behalf of the employee or others in furtherance of a prosecution under this section (including investigation for, initiation of, testimony for, or assistance in such prosecution), and

(2) was not a participant in the unlawful activity that is the subject of said prosecution, may, in a civil action, obtain all relief necessary to make such individual whole. Such relief shall include reinstatement with the same seniority status such individual would have had but for the discrimination, two times the amount of back pay, interest on the back pay, and compensation for any special damages sustained as a result of the discrimination, including litigation costs and reasonable attorney's fees.

18 U.S.C. § 1341. FRAUDS AND SWINDLES

Whoever, having devised or intending to devise any scheme or artifice to defraud, or for obtaining money or property by means of false or fraudulent pretenses, representations, or promises, or to sell, dispose of, loan, exchange, alter, give away, distribute, supply, or furnish or procure for unlawful use any counterfeit or spurious coin, obligation, security, or other article, or anything represented to be or intimated or held out to be such counterfeit or spurious article, for the purpose of executing such scheme or artifice or attempting so to do, places in any post office or authorized depository for mail matter, any matter or thing whatever to be sent or delivered by the Postal Service, or deposits or causes to be deposited any matter or thing whatever to be sent or delivered by any private or commercial interstate carrier, or takes or receives therefrom, any such matter or thing, or knowingly causes to be delivered by mail or such carrier according to the direction thereon, or at the place at which it is directed to be delivered by the person to whom it is addressed, any such matter or thing, shall be fined under this title or imprisoned not more than 20 years, or both. If the violation occurs in relation to, or involving any benefit authorized, transported, transmitted, transferred, disbursed, or paid in connection with, a presidentially declared major disaster or emergency (as those terms are defined in section 102 of the Robert T. Stafford Disaster Relief and Emergency Assistance Act (42 U.S.C. 5122)), or affects a financial institution, such person shall be fined not more than $1,000,000 or imprisoned not more than 30 years, or both.

18 U.S.C. § 1343. FRAUD BY WIRE, RADIO, OR TELEVISION

Whoever, having devised or intending to devise any scheme or artifice to defraud, or for obtaining money or property by means of false or fraudulent pretenses, representations, or promises, transmits or causes to be transmitted by means of wire, radio, or television communication in interstate or foreign commerce, any writings, signs, signals, pictures, or sounds for the purpose of executing such scheme or artifice, shall be fined under this title or imprisoned not more than 20 years, or both. If the violation occurs in relation to, or involving any benefit authorized, transported, transmitted, transferred, disbursed, or paid in connection with, a presidentially declared major disaster or emergency (as those terms are defined in section 102 of the Robert T. Stafford Disaster Relief and Emergency Assistance Act

(42 U.S.C. 5122)), or affects a financial institution, such person shall be fined not more than $1,000,000 or imprisoned not more than 30 years, or both.

18 U.S.C. § 1344. BANK FRAUD
Whoever knowingly executes, or attempts to execute, a scheme or artifice—

(1) to defraud a financial institution; or

(2) to obtain any of the moneys, funds, credits, assets, securities, or other property owned by, or under the custody or control of, a financial institution, by means of false or fraudulent pretenses, representations, or promises;

shall be fined not more than $1,000,000 or imprisoned not more than 30 years, or both.

18 U.S.C. § 1346. DEFINITION OF "SCHEME OR ARTIFICE TO DEFRAUD"
For the purposes of this chapter, the term "scheme or artifice to defraud" includes a scheme or artifice to deprive another of the intangible right of honest services.

18 U.S.C. § 1348. SECURITIES AND COMMODITIES FRAUD
Whoever knowingly executes, or attempts to execute, a scheme or artifice—

(1) to defraud any person in connection with any commodity for future delivery, or any option on a commodity for future delivery, or any security of an issuer with a class of securities registered under section 12 of the Securities Exchange Act of 1934 (15 U.S.C. § 78*l*) or that is required to file reports under section 15(d) of the Securities Exchange Act of 1934 (15 U.S.C. § 78*o*(d)); or

(2) to obtain, by means of false or fraudulent pretenses, representations, or promises, any money or property in connection with the purchase or sale of any commodity for future delivery, or any option on a commodity for future delivery, any security of an issuer with a class of securities registered under section 12 of the

Securities Exchange Act of 1934 (15 U.S.C. § 78*l*) or that is required to file reports under section 15(d) of the Securities Exchange Act of 1934 (15 U.S.C. § 78*o*(d));

shall be fined under this title, or imprisoned not more than 25 years, or both.

18 U.S.C. § 1349. ATTEMPT AND CONSPIRACY

Any person who attempts or conspires to commit any offense under this chapter shall be subject to the same penalties as those prescribed for the offense, the commission of which was the object of the attempt or conspiracy.

18 U.S.C. § 1350. FAILURE OF CORPORATE OFFICERS TO CERTIFY FINANCIAL REPORTS

(a) Certification of periodic financial reports.—Each periodic report containing financial statements filed by an issuer with the Securities Exchange Commission pursuant to section 13(a) or 15(d) of the Securities Exchange Act of 1934 (15 U.S.C. § 78m(a) or 78*o*(d)) shall be accompanied by a written statement by the chief executive officer and chief financial officer (or equivalent thereof) of the issuer.

(b) Content. The statement required under subsection (a) shall certify that the periodic report containing the financial statements fully complies with the requirements of section 13(a) or 15(d) of the Securities Exchange Act [of] 1934 (15 U.S.C. §§ 78m or 78*o*(d)) and that information contained in the periodic report fairly presents, in all material respects, the financial condition and results of operations of the issuer.

(c) Criminal penalties.—Whoever—

(1) certifies any statement as set forth in subsections (a) and (b) of this section knowing that the periodic report accompanying the statement does not comport with all the requirements set forth in this section shall be fined not more than $1,000,000 or imprisoned not more than 10 years, or both; or

(2) willfully certifies any statement as set forth in subsections (a) and (b) of this section knowing that the periodic report

accompanying the statement does not comport with all the requirements set forth in this section shall be fined not more than $5,000,000, or imprisoned not more than 20 years, or both.

18 U.S.C. § 1503. INFLUENCING OR INJURING OFFICER OR JUROR GENERALLY

(a) Whoever corruptly, or by threats or force, or by any threatening letter or communication, endeavors to influence, intimidate, or impede any grand or petit juror, or officer in or of any court of the United States, or officer who may be serving at any examination or other proceeding before any United States magistrate judge or other committing magistrate, in the discharge of his duty, or injures any such grand or petit juror in his person or property on account of any verdict or indictment assented to by him, or on account of his being or having been such juror, or injures any such officer, magistrate judge, or other committing magistrate in his person or property on account of the performance of his official duties, or corruptly or by threats or force, or by any threatening letter or communication, influences, obstructs, or impedes, or endeavors to influence, obstruct, or impede, the due administration of justice, shall be punished as provided in subsection (b). If the offense under this section occurs in connection with a trial of a criminal case, and the act in violation of this section involves the threat of physical force or physical force, the maximum term of imprisonment which may be imposed for the offense shall be the higher of that otherwise provided by law or the maximum term that could have been imposed for any offense charged in such case.

(b) The punishment for an offense under this section is—

(1) in the case of a killing, the punishment provided in sections 1111 and 1112;

(2) in the case of an attempted killing, or a case in which the offense was committed against a petit juror and in which a class A or B felony was charged, imprisonment for not more than 20 years, a fine under this title, or both; and

(3) in any other case, imprisonment for not more than 10 years, a fine under this title, or both.

18 U.S.C. § 1505. OBSTRUCTION OF PROCEEDINGS BEFORE DEPARTMENTS, AGENCIES, AND COMMITTEES

Whoever, with intent to avoid, evade, prevent, or obstruct compliance, in whole or in part, with any civil investigative demand duly and properly made under the Antitrust Civil Process Act, willfully withholds, misrepresents, removes from any place, conceals, covers up, destroys, mutilates, alters, or by other means falsifies any documentary material, answers to written interrogatories, or oral testimony, which is the subject of such demand; or attempts to do so or solicits another to do so; or

Whoever corruptly, or by threats or force, or by any threatening letter or communication influences, obstructs, or impedes or endeavors to influence, obstruct, or impede the due and proper administration of the law under which any pending proceeding is being had before any department or agency of the United States, or the due and proper exercise of the power of inquiry under which any inquiry or investigation is being had by either House, or any committee of either House or any joint committee of the Congress—

Shall be fined under this title, imprisoned not more than 5 years or, if the offense involves international or domestic terrorism (as defined in section 2331), imprisoned not more than 8 years, or both.

18 U.S.C. § 1510. OBSTRUCTION OF CRIMINAL INVESTIGATIONS

(a) Whoever willfully endeavors by means of bribery to obstruct, delay, or prevent the communication of information relating to a violation of any criminal statute of the United States by any person to a criminal investigator shall be fined under this title, or imprisoned not more than five years, or both.

(b)(1) Whoever, being an officer of a financial institution, with the intent to obstruct a judicial proceeding, directly or indirectly notifies any other person about the existence or contents of a subpoena for records of that financial institution, or information that has been furnished in response to that subpoena, shall be fined under this title or imprisoned not more than 5 years, or both.

(2) Whoever, being an officer of a financial institution, directly or indirectly notifies—

(A) a customer of that financial institution whose records are sought by a subpoena for records; or

(B) any other person named in that subpoena;

about the existence or contents of that subpoena or information that has been furnished in response to that subpoena, shall be fined under this title or imprisoned not more than one year, or both.

(3) As used in this subsection—

(A) the term "an officer of a financial institution" means an officer, director, partner, employee, agent, or attorney of or for a financial institution; and

(B) the term "subpoena for records" means a Federal grand jury subpoena or a Department of Justice subpoena (issued under section 3486 of title 18), for customer records that has been served relating to a violation of, or a conspiracy to violate—

(i) section 215, 656, 657, 1005, 1006, 1007, 1014, 1344, 1956, 1957, or chapter 53 of title 31; or

(ii) section 1341 or 1343 affecting a financial institution.

(c) As used in this section, the term "criminal investigator" means any individual duly authorized by a department, agency, or armed force of the United States to conduct or engage in investigations of or prosecutions for violations of the criminal laws of the United States. . . .

18 U.S.C. § 1512. TAMPERING WITH A WITNESS, VICTIM, OR AN INFORMANT

(a)(1) Whoever kills or attempts to kill another person, with intent to—

(A) prevent the attendance or testimony of any person in an official proceeding;

(B) prevent the production of a record, document, or other object, in an official proceeding; or

(C) prevent the communication by any person to a law enforcement officer or judge of the United States of information relating to the commission or possible commission of a Federal offense or a violation of conditions of probation, parole, or release pending judicial proceedings;

shall be punished as provided in paragraph (3).

(2) Whoever uses physical force or the threat of physical force against any person, or attempts to do so, with intent to—

(A) influence, delay, or prevent the testimony of any person in an official proceeding;

(B) cause or induce any person to—

(i) withhold testimony, or withhold a record, document, or other object, from an official proceeding;

(ii) alter, destroy, mutilate, or conceal an object with intent to impair the integrity or availability of the object for use in an official proceeding;

(iii) evade legal process summoning that person to appear as a witness, or to produce a record, document, or other object, in an official proceeding; or

(iv) be absent from an official proceeding to which that person has been summoned by legal process; or

(C) hinder, delay, or prevent the communication to a law enforcement officer or judge of the United States of information relating to the commission or possible commission of a Federal offense or a violation of conditions of probation, supervised release, parole, or release pending judicial proceedings;

shall be punished as provided in paragraph (3).

(3) The punishment for an offense under this subsection is--

(A) in the case of a killing, the punishment provided in sections 1111 and 1112;

(B) in the case of—

(i) an attempt to murder; or

(ii) the use or attempted use of physical force against any person;

imprisonment for not more than 30 years; and

(C) in the case of the threat of use of physical force against any person, imprisonment for not more than 20 years.

(b) Whoever knowingly uses intimidation, threatens, or corruptly persuades another person, or attempts to do so, or engages in misleading conduct toward another person, with intent to—

(1) influence, delay or prevent the testimony of any person in an official proceeding;

(2) cause or induce any person to—

(A) withhold testimony, or withhold a record, document, or other object, from an official proceeding;

(B) alter, destroy, mutilate, or conceal an object with intent to impair the object's integrity or availability for use in an official proceeding;

(C) evade legal process summoning that person to appear as a witness, or to produce a record, document, or other object, in an official proceeding; or

(D) be absent from an official proceeding to which such person has been summoned by legal process; or

(3) hinder, delay, or prevent the communication to a law enforcement officer or judge of the United States of information relating to the commission or possible commission of a Federal offense or a violation of conditions of probation, supervised release, parole, or release pending judicial proceedings;

shall be fined under this title or imprisoned not more than 20 years, or both.

(c) Whoever corruptly—

(1) alters, destroys, mutilates, or conceals a record, document, or other object, or attempts to do so, with the intent to impair the object's integrity or availability for use in an official proceeding; or

(2) otherwise obstructs, influences, or impedes any official proceeding, or attempts to do so,

shall be fined under this title or imprisoned not more than 20 years, or both.

(d) Whoever intentionally harasses another person and thereby hinders, delays, prevents, or dissuades any person from—

(1) attending or testifying in an official proceeding;

(2) reporting to a law enforcement officer or judge of the United States the commission or possible commission of a Federal offense or a violation of conditions of probation, supervised release, parole, or release pending judicial proceedings;

(3) arresting or seeking the arrest of another person in connection with a Federal offense; or

(4) causing a criminal prosecution, or a parole or probation revocation proceeding, to be sought or instituted, or assisting in such prosecution or proceeding;

or attempts to do so, shall be fined under this title or imprisoned not more than 3 years, or both.

(e) In a prosecution for an offense under this section, it is an affirmative defense, as to which the defendant has the burden of proof by a preponderance of the evidence, that the conduct consisted solely of lawful conduct and that the defendant's sole intention was to encourage, induce, or cause the other person to testify truthfully.

(f) For the purposes of this section—

(1) an official proceeding need not be pending or about to be instituted at the time of the offense; and

(2) the testimony, or the record, document, or other object need not be admissible in evidence or free of a claim of privilege.

(g) In a prosecution for an offense under this section, no state of mind need be proved with respect to the circumstance—

(1) that the official proceeding before a judge, court, magistrate judge, grand jury, or government agency is before a judge or court of the United States, a United States magistrate judge, a bankruptcy judge, a Federal grand jury, or a Federal Government agency; or

(2) that the judge is a judge of the United States or that the law enforcement officer is an officer or employee of the Federal Government or a person authorized to act for or on behalf of the Federal Government or serving the Federal Government as an adviser or consultant.

(h) There is extraterritorial Federal jurisdiction over an offense under this section.

(i) A prosecution under this section or section 1503 may be brought in the district in which the official proceeding (whether or not pending or about to be instituted) was intended to be affected or in the district in which the conduct constituting the alleged offense occurred.

(j) If the offense under this section occurs in connection with a trial of a criminal case, the maximum term of imprisonment which may be imposed for the offense shall be the higher of that otherwise provided by law or the maximum term that could have been imposed for any offense charged in such case.

(k) Whoever conspires to commit any offense under this section shall be subject to the same penalties as those prescribed for the offense the commission of which was the object of the conspiracy.

18 U.S.C. § 1513. RETALIATING AGAINST A WITNESS, VICTIM, OR AN INFORMANT

(a)(1) Whoever kills or attempts to kill another person with intent to retaliate against any person for—

> (A) the attendance of a witness or party at an official proceeding, or any testimony given or any record, document, or other object produced by a witness in an official proceeding; or

> (B) providing to a law enforcement officer any information relating to the commission or possible commission of a Federal offense or a violation of conditions of probation, supervised release, parole, or release pending judicial proceedings,

shall be punished as provided in paragraph (2).

(2) The punishment for an offense under this subsection is—

> (A) in the case of a killing, the punishment provided in sections 1111 and 1112; and

> (B) in the case of an attempt, imprisonment for not more than 30 years.

(b) Whoever knowingly engages in any conduct and thereby causes bodily injury to another person or damages the tangible property of another person, or threatens to do so, with intent to retaliate against any person for—

(1) the attendance of a witness or party at an official proceeding, or any testimony given or any record, document, or other object produced by a witness in an official proceeding; or

(2) any information relating to the commission or possible commission of a Federal offense or a violation of conditions of probation, supervised release, parole, or release pending judicial proceedings given by a person to a law enforcement officer; or attempts to do so, shall be fined under this title or imprisoned not more than 20 years, or both.

(c) If the retaliation occurred because of attendance at or testimony in a criminal case, the maximum term of imprisonment which may be imposed for the offense under this section shall be the higher of that otherwise provided by law or the maximum term that could have been imposed for any offense charged in such case.

(d) There is extraterritorial Federal jurisdiction over an offense under this section.

(e) Whoever knowingly, with the intent to retaliate, takes any action harmful to any person, including interference with the lawful employment or livelihood of any person, for providing to a law enforcement officer any truthful information relating to the commission or possible commission of any Federal offense, shall be fined under this title or imprisoned not more than 10 years, or both.

. . .

18 U.S.C. § 1515. DEFINITIONS FOR CERTAIN PROVISIONS; GENERAL PROVISION

(a) As used in sections 1512 and 1513 of this title and in this section—

(1) the term "official proceeding" means—

(A) a proceeding before a judge or court of the United States, a United States magistrate judge, a bankruptcy judge, a judge of the United States Tax Court, a special trial judge of the Tax Court, a judge of the United States Court of Federal Claims, or a Federal grand jury;

(B) a proceeding before the Congress;

(C) a proceeding before a Federal Government agency which is authorized by law; or

(D) a proceeding involving the business of insurance whose activities affect interstate commerce before any insurance regulatory official or agency or any agent or examiner appointed by such official or agency to examine the affairs of any person engaged in the business of insurance whose activities affect interstate commerce;

(2) the term "physical force" means physical action against another, and includes confinement;

(3) the term "misleading conduct" means—

(A) knowingly making a false statement;

(B) intentionally omitting information from a statement and thereby causing a portion of such statement to be misleading, or intentionally concealing a material fact, and thereby creating a false impression by such statement;

(C) with intent to mislead, knowingly submitting or inviting reliance on a writing or recording that is false, forged, altered, or otherwise lacking in authenticity;

(D) with intent to mislead, knowingly submitting or inviting reliance on a sample, specimen, map, photograph, boundary mark, or other object that is misleading in a material respect; or

(E) knowingly using a trick, scheme, or device with intent to mislead;

(4) the term "law enforcement officer" means an officer or employee of the Federal Government, or a person authorized to act for or on behalf of the Federal Government or serving the Federal Government as an adviser or consultant—

(A) authorized under law to engage in or supervise the prevention, detection, investigation, or prosecution of an offense; or

(B) serving as a probation or pretrial services officer under this title;

(5) the term "bodily injury" means—

(A) a cut, abrasion, bruise, burn, or disfigurement;

(B) physical pain;

(C) illness;

(D) impairment of the function of a bodily member, organ, or mental faculty; or

(E) any other injury to the body, no matter how temporary; and

(6) the term "corruptly persuades" does not include conduct which would be misleading conduct but for a lack of a state of mind.

(b) As used in section 1505, the term "corruptly" means acting with an improper purpose, personally or by influencing another, including making a false or misleading statement, or withholding, concealing, altering, or destroying a document or other information.

(c) This chapter does not prohibit or punish the providing of lawful, bona fide, legal representation services in connection with or anticipation of an official proceeding.

18 U.S.C. § 1519. DESTRUCTION, ALTERATION, OR FALSIFICATION OF RECORDS IN FEDERAL INVESTIGATIONS AND BANKRUPTCY

Whoever knowingly alters, destroys, mutilates, conceals, covers up, falsifies, or makes a false entry in any record, document, or tangible object with the intent to impede, obstruct, or influence the investigation or proper administration of any matter within the jurisdiction of any department or agency of the United States or any case filed under title 11, or in relation to or contemplation of any such matter or case, shall be fined under this title, imprisoned not more than 20 years, or both.

18 U.S.C. § 1520. DESTRUCTION OF CORPORATE AUDIT RECORDS

(a)(1) Any accountant who conducts an audit of an issuer of securities to which section 10A(a) of the Securities Exchange Act of 1934 (15 U.S.C. § 78j-1(a)) applies, shall maintain all audit or review workpapers for a period of 5 years from the end of the fiscal period in which the audit or review was concluded.

(2) The Securities and Exchange Commission shall promulgate, within 180 days, after adequate notice and an opportunity for comment, such rules and regulations, as are reasonably necessary, relating to the retention of relevant records such as workpapers, documents that form the basis of an audit or review, memoranda, correspondence, communications, other documents, and records (including electronic records) which are created, sent, or received in connection with an audit or review and contain conclusions, opinions, analyses, or financial data relating to such an audit or review, which is conducted by any accountant who conducts an audit of an issuer of securities to which section 10A(a) of the Securities Exchange Act of 1934 (15 U.S.C. § 78j-1(a)) applies. The Commission may, from time to time, amend or supplement the rules and regulations that it is required to promulgate under this section, after adequate notice and an opportunity for comment, in order to ensure that such rules and regulations adequately comport with the purposes of this section.

(b) Whoever knowingly and willfully violates subsection (a)(1), or any rule or regulation promulgated by the Securities and Exchange Commission under subsection (a)(2), shall be fined under this title, imprisoned not more than 10 years, or both.

(c) Nothing in this section shall be deemed to diminish or relieve any person of any other duty or obligation imposed by Federal or State law or regulation to maintain, or refrain from destroying, any document.

18 U.S.C. § 1621. PERJURY GENERALLY
Whoever—

(1) having taken an oath before a competent tribunal, officer, or person, in any case in which a law of the United States authorizes an oath to be administered, that he will testify, declare, depose, or certify truly, or that any written testimony, declaration, deposition, or certificate by him subscribed, is true, willfully and contrary to such oath states or subscribes any material matter which he does not believe to be true; or

(2) in any declaration, certificate, verification, or statement under penalty of perjury as permitted under section 1746 of title 28, United States Code, willfully subscribes as true any material matter which he does not believe to be true;

is guilty of perjury and shall, except as otherwise expressly provided by law, be fined under this title or imprisoned not more than five years, or both. This section is applicable whether the statement or subscription is made within or without the United States.

18 U.S.C. § 1622. SUBORNATION OF PERJURY
Whoever procures another to commit any perjury is guilty of subornation of perjury, and shall be fined under this title or imprisoned not more than five years, or both.

18 U.S.C. § 1623. FALSE DECLARATIONS BEFORE GRAND JURY OR COURT
(a) Whoever under oath (or in any declaration, certificate, verification, or statement under penalty of perjury as permitted under section 1746 of title 28, United States Code) in any proceeding before or ancillary to any court or grand jury of the United States knowingly makes any false material declaration or makes or uses any other information, including any book, paper, document, record, recording, or other material, knowing the same to contain any false material declaration, shall be fined under this title or imprisoned not more than five years, or both.

(b) This section is applicable whether the conduct occurred within or without the United States.

(c) An indictment or information for violation of this section alleging that, in any proceedings before or ancillary to any court or grand jury of the United States, the defendant under oath has knowingly made two or more declarations, which are inconsistent to the degree that one of them is necessarily false, need not specify which declaration is false if—

(1) each declaration was material to the point in question, and

(2) each declaration was made within the period of the statute of limitations for the offense charged under this section.

In any prosecution under this section, the falsity of a declaration set forth in the indictment or information shall be established sufficient for conviction by proof that the defendant while under oath made irreconcilably contradictory declarations material to the point in question in any proceeding before or ancillary to any court or grand jury. It shall be a defense to an indictment or information made pursuant to the first sentence of this subsection that the defendant at the time he made each declaration believed the declaration was true.

(d) Where, in the same continuous court or grand jury proceeding in which a declaration is made, the person making the declaration admits such declaration to be false, such admission shall bar prosecution under this section if, at the time the admission is made, the declaration has not substantially affected the proceeding, or it has not become manifest that such falsity has been or will be exposed.

(e) Proof beyond a reasonable doubt under this section is sufficient for conviction. It shall not be necessary that such proof be made by any particular number of witnesses or by documentary or other type of evidence.

18 U.S.C. § 1956. LAUNDERING OF MONETARY INSTRUMENTS

(a)(1) Whoever, knowing that the property involved in a financial transaction represents the proceeds of some form of unlawful activity, conducts or attempts to conduct such a financial transaction which in fact involves the proceeds of specified unlawful activity—

 (A)(i) with the intent to promote the carrying on of specified unlawful activity; or

  (ii) with intent to engage in conduct constituting a violation of section 7201 or 7206 of the Internal Revenue Code of 1986; or

 (B) knowing that the transaction is designed in whole or in part—

  (i) to conceal or disguise the nature, the location, the source, the ownership, or the control of the proceeds of specified unlawful activity; or

  (ii) to avoid a transaction reporting requirement under State or Federal law,

shall be sentenced to a fine of not more than $500,000 or twice the value of the property involved in the transaction, whichever is greater, or imprisonment for not more than twenty years, or both.

 (2) Whoever transports, transmits, or transfers, or attempts to transport, transmit, or transfer a monetary instrument or funds from a place in the United States to or through a place outside the United States or to a place in the United States from or through a place outside the United States—

 (A) with the intent to promote the carrying on of specified unlawful activity; or

 (B) knowing that the monetary instrument or funds involved in the transportation, transmission, or transfer represent the proceeds of some form of unlawful activity and knowing that such transportation, transmission, or transfer is designed in whole or in part—

  (i) to conceal or disguise the nature, the location, the source, the ownership, or the control of the proceeds of specified unlawful activity; or

  (ii) to avoid a transaction reporting requirement under State or Federal law,

shall be sentenced to a fine of not more than $500,000 or twice the value of the monetary instrument or funds involved in the transportation, transmission, or transfer whichever is greater, or imprisonment for not more than twenty years, or both. For the purpose of the offense described in subparagraph (B), the defendant's knowledge may be established by proof that a law enforcement officer represented the matter specified in subparagraph (B) as true, and the defendant's subsequent statements or actions indicate that the defendant believed such representations to be true.

(3) Whoever, with the intent—

(A) to promote the carrying on of specified unlawful activity;

(B) to conceal or disguise the nature, location, source, ownership, or control of property believed to be the proceeds of specified unlawful activity; or

(C) to avoid a transaction reporting requirement under State or Federal law,

conducts or attempts to conduct a financial transaction involving property represented to be the proceeds of specified unlawful activity, or property used to conduct or facilitate specified unlawful activity, shall be fined under this title or imprisoned for not more than 20 years, or both. For purposes of this paragraph and paragraph (2), the term "represented" means any representation made by a law enforcement officer or by another person at the direction of, or with the approval of, a Federal official authorized to investigate or prosecute violations of this section.

(b) Penalties.—

(1) In general.—Whoever conducts or attempts to conduct a transaction described in subsection (a)(1) or (a)(3), or a transportation, transmission, or transfer described in subsection (a)(2), is liable to the United States for a civil penalty of not more than the greater of—

(A) the value of the property, funds, or monetary instruments involved in the transaction; or

(B) $10,000.

. . .

(c) As used in this section—

(1) the term "knowing that the property involved in a financial transaction represents the proceeds of some form of unlawful activity" means that the person knew the property involved in the transaction represented proceeds from some form, though not necessarily which form, of activity that constitutes a felony under State, Federal, or foreign law, regardless of whether or not such activity is specified in paragraph (7);

(2) the term "conducts" includes initiating, concluding, or participating in initiating, or concluding a transaction;

(3) the term "transaction" includes a purchase, sale, loan, pledge, gift, transfer, delivery, or other disposition, and with respect to a financial institution includes a deposit, withdrawal, transfer between accounts, exchange of currency, loan, extension of credit, purchase or sale of any stock, bond, certificate of deposit, or other monetary instrument, use of a safe deposit box, or any other payment, transfer, or delivery by, through, or to a financial institution, by whatever means effected;

(4) the term "financial transaction" means

(A) a transaction which in any way or degree affects interstate or foreign commerce

(i) involving the movement of funds by wire or other means[,] or

(ii) involving one or more monetary instruments, or

(iii) involving the transfer of title to any real property, vehicle, vessel, or aircraft, or

(B) a transaction involving the use of a financial institution which is engaged in, or the activities of which affect, interstate or foreign commerce in any way or degree;

(5) the term "monetary instruments" means (i) coin or currency of the United States or of any other country, travelers' checks, personal checks, bank checks, and money orders, or (ii) investment securities or negotiable instruments, in bearer form or otherwise in such form that title thereto passes upon delivery;

(6) the term "financial institution" includes—

(A) any financial institution, as defined in section 5312(a)(2) of title 31, United States Code, or the regulations promulgated thereunder; and

(B) any foreign bank, as defined in section 1 of the International Banking Act of 1978 (12 U.S.C. § 3101).

(7) the term "specified unlawful activity" means—

(A) any act or activity constituting an offense listed in section 1961(1) of this title except an act which is indictable under subchapter II of chapter 53 of title 31;

(B) with respect to a financial transaction occurring in whole or in part in the United States, an offense against a foreign nation involving—

(i) the manufacture, importation, sale, or distribution of a controlled substance (as such term is defined for the purposes of the Controlled Substances Act);

(ii) murder, kidnapping, robbery, extortion, or destruction of property by means of explosive or fire;

(iii) fraud, or any scheme or attempt to defraud, by or against a foreign bank (as defined in paragraph 7 of section 1(b) of the International Banking Act of 1978;

(iv) bribery of a public official, or the misappropriation, theft, or embezzlement of public funds by or for the benefit of a public official;

(v) smuggling or export control violations involving—

(I) an item controlled on the United States Munitions List established under section 38 of the Arms Export Control Act (22 U.S.C. § 2778); or

(II) an item controlled under regulations under the Export Administration Regulations (15 C.F.R. Parts 730-774); or

(vi) an offense with respect to which the United States would be obligated by a multilateral treaty, either to extradite the alleged offender or to submit the case for prosecution, if the offender were found within the territory of the United States;

(C) any act or acts constituting a continuing criminal enterprise, as that term is defined in section 408 of the Controlled Substances Act (21 U.S.C. § 848);

(D) an offense under section 32 (relating to the destruction of aircraft), section 37 (relating to violence at international airports), section 115 (relating to influencing, impeding, or retaliating against a Federal official by threatening or injuring a family member), section 152 (relating to concealment of assets; false oaths and claims; bribery), section 175c (relating to the variola virus), section 215 (relating to commissions or gifts for procuring loans), section 351 (relating to congressional or Cabinet officer assassination), any of sections 500 through 503 (relating to certain counterfeiting offenses), section 513 (relating to securities of States and private entities), section 541 (relating to goods falsely classified), section 542 (relating to entry of goods by means of false statements), section 545 (relating to smuggling goods into the United States), section 549 (relating to removing goods from Customs custody), section 554 (relating to smuggling goods from the United States), section 641 (relating to public money, property, or records), section 656 (relating to theft, embezzlement, or misapplication by bank officer or employee), section 657 (relating to lending, credit, and insurance institutions), section 658 (relating to property mortgaged or pledged to farm credit agencies), section 666 (relating to theft or bribery concerning programs receiving Federal funds), section 793, 794, or 798 (relating to espionage), section 831 (relating to prohibited transactions involving nuclear materials), section 844(f) or (i) (relating to destruction by explosives or fire of Government property or property affecting interstate or foreign commerce), section 875 (relating to interstate communications), section 922(1) (relating to the unlawful importation of firearms), section 924(n) (relating to firearms trafficking), section 956 (relating to conspiracy to kill, kidnap, maim, or injure certain property in a foreign country), section 1005 (relating to fraudulent bank entries), 1006 (relating to fraudulent Federal credit institution entries), 1007 (relating to fraudulent Federal Deposit Insurance transactions), 1014 (relating to fraudulent loan or credit applications), section 1030 (relating to computer fraud and abuse), 1032 (relating to concealment of assets from conservator, receiver, or liquidating agent of financial institution), section 1111 (relating to murder), section 1114 (relating to murder of United States law enforcement officials), section 1116 (relating to murder of foreign officials, official guests, or internationally protected persons), section 1201 (relating to kidnapping), section 1203 (relating to hostage taking), section 1361 (relating to willful injury of Government property), section 1363 (relating to destruction of property within the special maritime and territorial jurisdiction), section 1708 (theft from the mail), section 1751 (relating to Presidential assassination), section 2113 or 2114 (relating to bank and postal robbery and theft), section 2252A (relating to child pornography) where the child pornography contains a visual depiction of an actual minor engaging in sexually explicit conduct, section 2260 (production of child pornography for importation into the United States), section 2280 (relating to violence against maritime navigation), section 2281 (relating to violence against maritime fixed platforms), section 2319 (relating to copyright infringement), section 2320 (relating to trafficking in counterfeit goods and services), section 2332 (relating to terrorist acts abroad against United States nationals), section 2332a (relating to use of weapons of mass destruction), section 2332b (relating to international terrorist acts transcending national boundaries), section 2332g (relating to missile systems designed to destroy aircraft), section 2332h (relating to radiological dispersal devices), section 2339A or 2339B (relating to providing material support to terrorists), section 2339C (relating to financing of terrorism), or section 2339D (relating to receiving military-type training from a foreign terrorist organization) of this title, section 46502 of title 49, United States Code, a felony violation of the Chemical Diversion and Trafficking Act of 1988 (relating to precursor and essential chemicals), section 590 of the Tariff Act of 1930 (19 U.S.C. § 1590) (relating to aviation smuggling), section 422 of the Controlled Substances Act (relating to transportation of drug paraphernalia), section 38(c) (relating to criminal violations) of the Arms Export Control Act, section 11 (relating to violations) of the Export Administration Act of 1979, section 206 (relating to penalties) of the International Emergency Economic Powers Act, section 16 (relating to offenses and punishment) of the Trading with the Enemy Act, any felony violation of section 15 of the Food and Nutrition Act of 2008 (relating to supplemental nutrition assistance program benefits fraud) involving a quantity of benefits having a value of not less than $5,000, any violation of section 543(a)(1) of the Housing Act of 1949 (relating to equity skimming), any felony violation of the Foreign Corrupt Practices Act, section 92 of the Atomic Energy Act of 1954 (relating to prohibitions governing atomic weapons)[;]

(E) a felony violation of the Federal Water Pollution Control Act (33 U.S.C. §§ 1251 et seq.), the Ocean Dumping Act (33 U.S.C. §§ 1401 et seq.), the Act to Prevent Pollution from Ships (33 U.S.C. §§ 1901 et seq.), the Safe Drinking Water Act (42 U.S.C. §§ 300f et seq.), or the Resource[] Conservation and Recovery Act (42 U.S.C. §§ 6901 et seq.).

(F) Any act or activity constituting an offense involving a Federal health care offense.

(8) the term "State" includes a State of the United States, the District of Columbia, and any commonwealth, territory, or possession of the United States; and

(9) the term "proceeds" means any property derived from or obtained or retained, directly or indirectly, through some form of unlawful activity, including the gross receipts of such activity.

(d) Nothing in this section shall supersede any provision of Federal, State, or other law imposing criminal penalties or affording civil remedies in addition to those provided for in this section.

(e) Violations of this section may be investigated by such components of the Department of Justice as the Attorney General may direct, and by such components of the Department of the Treasury as the Secretary of the Treasury may direct, as appropriate and, with respect to offenses over which the United States Postal Service has jurisdiction, by the Postal Service. Such authority of the Secretary of the Treasury and the Postal Service shall be exercised in accordance with an agreement which shall be entered into by the Secretary of the Treasury, the Postal Service, and the Attorney General. Violations of this section involving offenses described in paragraph (c)(7)(E) may be investigated by such components of the Department of Justice as the Attorney General may direct, and the National Enforcement Investigations Center of the Environmental Protection Agency.

(f) There is extraterritorial jurisdiction over the conduct prohibited by this section if—

(1) the conduct is by a United States citizen or, in the case of a non-United States citizen, the conduct occurs in part in the United States; and

(2) the transaction or series of related transactions involves funds or monetary instruments of a value exceeding $10,000.

. . .

(h) Any person who conspires to commit any offense defined in this section or section 1957 shall be subject to the same penalties as those prescribed for the offense the commission of which was the object of the conspiracy.

18 U.S.C. § 1957. ENGAGING IN MONETARY TRANSACTIONS IN PROPERTY DERIVED FROM SPECIFIED UNLAWFUL ACTIVITY

(a) Whoever, in any of the circumstances set forth in subsection (d), knowingly engages or attempts to engage in a monetary transaction in criminally derived property of a value greater than

$10,000 and is derived from specified unlawful activity, shall be punished as provided in subsection (b).

(b)(1) Except as provided in paragraph (2), the punishment for an offense under this section is a fine under title 18, United States Code, or imprisonment for not more than ten years or both.

(2) The court may impose an alternate fine to that imposable under paragraph (1) of not more than twice the amount of the criminally derived property involved in the transaction.

(c) In a prosecution for an offense under this section, the Government is not required to prove the defendant knew that the offense from which the criminally derived property was derived was specified unlawful activity.

(d) The circumstances referred to in subsection (a) are—

(1) that the offense under this section takes place in the United States or in the special maritime and territorial jurisdiction of the United States; or

(2) that the offense under this section takes place outside the United States and such special jurisdiction, but the defendant is a United States person (as defined in section 3077 of this title, but excluding the class described in paragraph (2)(D) of such section).

(e) Violations of this section may be investigated by such components of the Department of Justice as the Attorney General may direct, and by such components of the Department of the Treasury as the Secretary of the Treasury may direct, as appropriate and, with respect to offenses over which the United States Postal Service has jurisdiction, by the Postal Service. Such authority of the Secretary of the Treasury and the Postal Service shall be exercised in accordance with an agreement which shall be entered into by the Secretary of the Treasury, the Postal Service, and the Attorney General.

(f) As used in this section—

(1) the term "monetary transaction" means the deposit, withdrawal, transfer, or exchange, in or affecting interstate or foreign commerce, of funds or a monetary instrument (as defined in section 1956(c)(5) of this title) by, through, or to a financial institution (as defined in section 1956 of this title), including any

transaction that would be a financial transaction under section 1956(c)(4)(B) of this title, but such term does not include any transaction necessary to preserve a person's right to representation as guaranteed by the sixth amendment to the Constitution;

(2) the term "criminally derived property" means any property constituting, or derived from, proceeds obtained from a criminal offense; and

(3) the terms "specified unlawful activity" and "proceeds" shall have the meaning given those terms in section 1956 of this title.

18 U.S.C. § 1961. DEFINITIONS

As used in this chapter—

(1) "racketeering activity" means

(A) any act or threat involving murder, kidnapping, gambling, arson, robbery, bribery, extortion, dealing in obscene matter, or dealing in a controlled substance or listed chemical (as defined in section 102 of the Controlled Substances Act, which is chargeable under State law and punishable by imprisonment for more than one year;

(B) any act which is indictable under any of the following provisions of title 18, United States Code: Section 201 (relating to bribery), section 224 (relating to sports bribery), sections 471, 472, and 473 (relating to counterfeiting), section 659 (relating to theft from interstate shipment) if the act indictable under section 659 is felonious, section 664 (relating to embezzlement from pension and welfare funds), sections 891-894 (relating to extortionate credit transactions), section 1028 (relating to fraud and related activity in connection with identification documents) if the act indictable under section 1028 was committed for the purpose of financial gain, section 1029 (relating to fraud and related activity in connection with access devices), section 1084 (relating to the transmission of gambling information), section 1341 (relating to mail fraud), section 1343 (relating to wire fraud), section 1344 (relating to financial institution fraud), section 1425 (relating to the procurement of citizenship or nationalization unlawfully), section 1426 (relating to the reproduction of naturalization or citizenship papers), section 1427 (relating to the sale of naturalization or citizenship papers), sections 1461-1465 (relating to obscene matter), section 1503 (relating to obstruction of justice), section 1510 (relating to obstruction of criminal investigations), section 1511 (relating to the obstruction of State or local law enforcement), section 1512 (relating to tampering with a witness, victim, or an informant), section 1513 (relating to retaliating against a witness, victim, or an informant), section 1542 (relating to false statement in application and use of passport) if the act indictable under section 1542 was committed for the purpose of financial gain, section 1543 (relating to forgery or false use of passport) if the act indictable under section 1543 was committed for the purpose of financial gain, section 1544 (relating to misuse of passport) if the act indictable under section 1544 was committed for the purpose of financial gain, section 1546 (relating to fraud and misuse of visas, permits, and other documents) if the act indictable under section 1546 was committed for the purpose of financial gain, sections 1581-1592 (relating to peonage, slavery, and trafficking in persons), section 1951 (relating to interference with commerce, robbery, or extortion), section 1952 (relating to racketeering), section 1953 (relating to interstate transportation of wagering paraphernalia), section 1954 (relating to unlawful welfare fund payments), section 1955 (relating to the prohibition of illegal gambling businesses), section 1956 (relating to the laundering of monetary instruments), section 1957 (relating to engaging in monetary transactions in property derived from specified unlawful activity), section 1958 (relating to use of interstate commerce facilities in the commission of murder-for-hire), section 1960 (relating to illegal money transmitters), sections 2251, 2251A, 2252, and 2260 (relating to sexual exploitation of children), sections 2312 and 2313 (relating to interstate transportation of stolen motor vehicles), sections 2314 and 2315 (relating to interstate transportation of stolen property), section 2318 (relating to trafficking in counterfeit labels for phonorecords, computer programs or computer program documentation or packaging and copies of motion pictures or other audiovisual works), section 2319 (relating to criminal infringement of a copyright), section 2319A (relating to unauthorized fixation of and trafficking in sound recordings and music videos of live musical performances), section 2320 (relating to trafficking in goods or services bearing counterfeit marks), section 2321 (relating to trafficking in certain motor vehicles or motor vehicle parts), sections 2341-2346 (relating to trafficking in contraband cigarettes), sections 2421-24 (relating to white slave traffic), sections 175-178 (relating to biological weapons), sections 229-229F (relating to chemical weapons), section 831 (relating to nuclear materials),

(C) an act which is indictable under title 29, United States Code, section 186 (dealing with restrictions on payments and loans to labor organizations) or section 501(c) (relating to embezzlement from union funds),

(D) any offense involving fraud connected with a case under title 11 (except a case under section 157 of this title), fraud in the sale of securities, or the felonious manufacture, importation, receiving, concealment, buying, selling, or otherwise dealing in a controlled substance or listed chemical (as defined in section 102 of the Controlled Substances Act), punishable under any law of the United States,

(E) any act which is indictable under the Currency and Foreign Transactions Reporting Act,

(F) any act which is indictable under the Immigration and Nationality Act, section 274 (relating to bringing in and harboring certain aliens), section 277 (relating to aiding or assisting certain aliens to enter the United States), or section 278 (relating to importation of alien for immoral purpose) if the act indictable under such section of such Act was committed for the purpose of financial gain, or

(G) any act that is indictable under any provision listed in section 23326(g)(5)(B);

(2) "State" means any State of the United States, the District of Columbia, the Commonwealth of Puerto Rico, any territory or possession of the United States, any political subdivision, or any department, agency, or instrumentality thereof;

(3) "person" includes any individual or entity capable of holding a legal or beneficial interest in property;

(4) "enterprise" includes any individual, partnership, corporation, association, or other legal entity, and any union or group of individuals associated in fact although not a legal entity;

(5) "pattern of racketeering activity" requires at least two acts of racketeering activity, one of which occurred after the effective date of this chapter and the last of which occurred within ten years (excluding any period of imprisonment) after the commission of a prior act of racketeering activity;

(6) "unlawful debt" means a debt

(A) incurred or contracted in gambling activity which was in violation of the law of the United States, a State or political subdivision thereof, or which is unenforceable under State or Federal law in whole or in part as to principal or interest because of the laws relating to usury, and

(B) which was incurred in connection with the business of gambling in violation of the law of the United States, a State or political subdivision thereof, or the business of lending money or a thing of value at a rate usurious under State or Federal law, where the usurious rate is at least twice the enforceable rate;

. . .

18 U.S.C. § 1962. PROHIBITED ACTIVITIES

(a) It shall be unlawful for any person who has received any income derived, directly or indirectly, from a pattern of racketeering activity or through collection of an unlawful debt in which such person has participated as a principal within the meaning of section 2, title 18, United States Code, to use or invest, directly or indirectly, any part of such income, or the proceeds of such income, in acquisition of any interest in, or the establishment or operation of, any enterprise which is engaged in, or the activities of which affect, interstate or foreign commerce. A purchase of securities on the open market for purposes of investment, and without the intention of controlling or participating in the control of the issuer, or of assisting another to do so, shall not be unlawful under this subsection if the securities of the issuer held by the purchaser, the members of his immediate family, and his or their accomplices in any pattern or racketeering activity or the collection of an unlawful debt after such purchase do not amount in the aggregate to one percent of the outstanding securities of any one class, and do not confer, either in law or in fact, the power to elect one or more directors of the issuer.

(b) It shall be unlawful for any person through a pattern of racketeering activity or through collection of an unlawful debt to acquire or maintain, directly or indirectly, any interest in or control of any enterprise which is engaged in, or the activities of which affect, interstate or foreign commerce.

(c) It shall be unlawful for any person employed by or associated with any enterprise engaged in, or the activities of which affect, interstate or foreign commerce, to conduct or participate, directly or indirectly, in the conduct of such enterprise's affairs through a pattern of racketeering activity or collection of unlawful debt.

(d) It shall be unlawful for any person to conspire to violate any of the provisions of subsection (a), (b), or (c) of this section.

18 U.S.C. § 1963. CRIMINAL PENALTIES

(a) Whoever violates any provision of section 1962 of this chapter shall be fined under this title or imprisoned not more than 20 years (or for life if the violation is based on a racketeering activity for which the maximum penalty includes life imprisonment), or both, and shall forfeit to the United States, irrespective of any provision of State law—

   (1) any interest the person has acquired or maintained in violation of section 1962;
   (2) any—
        (A) interest in;
        (B) security of;
        (C) claim against; or

(D) property or contractual right of any kind affording a source of influence over;

any enterprise which the person has established, operated, controlled, conducted, or participated in the conduct of, in violation of section 1962; and

(3) any property constituting, or derived from, any proceeds which the person obtained, directly or indirectly, from racketeering activity or unlawful debt collection in violation of section 1962.

The court, in imposing sentence on such person shall order, in addition to any other sentence imposed pursuant to this section, that the person forfeit to the United States all property described in this subsection. In lieu of a fine otherwise authorized by this section, a defendant who derives profits or other proceeds from an offense may be fined not more than twice the gross profits or other proceeds.

(b) Property subject to criminal forfeiture under this section includes—

(1) real property, including things growing on, affixed to, and found in land; and

(2) tangible and intangible personal property, including rights, privileges, interests, claims, and securities.

(c) All right, title, and interest in property described in subsection (a) vests in the United States upon the commission of the act giving rise to forfeiture under this section. Any such property that is subsequently transferred to a person other than the defendant may be the subject of a special verdict of forfeiture and thereafter shall be ordered forfeited to the United States, unless the transferee establishes in a hearing pursuant to subsection (*l*) that he is a bona fide purchaser for value of such property who at the time of purchase was reasonably without cause to believe that the property was subject to forfeiture under this section.

(d)(1) Upon application of the United States, the court may enter a restraining order or injunction, require the execution of a satisfactory performance bond, or take any other action to preserve the availability of property described in subsection (a) for forfeiture under this section—

(A) upon the filing of an indictment or information charging a violation of section 1962 of this chapter and alleging that the property with respect to which the order is sought would, in the event of conviction, be subject to forfeiture under this section; or

(B) prior to the filing of such an indictment or information, if, after notice to persons appearing to have an interest in the property and opportunity for a hearing, the court determines that—

(i) there is a substantial probability that the United States will prevail on the issue of forfeiture and that failure to enter the order will result in the property being destroyed, removed from the jurisdiction of the court, or otherwise made unavailable for forfeiture; and

(ii) the need to preserve the availability of the property through the entry of the requested order outweighs the hardship on any party against whom the order is to be entered:

Provided, however, that an order entered pursuant to subparagraph (B) shall be effective for not more than ninety days, unless extended by the court for good cause shown or unless an indictment or information described in subparagraph (A) has been filed.

(2) A temporary restraining order under this subsection may be entered upon application of the United States without notice or opportunity for a hearing when an information or indictment has not yet been filed with respect to the property, if the United States demonstrates that there is probable cause to believe that the property with respect to which the order is sought would, in the event of conviction, be subject to forfeiture under this section and that provision of notice will jeopardize the availability of the property for forfeiture. Such a temporary order shall expire not more than fourteen days after the date on which it is entered, unless extended for good cause shown or unless the party against whom it is entered consents to an extension for a longer period. A hearing requested concerning an order entered under this

paragraph shall be held at the earliest possible time, and prior to the expiration of the temporary order.

(3) The court may receive and consider, at a hearing held pursuant to this subsection, evidence and information that would be inadmissible under the Federal Rules of Evidence.

(e) Upon conviction of a person under this section, the court shall enter a judgment of forfeiture of the property to the United States and shall also authorize the Attorney General to seize all property ordered forfeited upon such terms and conditions as the court shall deem proper. Following the entry of an order declaring the property forfeited, the court may, upon application of the United States, enter such appropriate restraining orders or injunctions, require the execution of satisfactory performance bonds, appoint receivers, conservators, appraisers, accountants, or trustees, or take any other action to protect the interest of the United States in the property ordered forfeited. Any income accruing to, or derived from, an enterprise or an interest in an enterprise which has been ordered forfeited under this section may be used to offset ordinary and necessary expenses to the enterprise which are required by law, or which are necessary to protect the interests of the United States or third parties.

(f) Following the seizure of property ordered forfeited under this section, the Attorney General shall direct the disposition of the property by sale or any other commercially feasible means, making due provision for the rights of any innocent persons. Any property right or interest not exercisable by, or transferable for value to, the United States shall expire and shall not revert to the defendant, nor shall the defendant or any person acting in concert with or on behalf of the defendant be eligible to purchase forfeited property at any sale held by the United States. Upon application of a person, other than the defendant or a person acting in concert with or on behalf of the defendant, the court may restrain or stay the sale or disposition of the property pending the conclusion of any appeal of the criminal case giving rise to the forfeiture, if the applicant demonstrates that proceeding with the sale or disposition of the property will result in irreparable injury, harm or loss to him. Notwithstanding 31 U.S.C.

§ 3302(b), the proceeds of any sale or other disposition of property forfeited under this section and any moneys forfeited shall be used to pay all proper expenses for the forfeiture and the sale, including expenses of seizure, maintenance and custody of the property pending its disposition, advertising and court costs. The Attorney General shall deposit in the Treasury any amounts of such proceeds or moneys remaining after the payment of such expenses.

(g) With respect to property ordered forfeited under this section, the Attorney General is authorized to—

    (1) grant petitions for mitigation or remission of forfeiture, restore forfeited property to victims of a violation of this chapter, or take any other action to protect the rights of innocent persons which is in the interest of justice and which is not inconsistent with the provisions of this chapter;

    (2) compromise claims arising under this section;

    (3) award compensation to persons providing information resulting in a forfeiture under this section;

    (4) direct the disposition by the United States of all property ordered forfeited under this section by public sale or any other commercially feasible means, making due provision for the rights of innocent persons; and

    (5) take appropriate measures necessary to safeguard and maintain property ordered forfeited under this section pending its disposition.

(h) The Attorney General may promulgate regulations with respect to—

    (1) making reasonable efforts to provide notice to persons who may have an interest in property ordered forfeited under this section;

    (2) granting petitions for remission or mitigation of forfeiture;

    (3) the restitution of property to victims of an offense petitioning for remission or mitigation of forfeiture under this chapter;

    (4) the disposition by the United States of forfeited property by public sale or other commercially feasible means;

(5) the maintenance and safekeeping of any property forfeited under this section pending its disposition; and

(6) the compromise of claims arising under this chapter.

Pending the promulgation of such regulations, all provisions of law relating to the disposition of property, or the proceeds from the sale thereof, or the remission or mitigation of forfeitures for violation of the customs laws, and the compromise of claims and the award of compensation to informers in respect of such forfeitures shall apply to forfeitures incurred, or alleged to have been incurred, under the provisions of this section, insofar as applicable and not inconsistent with the provisions hereof. Such duties as are imposed upon the Customs Service or any person with respect to the disposition of property under the customs law shall be performed under this chapter by the Attorney General.

(i) Except as provided in subsection (*l*), no party claiming an interest in property subject to forfeiture under this section may—

(1) intervene in a trial or appeal of a criminal case involving the forfeiture of such property under this section; or

(2) commence an action at law or equity against the United States concerning the validity of his alleged interest in the property subsequent to the filing of an indictment or information alleging that the property is subject to forfeiture under this section.

(j) The district courts of the United States shall have jurisdiction to enter orders as provided in this section without regard to the location of any property which may be subject to forfeiture under this section or which has been ordered forfeited under this section.

(k) In order to facilitate the identification or location of property declared forfeited and to facilitate the disposition of petitions for remission or mitigation of forfeiture, after the entry of an order declaring property forfeited to the United States the court may, upon application of the United States, order that the testimony of any witness relating to the property forfeited be taken by deposition and that any designated book, paper, document, record, recording, or other material not privileged be produced at the same time and place, in the same manner as provided for the taking of depositions under Rule 15 of the Federal Rules of Criminal Procedure.

(*l*)(1) Following the entry of an order of forfeiture under this section, the United States shall publish notice of the order and of its intent to dispose of the property in such manner as the Attorney General may direct. The Government may also, to the extent practicable, provide direct written notice to any person known to have alleged an interest in the property that is the subject of the order of forfeiture as a substitute for published notice as to those persons so notified.

(2) Any person, other than the defendant, asserting a legal interest in property which has been ordered forfeited to the United States pursuant to this section may, within thirty days of the final publication of notice or his receipt of notice under paragraph (*1*), whichever is earlier, petition the court for a hearing to adjudicate the validity of his alleged interest in the property. The hearing shall be held before the court alone, without a jury.

(3) The petition shall be signed by the petitioner under penalty of perjury and shall set forth the nature and extent of the petitioner's right, title, or interest in the property, the time and circumstances of the petitioner's acquisition of the right, title, or interest in the property, any additional facts supporting the petitioner's claim, and the relief sought.

(4) The hearing on the petition shall, to the extent practicable and consistent with the interests of justice, be held within thirty days of the filing of the petition. The court may consolidate the hearing on the petition with a hearing on any other petition filed by a person other than the defendant under this subsection.

(5) At the hearing, the petitioner may testify and present evidence and witnesses on his own behalf, and cross-examine witnesses who appear at the hearing. The United States may present evidence and witnesses in rebuttal and in defense of its claim to the property and cross-examine witnesses who appear at the hearing. In addition to testimony and evidence presented at the hearing, the court shall consider the relevant portions of the

record of the criminal case which resulted in the order of forfeiture.

(6) If, after the hearing, the court determines that the petitioner has established by a preponderance of the evidence that—

(A) the petitioner has a legal right, title, or interest in the property, and such right, title, or interest renders the order of forfeiture invalid in whole or in part because the right, title, or interest was vested in the petitioner rather than the defendant or was superior to any right, title, or interest of the defendant at the time of the commission of the acts which gave rise to the forfeiture of the property under this section; or

(B) the petitioner is a bona fide purchaser for value of the right, title, or interest in the property and was at the time of purchase reasonably without cause to believe that the property was subject to forfeiture under this section;

the court shall amend the order of forfeiture in accordance with its determination.

(7) Following the court's disposition of all petitions filed under this subsection, or if no such petitions are filed following the expiration of the period provided in paragraph (2) for the filing of such petitions, the United States shall have clear title to property that is the subject of the order of forfeiture and may warrant good title to any subsequent purchaser or transferee.

(m) If any of the property described in subsection (a), as a result of any act or omission of the defendant—

(1) cannot be located upon the exercise of due diligence;

(2) has been transferred or sold to, or deposited with, a third party;

(3) has been placed beyond the jurisdiction of the court;

(4) has been substantially diminished in value; or

(5) has been commingled with other property which cannot be divided without difficulty;

the court shall order the forfeiture of any other property of the defendant up to the value of any property described in paragraphs (1) through (5).

18 U.S.C. § 1964. CIVIL REMEDIES

(a) The district courts of the United States shall have jurisdiction to prevent and restrain violations of section 1962 of this chapter by issuing appropriate orders, including, but not limited to: ordering any person to divest himself of any interest, direct or indirect, in any enterprise; imposing reasonable restrictions on the future activities or investments of any person, including, but not limited to, prohibiting any person from engaging in the same type of endeavor as the enterprise engaged in, the activities of which affect interstate or foreign commerce; or ordering dissolution or reorganization of any enterprise, making due provision for the rights of innocent persons.

(b) The Attorney General may institute proceedings under this section. Pending final determination thereof, the court may at any time enter such restraining orders or prohibitions, or take such other actions, including the acceptance of satisfactory performance bonds, as it shall deem proper.

(c) Any person injured in his business or property by reason of a violation of section 1962 of this chapter may sue therefor in any appropriate United States district court and shall recover threefold the damages he sustains and the cost of the suit, including a reasonable attorney's fee, except that no person may rely upon any conduct that would have been actionable as fraud in the purchase or sale of securities to establish a violation of section 1962. The exception contained in the preceding sentence does not apply to an action against any person that is criminally convicted in connection with the fraud, in which case the statute of limitations shall start to run on the date on which the conviction becomes final.

(d) A final judgment or decree rendered in favor of the United States in any criminal proceeding brought by the United States under this chapter shall estop the defendant from denying the essential allegations of the criminal offense in any subsequent civil proceeding brought by the United States.

18 U.S.C. § 3559. SENTENCING CLASSIFICATION OF OFFENSES

(a) Classification.—An offense that is not specifically classified by a letter grade in the section defining it, is classified if the maximum term of imprisonment authorized is—

(1) life imprisonment, or if the maximum penalty is death, as a Class A felony;

(2) twenty-five years or more, as a Class B felony;

(3) less than twenty-five years but ten or more years, as a Class C felony;

(4) less than ten years but five or more years, as a Class D felony;

(5) less than five years but more than one year, as a Class E felony;

(6) one year or less but more than six months, as a Class A misdemeanor;

(7) six months or less but more than thirty days, as a Class B misdemeanor;

(8) thirty days or less but more than five days, as a Class C misdemeanor; or

(9) five days or less, or if no imprisonment is authorized, as an infraction.

(b) Effect of classification.—Except as provided in subsection (c), an offense classified under subsection (a) carries all the incidents assigned to the applicable letter designation, except that, the maximum term of imprisonment is the term authorized by the law describing the offense.

. . .

18 U.S.C. § 3561. SENTENCE OF PROBATION

(a) In general.—A defendant who has been found guilty of an offense may be sentenced to a term of probation unless—

(1) the offense is a Class A or Class B felony and the defendant is an individual;

(2) the offense is an offense for which probation has been expressly precluded; or

(3) the defendant is sentenced at the same time to a term of imprisonment for the same or a different offense that is not a petty offense.

(b) Domestic violence offenders.—A defendant who has been convicted for the first time of a domestic violence crime shall be sentenced to a term of probation if not sentenced to a term of imprisonment. The term "domestic violence crime" means a crime of violence for which the defendant may be prosecuted in a court of the United States in which the victim or intended victim is the spouse, former spouse, intimate partner, former intimate partner, child, or former child of the defendant, or any other relative of the defendant.

(c) Authorized terms.—The authorized terms of probation are—

(1) for a felony, not less than one nor more than five years;

(2) for a misdemeanor, not more than five years; and

(3) for an infraction, not more than one year.

18 U.S.C. § 3571. SENTENCE OF FINE

(a) In general.—A defendant who has been found guilty of an offense may be sentenced to pay a fine.

(b) Fines for individuals.—Except as provided in subsection (e) of this section, an individual who has been found guilty of an offense may be fined not more than the greatest of—

(1) the amount specified in the law setting forth the offense;

(2) the applicable amount under subsection (d) of this section;

(3) for a felony, not more than $250,000;

(4) for a misdemeanor resulting in death, not more than $250,000;

(5) for a Class A misdemeanor that does not result in death, not more than $100,000;

(6) for a Class B or C misdemeanor that does not result in death, not more than $5,000; or

(7) for an infraction, not more than $5,000.

(c) Fines for organizations.—Except as provided in subsection (e) of this section, an organization that has been found guilty of an offense may be fined not more than the greatest of—

(1) the amount specified in the law setting forth the offense;

(2) the applicable amount under subsection (d) of this section;

(3) for a felony, not more than $500,000;

(4) for a misdemeanor resulting in death, not more than $500,000;

(5) for a Class A misdemeanor that does not result in death, not more than $200,000;

(6) for a Class B or C misdemeanor that does not result in death, not more than $10,000; or

(7) for an infraction, not more than $10,000.

(d) Alternative fine based on gain or loss.—If any person derives pecuniary gain from the offense, or if the offense results in pecuniary loss to a person other than the defendant, the defendant may be fined not more than the greater of twice the gross gain or twice the gross loss, unless imposition of a fine under this subsection would unduly complicate or prolong the sentencing process.

(e) Special rule for lower fine specified in substantive provision.—If a law setting forth an offense specifies no fine or a fine that is lower than the fine otherwise applicable under this section and such law, by specific reference, exempts the offense from the applicability of the fine otherwise applicable under this section, the defendant may not be fined more than the amount specified in the law setting forth the offense.

18 U.S.C. § 3572. IMPOSITION OF A SENTENCE OF FINE AND RELATED MATTERS

(a) Factors to be considered.—In determining whether to impose a fine, and the amount, time for payment, and method of payment of a fine, the court shall consider, in addition to the factors set forth in section 3553(a)—

(1) the defendant's income, earning capacity, and financial resources;

(2) the burden that the fine will impose upon the defendant, any person who is financially dependent on the defendant, or any other person (including a government) that would be responsible for the welfare of any person financially dependent on the

defendant, relative to the burden that alternative punishments would impose;

(3) any pecuniary loss inflicted upon others as a result of the offense;

(4) whether restitution is ordered or made and the amount of such restitution;

(5) the need to deprive the defendant of illegally obtained gains from the offense;

(6) the expected costs to the government of any imprisonment, supervised release, or probation component of the sentence;

(7) whether the defendant can pass on to consumers or other persons the expense of the fine; and

(8) if the defendant is an organization, the size of the organization and any measure taken by the organization to discipline any officer, director, employee, or agent of the organization responsible for the offense and to prevent a recurrence of such an offense.

(b) Fine not to impair ability to make restitution.—If, as a result of a conviction, the defendant has the obligation to make restitution to a victim of the offense, other than the United States, the court shall impose a fine or other monetary penalty only to the extent that such fine or penalty will not impair the ability of the defendant to make restitution.

. . .

(d) Time, method of payment, and related items.

(1) A person sentenced to pay a fine or other monetary penalty, including restitution, shall make such payment immediately, unless, in the interest of justice, the court provides for payment on a date certain or in installments. If the court provides for payment in installments, the installments shall be in equal monthly payments over the period provided by the court, unless the court establishes another schedule.

(2) If the judgment, or, in the case of a restitution order, the order, permits other than immediate payment, the length of time over which scheduled payments will be made shall be set by the

court, but shall be the shortest time in which full payment can reasonably be made.

(3) A judgment for a fine which permits payments in installments shall include a requirement that the defendant will notify the court of any material change in the defendant's economic circumstances that might affect the defendant's ability to pay the fine. Upon receipt of such notice the court may, on its own motion or the motion of any party, adjust the payment schedule, or require immediate payment in full, as the interests of justice require.

(e) Alternative sentence precluded.—At the time a defendant is sentenced to pay a fine, the court may not impose an alternative sentence to be carried out if the fine is not paid.

(f) Responsibility for payment of monetary obligation relating to organization.—If a sentence includes a fine, special assessment, restitution, or other monetary obligation (including interest) with respect to an organization, each individual authorized to make disbursements for the organization has a duty to pay the obligation from assets of the organization. If such an obligation is imposed on a director, officer, shareholder, employee, or agent of an organization, payments may not be made, directly or indirectly, from assets of the organization, unless the court finds that such payment is expressly permissible under applicable State law.

. . .

18 U.S.C. § 3581. SENTENCE OF IMPRISONMENT

(a) In general.—A defendant who has been found guilty of an offense may be sentenced to a term of imprisonment.

(b) Authorized terms.—The authorized terms of imprisonment are—

(1) for a Class A felony, the duration of the defendant's life or any period of time;

(2) for a Class B felony, not more than twenty-five years;

(3) for a Class C felony, not more than twelve years;

(4) for a Class D felony, not more than six years;

(5) for a Class E felony, not more than three years;

(6) for a Class A misdemeanor, not more than one year;

(7) for a Class B misdemeanor, not more than six months;

(8) for a Class C misdemeanor, not more than thirty days; and

(9) for an infraction, not more than five days.

18 U.S.C. § 3582. IMPOSITION OF A SENTENCE OF IMPRISONMENT

(a) Factors to be considered in imposing a term of imprisonment.—The court, in determining whether to impose a term of imprisonment, and, if a term of imprisonment is to be imposed, in determining the length of the term, shall consider the factors set forth in section 3553(a) to the extent that they are applicable, recognizing that imprisonment is not an appropriate means of promoting correction and rehabilitation. In determining whether to make a recommendation concerning the type of prison facility appropriate for the defendant, the court shall consider any pertinent policy statements issued by the Sentencing Commission pursuant to 28 U.S.C. § 994(a)(2).

. . .

18 U.S.C. § 6002. IMMUNITY GENERALLY

Whenever a witness refuses, on the basis of his privilege against self-incrimination, to testify or provide other information in a proceeding before or ancillary to—

(1) a court or grand jury of the United States,

(2) an agency of the United States, or

(3) either House of Congress, a joint committee of the two Houses, or a committee or a subcommittee of either House,

and the person presiding over the proceeding communicates to the witness an order issued under this title, the witness may not refuse to comply with the order on the basis of his privilege against self-incrimination; but no testimony or other information compelled under the order (or any information directly or indirectly derived from such testimony or other information) may be used against the witness in any criminal case, except a prosecution for perjury, giving a false statement, or otherwise failing to comply with the order.

TITLE 26
INTERNAL REVENUE CODE

26 U.S.C. § 6050I. RETURNS RELATING TO CASH RECEIVED IN TRADE OR BUSINESS, ETC.

(a) Cash receipts of more than $10,000. Any person—

(1) who is engaged in a trade or business, and

(2) who, in the course of such trade or business, receives more than $10,000 in cash in 1 transaction (or 2 or more related transactions),

shall make the return described in subsection (b) with respect to such transaction (or related transactions) at such time as the Secretary may by regulations prescribe.

(b) Form and manner of returns. A return is described in this subsection if such return—

(1) is in such form as the Secretary may prescribe,

(2) contains—

(A) the name, address, and TIN of the person from whom the cash was received,

(B) the amount of cash received,

(C) the date and nature of the transaction, and

(D) such other information as the Secretary may prescribe.

(c) Exceptions.

(1) Cash received by financial institutions. Subsection (a) shall not apply to—

(A) cash received in a transaction reported under title 31, United States Code, if the Secretary determines that reporting under this section would duplicate the reporting to the Treasury under title 31, United States Code, or

(B) cash received by any financial institution (as defined in subparagraphs (A), (B), (C), (D), (E), (F), (G), (J), (K), (R), and (S) of section 5312(a)(2) of title 31, United States Code).

(2) Transactions occurring outside the United States. Except to the extent provided in regulations prescribed by the

Secretary, subsection (a) shall not apply to any transaction if the entire transaction occurs outside the United States.

(d) Cash includes foreign currency and certain monetary instruments. For purposes of this section, the term 'cash' includes—

(1) foreign currency, and

(2) to the extent provided in regulations prescribed by the Secretary, any monetary instrument (whether or not in bearer form) with a face amount of not more than $10,000.

Paragraph (2) shall not apply to any check drawn on the account of the writer in a financial institution referred to in subsection (c)(1)(B).

(e) Statements to be furnished to persons with respect to whom information is required. Every person required to make a return under subsection (a) shall furnish to each person whose name is required to be set forth in such return a written statement showing—

(1) the name, address, and phone number of the information contact of the person required to make such return, and

(2) the aggregate amount of cash described in subsection (a) received by the person required to make such return.

The written statement required under the preceding sentence shall be furnished to the person on or before January 31 of the year following the calendar year for which the return under subsection (a) was required to be made.

(f) Structuring transactions to evade reporting requirements prohibited.

(1) In general. No person shall for the purpose of evading the return requirements of this section—

(A) cause or attempt to cause a trade or business to fail to file a return required under this section,

(B) cause or attempt to cause a trade or business to file a return required under this section that contains a material omission or misstatement of fact, or

(C) structure or assist in structuring, or attempt to structure or assist in structuring, any transaction with one or more trades or businesses.

(2) Penalties. A person violating paragraph (1) of this subsection shall be subject to the same civil and criminal sanctions applicable to a person which fails to file or completes a false or incorrect return under this section.

(g) Cash received by criminal court clerks.

(1) In general. Every clerk of a Federal or State criminal court who receives more than $10,000 in cash as bail for any individual charged with a specified criminal offense shall make a return described in paragraph (2) (at such time as the Secretary may by regulations prescribe) with respect to the receipt of such bail.

(2) Return. A return is described in this paragraph if such return—

(A) is in such form as the Secretary may prescribe, and

(B) contains—

(i) the name, address, and TIN of—

(I) the individual charged with the specified criminal offense, and

(II) each person posting the bail (other than a person licensed as a bail bondsman),

(ii) the amount of cash received,

(iii) the date the cash was received, and

(iv) such other information as the Secretary may prescribe.

(3) Specified criminal offense. For purposes of this subsection, the term "specified criminal offense" means—

(A) any Federal criminal offense involving a controlled substance,

(B) racketeering (as defined in section 1951, 1952, or 1955 of title 18, United States Code),

(C) money laundering (as defined in section 1956 or 1957 of such title), and

(D) any State criminal offense substantially similar to an offense described in subparagraph (A), (B), or (C).

(4) Information to federal prosecutors. Each clerk required to include on a return under paragraph (1) the information described in paragraph (2)(B) with respect to an individual described in

paragraph (2)(B)(i)(I) shall furnish (at such time as the Secretary may by regulations prescribe) a written statement showing such information to the United States Attorney for the jurisdiction in which such individual resides and the jurisdiction in which the specified criminal offense occurred.

(5) Information to payors of bail. Each clerk required to make a return under paragraph (1) shall furnish (at such time as the Secretary may by regulations prescribe) to each person whose name is required to be set forth in such return by reason of paragraph (2)(B)(i)(II) a written statement showing—

(A) the name and address of the clerk's office required to make the return, and

(B) the aggregate amount of cash described in paragraph (1) received by such clerk.

26 U.S.C. § 7201. ATTEMPT TO EVADE OR DEFEAT TAX

Any person who willfully attempts in any manner to evade or defeat any tax imposed by this title or the payment thereof shall, in addition to other penalties provided by law, be guilty of a felony and, upon conviction thereof, shall be fined not more than $100,000 ($500,000 in the case of a corporation), or imprisoned not more than 5 years, or both, together with the costs of prosecution.

26 U.S.C. § 7203. WILLFUL FAILURE TO FILE RETURN, SUPPLY INFORMATION, OR PAY TAX

Any person required under this title to pay any estimated tax or tax, or required by this title or by regulations made under authority thereof to make a return, keep any records, or supply any information, who willfully fails to pay such estimated tax or tax, make such return, keep such records, or supply such information, at the time or times required by law or regulations, shall, in addition to other penalties provided by law, be guilty of a misdemeanor and, upon conviction thereof, shall be fined not more than $25,000 ($100,000 in the case of a corporation), or imprisoned not more than 1 year, or both, together with the costs of prosecution. In the case of any person with respect to whom there is a failure to pay any estimated tax, this section shall not apply to such person with respect to such failure if there is no addition to tax under section 6654 or 6655 with respect to such failure. In the case of a willful violation of any provision of section 6050I, the first sentence of this section shall be applied by substituting "felony" for "misdemeanor" and "5 years" for "1 year".

26 U.S.C. § 7206. FRAUD AND FALSE STATEMENTS

Any person who—

(1) Declaration under penalties of perjury. Willfully makes and subscribes any return, statement, or other document, which contains or is verified by a written declaration that it is made under the penalties of perjury, and which he does not believe to be true and correct as to every material matter; or

(2) Aid or assistance. Willfully aids or assists in, or procures, counsels, or advises the preparation or presentation under, or in connection with any matter arising under, the internal revenue laws, of a return, affidavit, claim, or other document, which is fraudulent or is false as to any material matter, whether or not such falsity or fraud is with the knowledge or consent of the person authorized or required to present such return, affidavit, claim, or document;

. . .

shall be guilty of a felony and, upon conviction thereof, shall be fined not more than $100,000 ($500,000 in the case of a corporation), or imprisoned not more than 3 years, or both, together with the costs of prosecution.

TITLE 31
MONEY AND FINANCE

31 U.S.C. § 5313.[1] REPORTS ON DOMESTIC COINS AND CURRENCY TRANSACTIONS

(a) When a domestic financial institution is involved in a transaction for the payment, receipt, or transfer of United States coins or currency (or other monetary instruments the Secretary of the Treasury prescribes), in an amount, denomination, or amount and denomination, or under circumstances the Secretary prescribes by regulation, the institution and any other participant in the transaction the Secretary may prescribe shall file a report on the transaction at the time and in the way the Secretary prescribes. A participant acting for another person shall make the report as the agent or bailee of the person and identify the person for whom the transaction is being made.

. . .

31 U.S.C. § 5314.[2] RECORDS AND REPORTS ON FOREIGN FINANCIAL AGENCY TRANSACTIONS

(a) Considering the need to avoid impeding or controlling the export or import of monetary instruments and the need to avoid burdening unreasonably a person making a transaction with a foreign financial agency, the Secretary of the Treasury shall require a resident or citizen of the United States or a person in, and doing business in, the United States, to keep records, file reports, or keep records and file reports, when the resident, citizen, or person makes a transaction or maintains a relation for any person with a foreign financial agency. The records and reports shall contain the following information in the way and to the extent the Secretary prescribes:

    (1) the identity and address of participants in a transaction or relationship.

    (2) the legal capacity in which a participant is acting.

---

[1]Formerly codified at 31 U.S.C. §§ 1081, 1082, 1083.—ED.
[2]Formerly codified at 31 U.S.C. §§ 1121, 1122.—ED.

(3) the identity of real parties in interest.

(4) a description of the transaction.

(b) The Secretary may prescribe—

(1) a reasonable classification of persons subject to or exempt from a requirement under this section or a regulation under this section;

(2) a foreign country to which a requirement or a regulation under this section applies if the Secretary decides applying the requirement or regulation to all foreign countries is unnecessary or undesirable;

(3) the magnitude of transactions subject to a requirement or a regulation under this section;

(4) the kind of transaction subject to or exempt from a requirement or a regulation under this section; and

(5) other matters the Secretary considers necessary to carry out this section or a regulation under this section.

(c) A person shall be required to disclose a record required to be kept under this section or under a regulation under this section only as required by law.

31 U.S.C. § 5316.[3] REPORTS ON EXPORTING AND IMPORTING MONETARY INSTRUMENTS

(a) Except as provided in subsection (c) of this section, a person or an agent or bailee of the person shall file a report under subsection (b) of this section when the person, agent, or bailee knowingly—

(1) transports, is about to transport, or has transported, monetary instruments of more than $10,000 at one time—

(A) from a place in the United States to or through a place outside the United States; or

(B) to a place in the United States from or through a place outside the United States; or

---

[3]Formerly codified at 31 U.S.C. § 1101.—ED.

(2) receives monetary instruments of more than $10,000 at one time transported into the United States from or through a place outside the United States.

(b) A report under this section shall be filed at the time and place the Secretary of the Treasury prescribes. The report shall contain the following information to the extent the Secretary prescribes:

(1) the legal capacity in which the person filing the report is acting.

(2) the origin, destination, and route of the monetary instruments.

(3) when the monetary instruments are not legally and beneficially owned by the person transporting the instruments, or if the person transporting the instruments personally is not going to use them, the identity of the person that gave the instruments to the person transporting them, the identity of the person who is to receive them, or both.

(4) the amount and kind of monetary instruments transported.

(5) additional information.

(c) This section or a regulation under this section does not apply to a common carrier of passengers when a passenger possesses a monetary instrument, or to a common carrier of goods if the shipper does not declare the instrument.

(d) Cumulation of closely related events.—The Secretary of the Treasury may prescribe regulations under this section defining the term "at one time" for purposes of subsection (a). Such regulations may permit the cumulation of closely related events in order that such events may collectively be considered to occur at one time for the purposes of subsection (a).

31 U.S.C. § 5322.[4]   CRIMINAL PENALTIES

(a) A person willfully violating this subchapter or a regulation prescribed or order issued under this subchapter (except section 5315 or 5324 of this title or a regulation prescribed under section 5315 or

---

[4]Formerly codified at 31 U.S.C. §§ 1058, 1059, 1054.—ED.

5324), or willfully violating a regulation prescribed under section 21 of the Federal Deposit Insurance Act or section 123 of Public Law 91-508, shall be fined not more than $250,000, or imprisoned for not more than five years, or both.

(b) A person willfully violating this subchapter or a regulation prescribed or order issued under this subchapter (except section 5315 or 5324 of this title or a regulation prescribed under section 5315 or 5324), or willfully violating a regulation prescribed under section 21 of the Federal Deposit Insurance Act or section 123 of Public Law 91-508, while violating another law of the United States or as part of a pattern of any illegal activity involving more than $100,000 in a 12-month period, shall be fined not more than $500,000, imprisoned for not more than 10 years, or both.

(c) For a violation of section 5318(a)(2) of this title or a regulation prescribed under section 5318(a)(2), a separate violation occurs for each day the violation continues and at each office, branch, or place of business at which a violation occurs or continues.

(d) A financial institution or agency that violates any provision of subsection (i) or (j) of section 5318, or any special measures imposed under section 5318A, or any regulation prescribed under subsection (i) or (j) of section 5318 or section 5318A, shall be fined in an amount equal to not less than 2 times the amount of the transaction, but not more than $1,000,000.

31 U.S.C. § 5323. REWARDS FOR INFORMANTS

(a) The Secretary may pay a reward to an individual who provides original information which leads to a recovery of a criminal fine, civil penalty, or forfeiture, which exceeds $50,000, for a violation of this chapter.

(b) The Secretary shall determine the amount of a reward under this section. The Secretary may not award more than 25 per centum of the net amount of the fine, penalty, or forfeiture collected or $150,000, whichever is less.

(c) An officer or employee of the United States, a State, or a local government who provides information described in subsection (a) in the performance of official duties is not eligible for a reward under this section.

(d) There are authorized to be appropriated such sums as may be necessary to carry out the provisions of this section.

31 U.S.C. § 5324. STRUCTURING TRANSACTIONS TO EVADE REPORTING REQUIREMENT PROHIBITED

(a) Domestic coin and currency transactions involving financial institutions.—No person shall, for the purpose of evading the reporting requirements of section 5313(a) or section 5325 or any regulation prescribed under such section, the reporting or recordkeeping requirements imposed by any order issued under section 5326, or the recordkeeping requirements imposed by any regulation prescribed under section 21 of the Federal Deposit Insurance Act or section 123 of Public Law 91-508—

(1) cause or attempt to cause a domestic financial institution to fail to file a report required under section 5313(a) or 5325 or any regulation prescribed under any such section, to file a report or to maintain a record required by any order issued under section 5326, or to maintain a record required pursuant to any regulation prescribed under section 5326, or to maintain a record required pursuant to any regulation prescribed under section 21 of the Federal Deposit Insurance Act or section 123 of Public Law 91-508;

(2) cause or attempt to cause a domestic financial institution to file a report required under section 5313(a) or section 5325 or any regulation prescribed under any such section, to file a report or to maintain a record required by any order issued under section 5326, or to maintain a record required pursuant to any regulation prescribed under section 5326, or to maintain a record required pursuant to any regulation prescribed under section 21 of the Federal Deposit Insurance Act or section 123 of Public Law 91-508, that contains a material omission or misstatement of fact; or

(3) structure or assist in structuring, or attempt to structure or assist in structuring, any transaction with one or more domestic financial institutions.

. . .

(d) Criminal penalty.—

(1) In general.—Whoever violates this section shall be fined in accordance with title 18, United States Code, imprisoned for not more than 5 years, or both.

(2) Enhanced penalty for aggravated cases.—Whoever violates this section while violating another law of the United States or as part of a pattern of any illegal activity involving more than $ 100,000 in a 12-month period shall be fined twice the amount provided in subsection (b)(3) or (c)(3) (as the case may be) of section 3571 of title 18, United States Code, imprisoned for not more than 10 years, or both.

TITLE 33
NAVIGATION AND NAVIGABLE WATERS

CHAPTER 9. PROTECTION OF NAVIGABLE WATERS AND OF HARBOR AND RIVER IMPROVEMENTS GENERALLY

33 U.S.C. § 407. DEPOSIT OF REFUSE IN NAVIGABLE WATERS GENERALLY

It shall not be lawful to throw, discharge, or deposit, or cause, suffer, or procure to be thrown, discharged, or deposited either from or out of any ship, barge, or other floating craft of any kind, or from the shore, wharf, manufacturing establishment, or mill of any kind, any refuse matter of any kind or description whatever other than that flowing from streets and sewers and passing therefrom in a liquid state, into any navigable water of the United States, or into any tributary of any navigable water from which the same shall float or be washed into such navigable water; and it shall not be lawful to deposit, or cause, suffer, or procure to be deposited material of any kind in any place on the bank of any navigable water, or on the bank of any tributary of any navigable water, where the same shall be liable to be washed into such navigable water, either by ordinary or high tides, or by storms or floods, or otherwise, whereby navigation shall or may be impeded or obstructed: Provided, That nothing herein contained shall extend to, apply to, or prohibit the operations in connection with the improvement of navigable waters or construction of public works, considered necessary and proper by the United States officers supervising such improvement or public work: And provided further, That the Secretary of the Army, whenever in the judgment of the Chief of Engineers anchorage and navigation will not be injured thereby, may permit the deposit of any material above mentioned in navigable waters, within limits to be defined and under conditions to be prescribed by him, provided application is made to him prior to depositing such material; and whenever any permit is so granted the conditions thereof shall be strictly complied with, and any violation thereof shall be unlawful.

CHAPTER 26. WATER POLLUTION PREVENTION AND CONTROL

33 U.S.C. § 1311. EFFLUENT LIMITATIONS

(a) Illegality of pollutant discharges except in compliance with law. Except as in compliance with this section and sections 302, 306, 307, 318, 402, and 404 of this Act [33 U.S.C. §§ 1312, 1316, 1317, 1328, 1342, 1344], the discharge of any pollutant by any person shall be unlawful.

. . .

33 U.S.C. § 1319. ENFORCEMENT

. . .

(c) **Criminal penalties.**

(1) **Negligent violations.**—Any person who—

(A) negligently violates section 301, 302, 306, 307, 308, 311(b)(3), 318, or 405 of this Act [33 U.S.C. §§ 1311, 1312, 1316, 1317, 1318, 1321(b)(3), 1328, or 1345], or any permit condition or limitation implementing any of such sections in a permit issued under section 402 of this Act by the Administrator or by a State, or any requirement imposed in a pretreatment program approved under section 402(a)(3) or 402(b)(8) of this Act [33 U.S.C. §§ 1342(a)(3) or (b)(8)] or in a permit issued under section 404 of this Act [33 U.S.C. § 1344] by the Secretary of the Army or by a State; or

(B) negligently introduces into a sewer system or into a publicly owned treatment works any pollutant or hazardous substance which such person knew or reasonably should have known could cause personal injury or property damage or, other than in compliance with all applicable Federal, State, or local requirements or permits, which causes such treatment works to violate any effluent limitation or condition in any permit issued to the treatment works under section 402 of this

Act [33 U.S.C. § 1342] by the Administrator or a State; shall be punished by a fine of not less than $2,500 nor more than $25,000 per day of violation, or by imprisonment for not more than 1 year, or by both. If a conviction of a person is for a violation committed after a first conviction of such person under this paragraph, punishment shall be by a fine of not more than $50,000 per day of violation, or by imprisonment of not more than 2 years, or by both.

(2) Knowing violations.—Any person who—

(A) knowingly violates section 301, 302, 306, 307, 308, 311(b)(3), 318, or 405 of this Act [33 U.S.C. §§ 1311, 1312, 1316, 1318, 1321(b)(3), 1328, or 1345], or any permit condition or limitation implementing any of such sections in a permit issued under section 402 of this Act [33 U.S.C. § 1342] by the Administrator or by a State, or any requirement imposed in a pretreatment program approved under section 402(a)(3) or 402(b)(8) of this Act [33 U.S.C. § 1342(a)(3) or (b)(8)] or in a permit issued under section 404 of this Act [33 U.S.C. § 1344] by the Secretary of the Army or by a State; or

(B) knowingly introduces into a sewer system or into a publicly owned treatment works any pollutant or hazardous substance which such person knew or reasonably should have known could cause personal injury or property damage or, other than in compliance with all applicable Federal, State, or local requirements or permits, which causes such treatment works to violate any effluent limitation or condition in a permit issued to the treatment works under section 402 of this Act [33 U.S.C. § 1342] by the Administrator or a State;

shall be punished by a fine of not less than $5,000 nor more than $50,000 per day of violation, or by imprisonment for not more than 3 years, or by both. If a conviction of a person is for a violation committed after a first conviction of such person under this paragraph, punishment shall be by a fine of not more than $100,000 per day of violation, or by imprisonment of not more than 6 years, or by both.

(3) Knowing endangerment.

(A) General rule.—Any person who knowingly violates section 301, 302, 303, 306, 307, 308, 311(b)(3), 318, or 405 of this Act [33 U.S.C. §§ 1311, 1312, 1313, 1316, 1317, 1318, 1321(b)(3), 1328, or 1345], or any permit condition or limitation implementing any of such sections in a permit issued under section 402 of this Act [33 U.S.C. § 1342] by the Administrator or by a State, or in a permit issued under section 404 of this Act [33 U.S.C. § 1344] by the Secretary of the Army or by a State, and who knows at that time that he thereby places another person in imminent danger of death or serious bodily injury, shall, upon conviction, be subject to a fine of not more than $250,000 or imprisonment of not more than 15 years, or both. A person which is an organization shall, upon conviction of violating this subparagraph, be subject to a fine of not more than $1,000,000. If a conviction of a person is for a violation committed after a first conviction of such person under this paragraph, the maximum punishment shall be doubled with respect to both fine and imprisonment.

(B) Additional provisions.—For the purpose of subparagraph (A) of this paragraph—

(i) in determining whether a defendant who is an individual knew that his conduct placed another person in imminent danger of death or serious bodily injury—

(I) the person is responsible only for actual awareness or actual belief that he possessed; and

(II) knowledge possessed by a person other than the defendant but not by the defendant himself may not be attributed to the defendant;

except that in proving the defendant's possession of actual knowledge, circumstantial evidence may be used, including evidence that the defendant took affirmative steps to shield himself from relevant information;

(ii) it is an affirmative defense to prosecution that the conduct charged was consented to by the person endangered and that the danger and conduct charged were reasonably foreseeable hazards of—

> (I) an occupation, a business, or a profession; or

> (II) medical treatment or medical or scientific experimentation conducted by professionally approved methods and such other person had been made aware of the risks involved prior to giving consent;

and such defense may be established under this subparagraph by a preponderance of the evidence;

> (iii) the term "organization" means a legal entity, other than a government, established or organized for any purpose, and such term includes a corporation, company, association, firm, partnership, joint stock company, foundation, institution, trust, society, union, or any other association of persons; and

> (iv) the term "serious bodily injury" means bodily injury which involves a substantial risk of death, unconsciousness, extreme physical pain, protracted and obvious disfigurement, or protracted loss or impairment of the function of a bodily member, organ, or mental faculty.

(4) False statements.—Any person who knowingly makes any false material statement, representation, or certification in any application, record, report, plan, or other document filed or required to be maintained under this Act or who knowingly falsifies, tampers with, or renders inaccurate any monitoring device or method required to be maintained under this Act, shall upon conviction, be punished by a fine of not more than $10,000, or by imprisonment for not more than 2 years, or by both. If a conviction of a person is for a violation committed after a first conviction of such person under this paragraph, punishment shall be by a fine of not more than $20,000 per day of violation, or by imprisonment of not more than 4 years, or by both.

(5) Treatment of single operational upset.—For purposes of this subsection, a single operational upset which leads to simultaneous violations of more than one pollutant parameter shall be treated as a single violation.

(6) Responsible corporate officer as "person".—For the purpose of this subsection, the term "person" means, in addition to the definition contained in section 502(5) of this Act [33 U.S.C. § 1365(5)], any responsible corporate officer.

(7) Hazardous substance defined.—For the purpose of this subsection, the term "hazardous substance" means

(A) any substance designated pursuant to section 311(b)(2)(A) of this Act [33 U.S.C. § 1321(b)(2)(A)],

(B) any element, compound, mixture, solution, or substance designated pursuant to section 102 of the Comprehensive Environmental Response, Compensation, and Liability Act of 1980,

(C) any hazardous waste having the characteristics identified under or listed pursuant to section 3001 of the Solid Waste Disposal Act (but not including any waste the regulation of which under the Solid Waste Disposal Act has been suspended by Act of Congress),

(D) any toxic pollutant listed under section 307(a) of this Act [33 U.S.C. § 1317(a)], and

(E) any imminently hazardous chemical substance or mixture with respect to which the Administrator has taken action pursuant to section 7 of the Toxic Substances Control Act.

. . .

TITLE 42
THE PUBLIC HEALTH AND WELFARE

CHAPTER 82. SOLID WASTE DISPOSAL

42 U.S.C. § 6928. FEDERAL ENFORCEMENT

. . .

(d) Criminal penalties.—Any person who—

(1) knowingly transports or causes to be transported any hazardous waste identified or listed under this subchapter to a facility which does not have a permit under this subchapter, or pursuant to title I of the Marine Protection, Research, and Sanctuaries Act (86 Stat. 1052),

(2) knowingly treats, stores, or disposes of any hazardous waste identified or listed under this subchapter—

(A) without a permit under this subchapter or pursuant to title I of the Marine Protection, Research, and Sanctuaries Act (86 Stat. 1052); or

(B) in knowing violation of any material condition or requirement of such permit; or

(C) in knowing violation of any material condition or requirement of any applicable interim status regulations or standards;

(3) knowingly omits material information or makes any false material statement or representation in any application, label, manifest, record, report, permit, or other document filed, maintained, or used for purposes of compliance with regulations promulgated by the Administrator (or by a State in the case of an authorized State program) under this subchapter;

(4) knowingly generates, stores, treats, transports, disposes of, exports, or otherwise handles any hazardous waste or any used oil not identified or listed as a hazardous waste under this subchapter (whether such activity took place before or takes place after the date of the enactment of this paragraph) and who knowingly destroys, alters, conceals, or fails to file any record, application,

manifest, report, or other document required to be maintained or filed for purposes of compliance with regulations promulgated by the Administrator (or by a State in the case of an authorized State program) under this subchapter;

(5) knowingly transports without a manifest, or causes to be transported without a manifest, any hazardous waste or any used oil not identified or listed as a hazardous waste under this subchapter required by regulations promulgated under this subchapter (or by a State in the case of a State program authorized under this subchapter) to be accompanied by a manifest;

(6) knowingly exports a hazardous waste identified or listed under this subchapter

(A) without the consent of the receiving country or,

(B) where there exists an international agreement between the United States and the government of the receiving country establishing notice, export, and enforcement procedures for the transportation, treatment, storage, and disposal of hazardous wastes, in a manner which is not in conformance with such agreement; or

(7) knowingly stores, treats, transports, or causes to be transported, disposes of, or otherwise handles any used oil not identified or listed as a hazardous waste under subchapter C of the Solid Waste Disposal Act—

(A) in knowing violation of any material condition or requirement of a permit under this subchapter C; or

(B) in knowing violation of any material condition or requirement of any applicable regulations or standards under this Chapter;

shall, upon conviction, be subject to a fine of not more than $50,000 for each day of violation, or imprisonment not to exceed two years (five years in the case of a violation of paragraph (1) or (2)), or both. If the conviction is for a violation committed after a first conviction of such person under this paragraph, the maximum punishment under the respective paragraph shall be doubled with respect to both fine and imprisonment.

(e) Knowing endangerment.—Any person who knowingly transports, treats, stores, disposes of, or exports any hazardous waste identified or listed under this subchapter or used oil not identified or listed as a hazardous waste under this subchapter in violation of paragraph (1), (2), (3), (4), (5), (6), or (7) of subsection (d) of this section who knows at that time that he thereby places another person in imminent danger of death or serious bodily injury, shall, upon conviction, be subject to a fine of not more than $250,000 or imprisonment for not more than fifteen years, or both. A defendant that is an organization shall, upon conviction of violating this subsection, be subject to a fine of not more than $1,000,000.

(f) Special rules.—For the purposes of subsection (e)—

(1) A person's state of mind is knowing with respect to—

(A) his conduct, if he is aware of the nature of his conduct;

(B) an existing circumstance, if he is aware or believes that the circumstance exists; or

(C) a result of his conduct, if he is aware or believes that his conduct is substantially certain to cause danger of death or serious bodily injury.

(2) In determining whether a defendant who is a natural person knew that his conduct placed another person in imminent danger of death or serious bodily injury—

(A) the person is responsible only for actual awareness or actual belief that he possessed; and

(B) knowledge possessed by a person other than the defendant but not by the defendant himself may not be attributed to the defendant;

Provided, That in proving the defendant's possession of actual knowledge, circumstantial evidence may be used, including evidence that the defendant took affirmative steps to shield himself from relevant information.

(3) It is an affirmative defense to a prosecution that the conduct charged was consented to by the person endangered and that the danger and conduct charged were reasonably foreseeable hazards of—

(A) an occupation, a business, or a profession; or

(B) medical treatment or medical or scientific experimentation conducted by professionally approved methods and such other person had been made aware of the risks involved prior to giving consent.

The defendant may establish an affirmative defense under this subsection by a preponderance of the evidence.

(4) All general defenses, affirmative defenses, and bars to prosecution that may apply with respect to other Federal criminal offenses may apply under subsection (e) and shall be determined by the courts of the United States according to the principles of common law as they may be interpreted in the light of reason and experience. Concepts of justification and excuse applicable under this section may be developed in the light of reason and experience.

(5) The term "organization" means a legal entity, other than a government, established or organized for any purpose, and such term includes a corporation, company, association, firm, partnership, joint stock company, foundation, institution, trust, society, union, or any other association of persons.

(6) The term "serious bodily injury" means—

(A) bodily injury which involves a substantial risk of death;

(B) unconsciousness;

(C) extreme physical pain;

(D) protracted and obvious disfigurement; or

(E) protracted loss or impairment of the function of a bodily member, organ, or mental faculty.

. . .

CHAPTER 85. AIR POLLUTION PREVENTION AND CONTROL

42 U.S.C. § 7413. FEDERAL ENFORCEMENT

. . .

(c) Criminal penalties.

(1) Any person who knowingly violates any requirement or prohibition of an applicable implementation plan (during any period of federally assumed enforcement or more than 30 days after having been notified under subsection (a)(1) of this section by the Administrator that such person is violating such requirement or prohibition), any order under subsection (a) of this section, requirement or prohibition of section 7411(e) of this title (relating to new source performance standards), section 7412 of this title, section 7414 of this title (relating to inspections, etc.), section 7429 of this title (relating to solid waste combustion), section 7475(a) of this title (relating to preconstruction requirements), an order under section 7477 of this title (relating to preconstruction requirements), an order under section 7603 of this title III (relating to emergency orders), section 7661a(a) or 7661(c) of this title (relating to permits), or any requirement or prohibition of subchapter IV-A of this chapter (relating to acid deposition control), or subchapter VI of this chapter (relating to stratospheric ozone control), including a requirement of any rule, order, waiver, or permit promulgated or approved under such sections or subchapters, and including any requirement for the payment of any fee owed the United States under this chapter (other than subchapter II of this chapter) shall, upon conviction, be punished by a fine pursuant to title 18 of the United States Code, or by imprisonment for not to exceed 5 years, or both. If a conviction of any person under this paragraph is for a violation committed after a first conviction of such person under this paragraph, the maximum punishment shall be doubled with respect to both the fine and imprisonment.

(2) Any person who knowingly—

(A) makes any false material statement, representation, or certification in, or omits material information from, or knowingly alters, conceals, or fails to file or maintain any notice, application, record, report, plan, or other document required pursuant to this chapter to be either filed or maintained (whether with respect to the requirements imposed by the Administrator or by a State);

(B) fails to notify or report as required under this chapter; or

(C) falsifies, tampers with, renders inaccurate, or fails to install any monitoring device or method required to be maintained or followed under this chapter

shall, upon conviction, be punished by a fine pursuant to title 18 of the United States Code, or by imprisonment for not more than 2 years, or both. If a conviction of any person under this paragraph is for a violation committed after a first conviction of such person under this paragraph, the maximum punishment shall be doubled with respect to both the fine and imprisonment.

(3) Any person who knowingly fails to pay any fee owed the United States under this subchapter, subchapter III, IV-A, V, or VI of this chapter, shall, upon conviction, be punished by a fine pursuant to title 18 of the United States Code, or by imprisonment for not more than 1 year, or both. If a conviction of any person under this paragraph is for a violation committed after a first conviction of such person under this paragraph, the maximum punishment shall be doubled with respect to both the fine and imprisonment.

(4) Any person who negligently releases into the ambient air any hazardous air pollutant listed pursuant to section 7412 of this title or any extremely hazardous substance listed pursuant to section 11002(a)(2) of this title that is not listed in section 7412 of this title, and who at the time negligently places another person in imminent danger of death or serious bodily injury shall, upon conviction, be punished by a fine under title 18 of the United States Code, or by imprisonment for not more than 1 year, or

both. If a conviction of any person under this paragraph is for a violation committed after a first conviction of such person under this paragraph, the maximum punishment shall be doubled with respect to both the fine and imprisonment.

(5)(A) Any person who knowingly releases into the ambient air any hazardous air pollutant listed pursuant to section 7412 of this title or any extremely hazardous substance listed pursuant to section 11002(a)(2) of this title that is not listed in section 7412 of this title, and who knows at the time that he thereby places another person in imminent danger of death or serious bodily injury shall, upon conviction, be punished by a fine under title 18, or by imprisonment of not more than 15 years, or both. Any person committing such violation which is an organization shall, upon conviction under this paragraph, be subject to a fine of not more than $1,000,000 for each violation. If a conviction of any person under this paragraph is for a violation committed after a first conviction of such person under this paragraph, the maximum punishment shall be doubled with respect to both the fine and imprisonment. For any air pollutant for which the Administrator has set an emissions standard or for any source for which a permit has been issued under subchapter V of this chapter, a release of such pollutant in accordance with that standard or permit shall not constitute a violation of this paragraph or paragraph (4).

(B) In determining whether a defendant who is an individual knew that the violation placed another person in imminent danger of death or serious bodily injury—

(i) the defendant is responsible only for actual awareness or actual belief possessed; and

(ii) knowledge possessed by a person other than the defendant, but not by the defendant, may not be attributed to the defendant;

except that in proving a defendant's possession of actual knowledge, circumstantial evidence may be used, including evidence that the defendant took affirmative steps to be shielded from relevant information.

(C) It is an affirmative defense to a prosecution that the conduct charged was freely consented to by the person endangered and that the danger and conduct charged were reasonably foreseeable hazards of—

(i) an occupation, a business, or a profession; or

(ii) medical treatment or medical or scientific experimentation conducted by professionally approved methods and such other person had been made aware of the risks involved prior to giving consent.

The defendant may establish an affirmative defense under this subparagraph by a preponderance of the evidence.

(D) All general defenses, affirmative defenses, and bars to prosecution that may apply with respect to other Federal criminal offenses may apply under subparagraph (A) of this paragraph and shall be determined by the courts of the United States according to the principles of common law as they may be interpreted in the light of reason and experience. Concepts of justification and excuse applicable under this section may be developed in the light of reason and experience.

(E) The term "organization" means a legal entity, other than a government, established or organized for any purpose, and such term includes a corporation, company, association, firm, partnership, joint stock company, foundation, institution, trust, society, union, or any other association of persons.

(F) The term "serious bodily injury" means bodily injury which involves a substantial risk of death, unconsciousness, extreme physical pain, protracted and obvious disfigurement or protracted loss or impairment of the function of a bodily member, organ, or mental faculty.

(6) For the purpose of this subsection, the term "person" includes, in addition to the entities referred to in section 7602(e) of this title, any responsible corporate officer.

. . .

(h) Operator.—For purposes of the provisions of this section and section 7420 of this chapter, the term "operator", as used in such provisions, shall include any person who is senior management personnel or a corporate officer. Except in the case of knowing and willful violations, such term shall not include any person who is a stationary engineer or technician responsible for the operation, maintenance, repair, or monitoring of equipment and facilities and who often has supervisory and training duties but who is not senior management personnel or a corporate officer. Except in the case of knowing and willful violations, for purposes of subsection (c)(4) of this section, the term "a person" shall not include an employee who is carrying out his normal activities and who is not a part of senior management personnel or a corporate officer. Except in the case of knowing and willful violations, for purposes of paragraphs (1), (2), (3), and (5) of subsection (c) of this section the term "a person" shall not include an employee who is carrying out his normal activities and who is acting under orders from the employer.

CHAPTER 103. COMPREHENSIVE ENVIRONMENTAL RESPONSE, COMPENSATION, AND LIABILITY

42 U.S.C. § 9603. NOTIFICATION REQUIREMENTS RESPECTING RELEASED SUBSTANCES

(a) Notice to National Response Center upon release from vessel or offshore or onshore facility by person in charge; conveyance of notice by Center.—Any person in charge of a vessel or an offshore or an onshore facility shall, as soon as he has knowledge of any release (other than a federally permitted release) of a hazardous substance from such vessel or facility in quantities equal to or greater than those determined pursuant to section 9602 of this title, immediately notify the National Response Center established under the Clean Water Act [33 U.S.C. §§ 1251 et seq.] of such release. The National Response Center shall convey the notification expeditiously to all appropriate Government agencies, including the Governor of any affected State.

(b) Penalties for failure to notify; use of notice or information pursuant to notice in criminal case.—Any person—

(1) in charge of a vessel from which a hazardous substance is released, other than a federally permitted release, into or upon the navigable waters of the United States, adjoining shorelines, or into or upon the waters of the contiguous zone, or

(2) in charge of a vessel from which a hazardous substance is released, other than a federally permitted release, which may affect natural resources belonging to, appertaining to, or under the exclusive management authority of the United States (including resources under the Magnuson-Stevens Fishery Conservation and Management Act [16 U.S.C. §§ 1801 et seq.]), and who is otherwise subject to the jurisdiction of the United States at the time of the release, or

(3) in charge of a facility from which a hazardous substance is released, other than a federally permitted release,

in a quantity equal to or greater than that determined pursuant to section 9602 of this title who fails to notify immediately the appropriate agency of the United States Government as soon as he has knowledge of such release or who submits in such a notification any information which he knows to be false or misleading shall, upon conviction, be fined in accordance with the applicable provisions of title 18 or imprisoned for not more than 3 years (or not more than 5 years in the case of a second or subsequent conviction), or both. Notification received pursuant to this subsection or information obtained by the exploitation of such notification shall not be used against any such person in any criminal case, except a prosecution for perjury or for giving a false statement.

(c) Notice to Administrator of EPA of existence of storage, etc., facility by owner or operator; exceptions; time, manner, and form of notice; penalties for failure to notify; use of notice or information pursuant to notice in criminal case.—Within one hundred and eighty days after Dec. 11, 1980, any person who owns or operates or who at the time of disposal owned or operated, or who accepted hazardous substances for transport and selected, a facility at which hazardous substances (as defined in section 9601(14)(C) of this title) are or have been stored, treated, or disposed of shall, unless such facility has a permit issued under, or has been accorded interim status under, subtitle C of the Solid Waste Disposal Act [42 U.S.C. §§ 6921 et seq.], notify the Administrator of the Environmental Protection Agency of the existence of such facility, specifying the amount and type of any hazardous substance to be found there, and any known, suspected, or likely releases of such substances from such facility. The Administrator may prescribe in greater detail the manner and form of the notice and the information included. The Administrator shall notify the affected State agency, or any department designated by the Governor to receive such notice, of the existence of such facility. Any person who knowingly fails to notify the Administrator of the existence of any such facility shall, upon conviction, be fined not more than $10,000, or imprisoned for not more than one year, or both. In addition, any such person who knowingly fails to provide the notice required by this subsection shall not be entitled to any limitation of liability or to any defenses to liability set out in section 9607 of this title: *Provided, however*, That notification under this subsection is not required for any facility which would be reportable hereunder solely as a result of any stoppage in transit which is temporary, incidental to the transportation movement, or at the ordinary operating convenience of a common or contract carrier, and such stoppage shall be considered as a continuity of movement and not as the storage of a hazardous substance. Notification received pursuant to this subsection or information obtained by the exploitation of such notification shall not be used against any such person in any criminal case, except a prosecution for perjury or for giving a false statement.

(d) Recordkeeping requirements; promulgation of rules and regulations by Administrator of EPA; penalties for violations; waiver of retention requirements.

(1) The Administrator of the Environmental Protection Agency is authorized to promulgate rules and regulations specifying, with respect to—

(A) the location, title, or condition of a facility, and

(B) the identity, characteristics, quantity, origin, or condition (including containerization and previous treatment) of any hazardous substances contained or deposited in a facility;

the records which shall be retained by any person required to provide the notification of a facility set out in subsection (c) of this section. Such specification shall be in accordance with the provisions of this subsection.

(2) Beginning with Dec. 11, 1980, for fifty years thereafter or for fifty years after the date of establishment of a record (whichever is later), or at any such earlier time as a waiver if obtained under paragraph (3) of this subsection, it shall be unlawful for any such person knowingly to destroy, mutilate, erase, dispose of, conceal, or otherwise render unavailable or unreadable or falsify any records identified in paragraph (1) of this subsection. Any person who violates this paragraph shall, upon conviction, be fined in accordance with the applicable provisions of title 18 or imprisoned for not more than 3 years (or not more than 5 years in the case of a second or subsequent conviction), or both.

. . .

(f) Exemptions from notice and penalty provisions for substances reported under other Federal law or in continuous release, etc.—No notification shall be required under subsection (a) or (b) of this section for any release of a hazardous substance—

(1) which is required to be reported (or specifically exempted from a requirement for reporting) under subtitle C of the Solid Waste Disposal Act [42 U.S.C. §§ 6921 et seq.] or regulations thereunder and which has been reported to the National Response Center, or

(2) which is a continuous release, stable in quantity and rate, and is—

(A) from a facility for which notification has been given under subsection (c) of this section, or

(B) a release of which notification has been given under subsections (a) and (b) of this section for a period sufficient to establish the continuity, quantity, and regularity of such release:

Provided, That notification in accordance with subsections (a) and (b) of this paragraph shall be given for releases subject to this paragraph annually, or at such time as there is any statistically significant increase in the quantity of any hazardous substance or constituent thereof released, above that previously reported or occurring.

Code of Federal Regulations

TITLE 17
COMMODITY AND SECURITIES EXCHANGE

17 C.F.R. § 240.10b-5. EMPLOYMENT OF MANIPULATIVE AND DECEPTIVE DEVICES

It shall be unlawful for any person, directly or indirectly, by the use of any means or instrumentality of interstate commerce, or of the mails or of any facility of any national securities exchange,

(a) To employ any device, scheme, or artifice to defraud,

(b) To make any untrue statement of a material fact or to omit to state a material fact necessary in order to make the statements made, in the light of the circumstances under which they were made, not misleading, or

(c) To engage in any act, practice, or course of business which operates or would operate as a fraud or deceit upon any person, in connection with the purchase or sale of any security.

17 C.F.R. § 240.10b5-1. TRADING "ON THE BASIS OF" MATERIAL NONPUBLIC INFORMATION IN INSIDER TRADING CASES

Preliminary Note to § 240.10b5-1: This provision defines when a purchase or sale constitutes trading "on the basis of" material nonpublic information in insider trading cases brought under Section 10(b) of the Act and Rule 10b-5 thereunder. The law of insider trading is otherwise defined by judicial opinions construing Rule 10b-5, and Rule 10b5-1 does not modify the scope of insider trading law in any other respect.

(a) *General.* The "manipulative and deceptive devices" prohibited by Section 10(b) of the Act (15 U.S.C. § 78j) and § 240.10b-5 thereunder include, among other things, the purchase or sale of a security of any issuer, on the basis of material nonpublic information about that security or issuer, in breach of a duty of trust or confidence that is owed directly, indirectly, or derivatively, to the issuer of that security or the shareholders of that issuer, or to any other person who is the source of the material nonpublic information.

(b) *Definition of "on the basis of."* Subject to the affirmative defenses in paragraph (c) of this section, a purchase or sale of a security of an issuer is "on the basis of" material nonpublic information about that security or issuer if the person making the purchase or sale was aware of the material nonpublic information when the person made the purchase or sale.

(c) *Affirmative defenses.*

(1)(i) Subject to paragraph (c)(1)(ii) of this section, a person's purchase or sale is not "on the basis of" material nonpublic information if the person making the purchase or sale demonstrates that:

(A) Before becoming aware of the information, the person had:

(1) Entered into a binding contract to purchase or sell the security,

(2) Instructed another person to purchase or sell the security for the instructing person's account, or

(3) Adopted a written plan for trading securities;

(B) The contract, instruction, or plan described in paragraph (c)(1)(i)(A) of this Section:

(1) Specified the amount of securities to be purchased or sold and the price at which and the date on which the securities were to be purchased or sold;

(2) Included a written formula or algorithm, or computer program, for determining the amount of securities to be purchased or sold and the price at which and the date on which the securities were to be purchased or sold; or

(3) Did not permit the person to exercise any subsequent influence over how, when, or whether to effect purchases or sales; provided, in addition, that any other person who, pursuant to the contract, instruction, or plan, did exercise such influence must not have been aware of the material nonpublic information when doing so; and

(C) The purchase or sale that occurred was pursuant to the contract, instruction, or plan. A purchase or sale is not "pursuant to a contract, instruction, or plan" if, among other things, the person who entered into the contract, instruction, or plan altered or deviated from the contract, instruction, or plan to purchase or sell securities (whether by changing the amount, price, or timing of the purchase or sale), or entered into or altered a corresponding or hedging transaction or position with respect to those securities.

(ii) Paragraph (c)(1)(i) of this section is applicable only when the contract, instruction, or plan to purchase or sell securities was given or entered into in good faith and not as part of a plan or scheme to evade the prohibitions of this section.

(iii) This paragraph (c)(1)(iii) defines certain terms as used in paragraph (c) of this Section.

(A) *Amount.* "Amount" means either a specified number of shares or other securities or a specified dollar value of securities.

(B) *Price.* "Price" means the market price on a particular date or a limit price, or a particular dollar price.

(C) *Date.* "Date" means, in the case of a market order, the specific day of the year on which the order is to be executed (or as soon thereafter as is practicable under ordinary principles of best execution). "Date" means, in the case of a limit order, a day of the year on which the limit order is in force.

(2) A person other than a natural person also may demonstrate that a purchase or sale of securities is not "on the basis of" material nonpublic information if the person demonstrates that:

(i) The individual making the investment decision on behalf of the person to purchase or sell the securities was not aware of the information; and

(ii) The person had implemented reasonable policies and procedures, taking into consideration the nature of the person's business, to ensure that individuals making investment decisions would not violate the laws prohibiting trading on the basis of material nonpublic information. These policies and procedures may include those that restrict any purchase, sale, and causing any purchase or sale of any security as to which the person has material nonpublic information, or those that prevent such individuals from becoming aware of such information.

17 C.F.R. § 240.10b5-2. DUTIES OF TRUST OR CONFIDENCE IN MISAPPROPRIATION INSIDER TRADING CASES

Preliminary Note to § 240.10b5-2: This section provides a non-exclusive definition of circumstances in which a person has a duty of trust or confidence for purposes of the "misappropriation" theory of insider trading under Section 10(b) of the Act and Rule 10b-5. The law of insider trading is otherwise defined by judicial opinions construing Rule 10b-5, and Rule 10b5-2 does not modify the scope of insider trading law in any other respect.

(a) *Scope of Rule*. This section shall apply to any violation of Section 10(b) of the Act (15 U.S.C. § 78j(b)) and § 240.10b-5 thereunder that is based on the purchase or sale of securities on the basis of, or the communication of, material nonpublic information misappropriated in breach of a duty of trust or confidence.

(b) *Enumerated "duties of trust or confidence."* For purposes of this section, a "duty of trust or confidence" exists in the following circumstances, among others:

(1) Whenever a person agrees to maintain information in confidence;

(2) Whenever the person communicating the material nonpublic information and the person to whom it is communicated have a history, pattern, or practice of sharing confidences, such that the recipient of the information knows or reasonably should know that the person communicating the material nonpublic information expects that the recipient will maintain its confidentiality; or

(3) Whenever a person receives or obtains material nonpublic information from his or her spouse, parent, child, or sibling; *provided*, however, that the person receiving or obtaining the information may demonstrate that no duty of trust or confidence existed with respect to the information, by establishing that he or she neither knew nor reasonably should have known that the person who was the source of the information expected that the person would keep the information confidential, because of the parties' history, pattern, or practice of sharing and maintaining confidences, and because there was no agreement or understanding to maintain the confidentiality of the information.

TITLE 26
INTERNAL REVENUE

26 C.F.R. § 1.6050I-1. RETURNS RELATING TO CASH IN EXCESS OF $10,000 RECEIVED IN A TRADE OR BUSINESS

(a) *Reporting requirement*—

(1) *Reportable transaction*—

(i) *In general.* Any person (as defined in section 7701(a)(1)) who, in the course of a trade or business in which such person is engaged, receives cash in excess of $10,000 in 1 transaction (or 2 or more related transactions) shall, except as otherwise provided, make a return of information with respect to the receipt of cash.

(ii) *Certain financial transactions.* Section 6050I of title 26 of the United States Code requires persons to report information about financial transactions to the Internal Revenue Service, and section 5331 of title 31 of the United States Code requires persons to report similar information about certain transactions to the Financial Crimes Enforcement Network. This information shall be reported on the same form as prescribed by the Secretary.

(2) *Cash received for the account of another.* Cash in excess of $10,000 received by a person for the account of another must be reported under this section. Thus, for example, a person who collects delinquent accounts receivable for an automobile dealer must report with respect to the receipt of cash in excess of $10,000 from the collection of a particular account even though the proceeds of the collection are credited to the account of the automobile dealer (i.e., where the rights to the proceeds from the account are retained by the automobile dealer and the collection is made on a fee-for-service basis).

(3) *Cash received by agents*—

(i) *General rule.* Except as provided in paragraph (a)(3)(ii) of this section, a person who in the course of a trade or business acts as an agent (or in some other similar capacity) and receives cash in excess of $10,000 from a principal, must report the receipt of cash under this section.

(ii) *Exception*. An agent who receives cash from a principal and uses all of the cash within 15 days in a cash transaction (the "second cash transaction") which is reportable under section 6050I or 5312 of title 31 of the United States Code and the regulations thereunder (31 C.F.R. Part 103), and who discloses the name, address, and taxpayer identification number of the principal to the recipient in the second cash transaction need not report the initial receipt of cash under this section. An agent will be deemed to have met the disclosure requirements of this paragraph (a)(3)(ii) if the agent discloses only the name of the principal and the agent knows that the recipient has the principal's address and taxpayer identification number.

(iii) *Example*. The following example illustrates the application of the rules in paragraphs (a)(3) (i) and (ii) of this section:

Example. B, the principal, gives D, an attorney, $75,000 in cash to purchase real property on behalf of B. Within 15 days D purchases real property for cash from E, a real estate developer, and discloses to E, B's name, address, and taxpayer identification number. Because the transaction qualifies for the exception provided in paragraph (a)(3)(ii) of this section, D need not report with respect to the initial receipt of cash under this section. The exception does not apply, however, if D pays E by means other than cash, or effects the purchase more than 15 days following receipt of the cash from B, or fails to disclose B's name, address, and taxpayer identification number (assuming D does not know that E already has B's address and taxpayer identification number), or purchases the property from a person whose sale of the property is not in the course of that person's trade or business. In any such case, D is required to report the receipt of cash from B under this section.

(b) *Multiple payments.* The receipt of multiple cash deposits or cash installment payments (or other similar payments or prepayments) on or after January 1, 1990, relating to a single transaction (or two or more related transactions), is reported as set forth in paragraphs (b)(1) through (b)(3) of this section.

(1) *Initial payment in excess of $10,000.* If the initial payment exceeds $10,000, the recipient must report the initial payment within 15 days of its receipt.

(2) *Initial payment of $10,000 or less.* If the initial payment does not exceed $10,000, the recipient must aggregate the initial payment and subsequent payments made within one year of the initial payment until the aggregate amount exceeds $10,000, and report with respect to the aggregate amount within 15 days after receiving the payment that causes the aggregate amount to exceed $10,000.

(3) *Subsequent payments.* In addition to any other required report, a report must be made each time that previously unreportable payments made within a 12-month period with respect to a single transaction (or two or more related transactions), individually or in the aggregate, exceed $10,000. The report must be made within 15 days after receiving the payment in excess of $10,000 or the payment that causes the aggregate amount received in the 12-month period to exceed $10,000. (If more than one report would otherwise be required for multiple cash payments within a 15-day period that relate to a single transaction (or two or more related transactions), the recipient may make a single combined report with respect to the payments. The combined report must be made no later than the date by which the first of the separate reports would otherwise be required to be made.) A report with respect to payments of $10,000 or less that are reportable under this paragraph (b)(3) and are received after December 31, 1989, but before July 10, 1990, is due July 24, 1990.

(4) *Example.* The following example illustrates the application of the rules in paragraphs (b)(1) through (b)(3) of this section:

Example. On January 10, 1991, M receives an initial cash payment of $11,000 with respect to a transaction. M receives subsequent cash payments with respect to the same transaction of $4,000 on February 15, 1991, $6,000 on March 20, 1991, and $12,000 on May 15, 1991. M must make a report with respect to the payment received on January 10, 1991, by January 25, 1991. M must also make a report with respect to the payments totalling $22,000 received from February 15, 1991, through May 15, 1991. This report must be made by May 30, 1991, that is, within 15 days of the date that the subsequent payments, all of which were received within a 12-month period, exceeded $10,000.

(c) *Meaning of terms.* The following definitions apply for purposes of this section—

(1) *Cash*—

(i) *Amounts received prior to February 3, 1992.* For amounts received prior to February 3, 1992, the term cash means the coin and currency of the United States or of any other country, which circulate in and are customarily used and accepted as money in the country in which issued.

(ii) *Amounts received on or after February 3, 1992.* For amounts received on or after February 3, 1992, the term cash means—

(A) The coin and currency of the United States or of any other country, which circulate in and are customarily used and accepted as money in the country in which issued; and

(B) A cashier's check (by whatever name called, including "treasurer's check" and "bank check"), bank draft, traveler's check, or money order having a face amount of not more than $10,000—

(1) Received in a designated reporting transaction as defined in paragraph (c)(1)(iii) of this section (except as provided in paragraphs (c)(1)(iv), (v), and (vi) of this section), or

(2) Received in any transaction in which the recipient knows that such instrument is being used in an attempt to avoid the reporting of the transaction under section 6050I and this section.

(iii) *Designated reporting transaction.* A designated reporting transaction is a retail sale (or the receipt of funds by a broker or other intermediary in connection with a retail sale) of—

(A) A consumer durable,

(B) A collectible, or

(C) A travel or entertainment activity.

. . .

(vii) *Examples.* The following examples illustrate the definition of "cash" set forth in paragraphs (c)(l)(ii) through (vi) of this section.

Example 1. D, an individual, purchases gold coins from M, a coin dealer, for $13,200. D tenders to M in payment United States currency in the amount of $6,200 and a cashier's check in the face amount of $7,000 which D had purchased. Because the sale is a designated reporting transaction, the cashier's check is treated as cash for purposes of section 6050I and this section. Therefore, because M has received more than $10,000 in cash with respect to the transaction, M must make the report required by section 6050I and this section.

. . .

Example 3. F, an individual, purchases an item of jewelry from S, a retail jeweler, for $12,000. F gives S traveler's checks totalling $2,400 and pays the balance with a personal check payable to S in the amount of $9,600. Because the sale is a designated reporting transaction, the traveler's checks are treated as cash for purposes of section 6050I and this section. However, because the personal check is not treated as cash for purposes of section 6050I and this section, S has not received more than $10,000 in cash in the transaction and no report is required to be filed under section 6050I and this section.

Example 4. G, an individual, purchases a boat from T, a boat dealer, for $16,500. G pays T with a cashier's check payable to T in the amount of $16,500. The cashier's check is not treated as cash because the face amount of the check is more than $10,000. Thus, no report is required to be made by T under section 6050I and this section.

Example 5. H, an individual, arranges with W, a travel agent, for the chartering of a passenger aircraft to transport a group of individuals to a sports event in another city. H also arranges with W for hotel accommodations for the group and for admission tickets to the sports event. In payment, H tenders to W money orders which H had previously purchased. The total amount of the money orders, none of which individually exceeds $10,000 in face amount, exceeds $10,000. Because the transaction is a designated reporting transaction, the money orders are treated as cash for purposes of section 6050I and this section. Therefore, because W has received more than $10,000 in cash with respect to the transaction, W must make the report required by section 6050I and this section.

(2) *Consumer durable.* The term *consumer durable* means an item of tangible personal property of a type that is suitable under ordinary usage for personal consumption or use, that can reasonably be expected to be useful for at least 1 year under ordinary usage, and that has a sales price of more than $10,000. Thus, for example, a $20,000 automobile is a consumer durable (whether or not it is sold for business use), but a $20,000 dump truck or a $20,000 factory machine is not.

(3) *Collectible.* The term *collectible* means an item described in paragraphs (A) through (D) of section 408(m)(2) (determined without regard to section 408(m)(3)).

(4) *Travel or entertainment activity.* The term *travel or entertainment activity* means an item of travel or entertainment (within the meaning of § 1.274-2(b)(1)) pertaining to a single trip or event where the aggregate sales price of the item and all other items pertaining to the same trip or event that are sold in the same transaction (or related transactions) exceeds $10,000.

(5) *Retail sale.* The term *retail sale* means any sale (whether for resale or for any other purpose) made in the course of a trade or business if that trade or business principally consists of making sales to ultimate consumers.

(6) *Trade or business.* The term *trade or business* has the same meaning as under section 162 of the Internal Revenue Code of 1954.

(7) *Transaction—*

(i) The term *transaction* means the underlying event precipitating the payer's transfer of cash to the recipient. Transactions include (but are not limited to) a sale of goods or services; a sale of real property; a sale of intangible property; a rental of real or personal property; an exchange of cash for other cash; the establishment or maintenance of or contribution to a custodial, trust, or escrow arrangement; a payment of a preexisting debt; a conversion of cash to a negotiable instrument; a reimbursement for expenses paid; or the making or repayment of a loan. A transaction may not be divided into multiple transactions in order to avoid reporting under this section.

(ii) The term *related transactions* means any transaction conducted between a payer (or its agent) and a recipient of cash in a 24-hour period. Additionally, transactions conducted between a payer (or its agent) and a cash recipient during a period of more than 24 hours are related if the recipient knows or has reason to know that each transaction is one of a series of connected transactions.

(iii) The following examples illustrate the definition of paragraphs (c)(7) (i) and (ii).

Example 1. A person has a tacit agreement with a gold dealer to purchase $36,000 in gold bullion. The $36,000 purchase represents a single transaction under paragraph (c)(7)(i) of this section and the reporting requirements of this section cannot be avoided by recasting the single sales transaction into 4 separate $9,000 sales transactions.

Example 2. An attorney agrees to represent a client in a criminal case with the attorney's fee to be determined on an hourly basis. In the first month in which the attorney represents the client, the bill for the attorney's services comes to $8,000 which the client pays in cash. In the second month in which the attorney represents the client, the bill for the attorney's services comes to $4,000, which the client again pays in cash. The aggregate amount of cash paid ($12,000) relates to a single transaction as defined in paragraph (c)(7)(i) of this section, the sale of legal services relating to the criminal case, and the receipt of cash must be reported under this section.

Example 3. A person intends to contribute a total of $45,000 to a trust fund, and the trustee of the fund knows or has reason to know of that intention. The $45,000 contribution is a single transaction under paragraph (c)(7)(i) of this section and the reporting requirement of this section cannot be avoided by the grantor's making five separate $9,000 cash contributions to a single fund or by making five $9,000 cash contributions to five separate funds administered by a common trustee.

Example 4. K, an individual, attends a one day auction and purchases for cash two items, at a cost of $9,240 and $1,732.50 respectively (tax and buyer's premium included). Because the transactions are related transactions as defined in paragraph (c)(7)(ii) of this section, the auction house is required to report the aggregate amount of cash received from the related sales ($10,972.50), even though the auction house accounts separately on its books for each item sold and presents the purchaser with separate bills for each item purchased.

Example 5. F, a coin dealer, sells for cash $9,000 worth of gold coins to an individual on three successive days. Under paragraph (c)(7)(ii) of this section the three $9,000 transactions are related transactions aggregating $27,000 if F knows, or has reason to know, that each transaction is one of a series of connected transactions.

(8) *Recipient.*

(i) The term *recipient* means the person receiving the cash. Except as provided in paragraph (c)(8)(ii) of this section, each store, division, branch, department, headquarters, or office ("branch") (regardless of physical location) comprising a portion of a person's trade or business shall for purposes of this section be deemed a separate recipient.

(ii) A branch that receives cash payments will not be deemed a separate recipient if the branch (or a central unit linking such branch with other branches) would in the ordinary course of business have reason to know the identity of payers making cash payments to other branches of such person.

(iii) *Examples.* The following examples illustrate the application of the rules in paragraphs (c)(8)(i) and (ii) of this section:

Example 1. N, an individual, purchases regulated futures contracts at a cost of $7,500 and $5,000, respectively, through two different branches of Commodities Broker X on the same day. N pays for each purchase with cash. Each branch of Commodities Broker X transmits the sales information regarding each of N's purchases to a central unit of Commodities Broker X (which settles the transactions against N's account). Under paragraph (c)(8)(ii) of this section the separate branches of Commodities Broker X are not deemed to be separate recipients; therefore. Commodities Broker X must report with respect to the two related regulated futures contracts sales in accordance with this section.

Example 2. P, a corporation, owns and operates a racetrack. P's racetrack contains 100 betting windows at which pari-mutuel wagers may be made. R, an individual, places cash wagers of $3,000 each at five separate betting windows. Assuming that in the ordinary course of business each betting window (or a central unit linking windows) does not have reason to know the identity of persons making wagers at other betting windows, each betting window would be deemed to be a separate cash recipient under paragraph (c)(8)(i) of this section. As no individual recipient received cash in excess of $10,000, no report need be made by P under this section.

(d) *Exceptions to the reporting requirements of section 6050I—*

(1) *Receipt of cash by certain financial institutions.* A financial institution as defined in subparagraphs (A), (B), (C), (D), (E), (F), (G), (J), (K), (R), and (S) of section 5312 (a)(2) of Title 31, United States Code is not required to report the receipt of cash exceeding $10,000 under section 6050I.

. . .

(3) *Receipt of cash not in the course of the recipient's trade or business.* The receipt of cash in excess of $10,000 by a person other than in the course of the person's trade or business is not reportable under section 6050I. Thus, for example, F, an individual in the trade or business of selling real estate, sells a motorboat for $12,000, the purchase price of which is paid in cash. F did not use the motorboat in any trade or business in which F was engaged. F is not required to report under section 6050I or these regulations because the exception provided in this paragraph (d)(3) applies.

. . .

(e) *Time, manner, and form of reporting—*

(1) *Time of reporting.* The reports required by this section must be filed with the Internal Revenue Service by the 15th day after the date the cash is received. However, in the case of

multiple payments relating to a single transaction (or two or more related transactions), see paragraph (b) of this section.

(2) *Form of reporting.* A report required by paragraph (a) of this section must be made on Form 8300. A return of information made in compliance with this paragraph must contain the name, address, and taxpayer identification number of the person from whom the cash was received; the name, address, and taxpayer identification number of the person on whose behalf the transaction was conducted (if the recipient knows or has reason to know that the person from whom the cash was received conducted the transaction as an agent for another person); the amount of cash received; the date and nature of the transaction; and any other information required by Form 8300. Form 8300 can be obtained from any Internal Revenue Service Forms Distribution Center.

. . .

(g) *Cross-reference to penalty provisions—*

. . .

(3) *Criminal penalties.* Any person who willfully fails to make a return or makes a false return under section 6050I and this section may be subject to criminal prosecution.

Federal Sentencing Guidelines

CHAPTER 1 - INTRODUCTION AND GENERAL APPLICATION PRINCIPLES

Part B - General Application Principles

§1B1.3. RELEVANT CONDUCT (FACTORS THAT DETERMINE THE GUIDELINE RANGE)

(a) Chapters Two (Offense Conduct) and Three (Adjustments). Unless otherwise specified, (i) the base offense level where the guideline specifies more than one base offense level, (ii) specific offense characteristics and (iii) cross references in Chapter Two, and (iv) adjustments in Chapter Three, shall be determined on the basis of the following:

(1)(A) all acts and omissions committed, aided, abetted, counseled, commanded, induced, procured, or willfully caused by the defendant; and

(B) in the case of a jointly undertaken criminal activity (a criminal plan, scheme, endeavor, or enterprise undertaken by the defendant in concert with others, whether or not charged as a conspiracy), all reasonably foreseeable acts and omissions of others in furtherance of the jointly undertaken criminal activity, that occurred during the commission of the offense of conviction, in preparation for that offense, or in the course of attempting to avoid detection or responsibility for that offense;

(2) solely with respect to offenses of a character for which §3D1.2(d) would require grouping of multiple counts, all acts and omissions described in subdivisions (1)(A) and (1)(B) above that were part of the same course of conduct or common scheme or plan as the offense of conviction;

(3) all harm that resulted from the acts and omissions specified in subsections (a)(1) and (a)(2) above, and all harm that was the object of such acts and omissions; and

(4) any other information specified in the applicable guideline.

(b) Chapters Four (Criminal History and Criminal Livelihood) and Five (Determining the Sentence). Factors in Chapters Four and Five that establish the guideline range shall be determined on the basis of the conduct and information specified in the respective guidelines.

CHAPTER 2 - OFFENSE CONDUCT

Part B - Basic Economic Offenses

§2B1.1. LARCENY, EMBEZZLEMENT, AND OTHER FORMS OF THEFT; OFFENSES INVOLVING STOLEN PROPERTY; PROPERTY DAMAGE OR DESTRUCTION; FRAUD AND DECEIT; FORGERY; OFFENSES INVOLVING ALTERED OR COUNTERFEIT INSTRUMENTS OTHER THAN COUNTERFEIT BEARER OBLIGATIONS OF THE UNITED STATES

    (a) Base Offense Level:

        (1) 7, if

            (A) the defendant was convicted of an offense referenced to this guideline; and

            (B) that offense of conviction has a statutory maximum term of imprisonment of 20 years or more; or

        (2) 6, otherwise.

    (b) Specific Offense Characteristics

        (1) If the loss exceeded $5,000, increase the offense level as follows:

Loss (Apply the Greatest)	*Increase in Level*
(A) $5,000 or less	No increase
(B) more than $5,000	add 2
(C) more than $10,000	add 4
(D) more than $30,000	add 6
(E) more than $70,000	add 8
(F) more than $120,000	add 10
(G) more than $200,000	add 12
(H) more than $400,000	add 14
(I) more than $1,000,000	add 16
(J) more than $2,500,000	add 18
(K) more than $7,000,000	add 20

(L)   more than $20,000,000   add 22
(M) more than $50,000,000   add 24
(N)   more than $100,000,000   add 26
(O)   more than $200,000,000   add 28
(P)   more than $400,000,000   add 30

(2) (Apply the greatest) If the offense—
(A)(i) involved 10 or more victims; or
(ii) was committed through mass-marketing, increase by 2 levels;
(B) involved 50 or more victims, increase by 4 levels; or
(C) involved 250 or more victims, increase by 6 levels.
(3) If the offense involved a theft from the person of another, increase by 2 levels.
(4) If the offense involved receiving stolen property, and the defendant was a person in the business of receiving and selling stolen property, increase by 2 levels.
(5) If the offense involved misappropriation of a trade secret and the defendant knew or intended that the offense would benefit a foreign government, foreign instrumentality, or foreign agent, increase by 2 levels.
(6) If the offense involved theft of, damage to, destruction of, or trafficking in, property from a national cemetery or veterans' memorial, increase by 2 levels.
(7) If
(A) the defendant was convicted of an offense under 18 U.S.C. § 1037; and
(B) the offense involved obtaining electronic mail addresses through improper means, increase by 2 levels.
(8) If the offense involved
(A) a misrepresentation that the defendant was acting on behalf of a charitable, educational, religious, or political organization, or a government agency;
(B) a misrepresentation or other fraudulent action during the course of a bankruptcy proceeding;

(C) a violation of any prior, specific judicial or administrative order, injunction, decree, or process not addressed elsewhere in the guidelines; or

(D) a misrepresentation to a consumer in connection with obtaining, providing, or furnishing financial assistance for an institution of higher education, increase by 2 levels. If the resulting offense level is less than level 10, increase to level 10.

(9) If

(A) the defendant relocated, or participated in relocating, a fraudulent scheme to another jurisdiction to evade law enforcement or regulatory officials;

(B) a substantial part of a fraudulent scheme was committed from outside the United States; or

(C) the offense otherwise involved sophisticated means, increase by 2 levels. If the resulting offense level is less than level 12, increase to level 12.

(10) If the offense involved

(A) the possession or use of any

(i) device-making equipment, or

(ii) authentication feature;

(B) the production or trafficking of any

(i) unauthorized access device or counterfeit access device, or

(ii) authentication feature; or

(C)(i) the unauthorized transfer or use of any means of identification unlawfully to produce or obtain any other means of identification; or

(ii) the possession of 5 or more means of identification that unlawfully were produced from, or obtained by the use of, another means of identification, increase by 2 levels. If the resulting offense level is less than level 12, increase to level 12.

(11) If the offense involved conduct described in 18 U.S.C. § 1040, increase by 2 levels. If the resulting offense level is less than level 12, increase to level 12.

(12) If the offense involved an organized scheme to steal or to receive stolen

(A) vehicles or vehicle parts; or

(B) goods or chattels that are part of a cargo shipment, increase by 2 levels. If the resulting offense level is less than level 14, increase to level 14.

(13) If the offense involved (A) the conscious or reckless risk of death or serious bodily injury; or (B) possession of a dangerous weapon (including a firearm) in connection with the offense, increase by 2 levels. If the resulting offense level is less than level 14, increase to level 14.

(14) (Apply the greater) If—

(A) the defendant derived more than $1,000,000 in gross receipts from one or more financial institutions as a result of the offense, increase by 2 levels; or

(B) the offense

(i) substantially jeopardized the safety and soundness of a financial institution;

(ii) substantially endangered the solvency or financial security of an organization that, at any time during the offense, (I) was a publicly traded company; or (II) had 1,000 or more employees; or

(iii) substantially endangered the solvency or financial security of 100 or more victims, increase by 4 levels.

(C) The cumulative adjustments from application of both subsections (b)(2) and (b)(14)(B) shall not exceed 8 levels, except as provided in subdivision (D).

(D) If the resulting offense level determined under subdivision (A) or (B) is less than level 24, increase to level 24.

(15) If (A) the defendant was convicted of an offense under 18 U.S.C. § 1030, and the offense involved an intent to obtain personal information, or (B) the offense involved the unauthorized public dissemination of personal information, increase by **2** levels.

(16)(A) (Apply the greatest) If the defendant was convicted of an offense under:

(i) 18 U.S.C. § 1030, and the offense involved a computer system used to maintain or operate a critical infrastructure, or used by or for a government entity in furtherance of the administration of justice, national defense, or national security increase by 2 levels.

(ii) 18 U.S.C. § 1030(a)(5)(A), increase by 4 levels.

(iii) 18 U.S.C. § 1030, and the offense caused a substantial disruption of a critical infrastructure, increase by 6 levels.

(B) If subdivision (A)(iii) applies, and the offense level is less than level 24, increase to level 24.

(17) If the offense involved—

(A) a violation of securities law and, at the time of the offense, the defendant was (i) an officer or a director of a publicly traded company; (ii) a registered broker or dealer, or a person associated with a broker or dealer; or (iii) an investment adviser, or a person associated with an investment adviser; or

(B) a violation of commodities law and, at the time of the offense, the defendant was (i) an officer or a director of a futures commission merchant or an introducing broker; (ii) a commodities trading advisor; or (iii) a commodity pool operator,

increase by 4 levels.

. . .

CHAPTER 3 - ADJUSTMENTS

Part B - Role in the Offense

§3B1.1. AGGRAVATING ROLE

Based on the defendant's role in the offense, increase the offense level as follows:

(a) If the defendant was an organizer or leader of a criminal activity that involved five or more participants or was otherwise extensive, increase by 4 levels.

(b) If the defendant was a manager or supervisor (but not an organizer or leader) and the criminal activity involved five or more participants or was otherwise extensive, increase by 3 levels.

(c) If the defendant was an organizer, leader, manager, or supervisor in any criminal activity other than described in (a) or (b), increase by 2 levels.

Part E - Acceptance of Responsibility

§3E1.1. ACCEPTANCE OF RESPONSIBILITY

(a) If the defendant clearly demonstrates acceptance of responsibility for his offense, decrease the offense level by 2 levels.

(b) If the defendant qualifies for a decrease under subsection (a), the offense level determined prior to the operation of subsection (a) is level 16 or greater, and upon motion of the government stating that the defendant has assisted authorities in the investigation or prosecution of his own misconduct by timely notifying authorities of his intention to enter a plea of guilty, thereby permitting the government to avoid preparing for trial and permitting the government and the court to allocate their resources efficiently, decrease the offense level by 1 additional level.

CHAPTER 5 - DETERMINING
THE SENTENCE

Part A - Sentencing Table

The Sentencing Table used to determine the guideline range follows:

SENTENCING TABLE
(in months of imprisonment)

Criminal History Category (Criminal History Points)

Offense Level	I (0 or 1)	II (2 or 3)	III (4, 5, 6)	IV (7, 8, 9)	V (10, 11, 12)	VI (13 or more)
1	0-6	0-6	0-6	0-6	0-6	0-6
2	0-6	0-6	0-6	0-6	0-6	1-7
3	0-6	0-6	0-6	0-6	2-8	3-9
4	0-6	0-6	0-6	2-8	4-10	6-12
5	0-6	0-6	1-7	4-10	6-12	9-15
6	0-6	1-7	2-8	6-12	9-15	12-18
7	0-6	2-8	4-10	8-14	12-18	15-21
8	0-6	4-10	6-12	10-16	15-21	18-24
9	4-10	6-12	8-14	12-18	18-24	21-27
10	6-12	8-14	10-16	15-21	21-27	24-30
11	8-14	10-16	12-18	18-24	24-30	27-33
12	10-16	12-18	15-21	21-27	27-33	30-37
13	12-18	15-21	18-24	24-30	30-37	33-41
14	15-21	18-24	21-27	27-33	33-41	37-46
15	18-24	21-27	24-30	30-37	37-46	41-51
16	21-27	24-30	27-33	33-41	41-51	46-57
17	24-30	27-33	30-37	37-46	46-57	51-63

Zone A covers offense levels 1-8.
Zone B covers offense levels 9-11.
Zone C covers offense levels 12-13.

	18	27-33	30-37	33-41	41-51	51-63	57-71
	19	30-37	33-41	37-46	46-57	57-71	63-78
	20	33-41	37-46	41-51	51-63	63-78	70-87
	21	37-46	41-51	46-57	57-71	70-87	77-96
	22	41-51	46-57	51-63	63-78	77-96	84-105
	23	46-57	51-63	57-71	70-87	84-105	92-115
	24	51-63	57-71	63-78	77-96	92-115	100-125
	25	57-71	63-78	70-87	84-105	100-125	110-137
	26	63-78	70-87	78-97	92-115	110-137	120-150
	27	70-87	78-97	87-108	100-125	120-150	130-162
Zone D	28	78-97	87-108	97-121	110-137	130-162	140-175
	29	87-108	97-121	108-135	121-151	140-175	151-188
	30	97-121	108-135	121-151	135-168	151-188	168-210
	31	108-135	121-151	135-168	151-188	168-210	188-235
	32	121-151	135-168	151-188	168-210	188-235	210-262
	33	135-168	151-188	168-210	188-235	210-262	235-293
	34	151-188	168-210	188-235	210-262	235-293	262-327
	35	168-210	188-235	210-262	235-293	262-327	292-365
	36	188-235	210-262	235-293	262-327	292-365	324-405
	37	210-262	235-293	262-327	292-365	324-405	360-life
	38	235-293	262-327	292-365	324-405	360-life	360-life
	39	262-327	292-365	324-405	360-life	360-life	360-life
	40	292-365	324-405	360-life	360-life	360-life	360-life
	41	324-405	360-life	360-life	360-life	360-life	360-life
	42	360-life	360-life	360-life	360-life	360-life	360-life
	43	life	life	life	life	life	life

Part B - Probation

§5B1.1. IMPOSITION OF A TERM OF PROBATION

(a) Subject to the statutory restrictions in subsection (b) below, a sentence of probation is authorized if:

(1) the applicable guideline range is in Zone A of the Sentencing Table; or

(2) the applicable guideline range is in Zone B of the Sentencing Table and the court imposes a condition or combination of conditions requiring intermittent confinement, community confinement, or home detention as provided in subsection (c)(3) of §5C1.1 (Imposition of a Term of Imprisonment).

(b) A sentence of probation may not be imposed in the event:

(1) the offense of conviction is a Class A or B felony, 18 U.S.C. § 3561(a)(1);

(2) the offense of conviction expressly precludes probation as a sentence, 18 U.S.C. § 3561(a)(2);

(3) the defendant is sentenced at the same time to a sentence of imprisonment for the same or a different offense, 18 U.S.C. § 3561(a)(3).

§5B1.2. TERM OF PROBATION

(a) When probation is imposed, the term shall be:

(1) at least one year but not more than five years if the offense level is 6 or greater;

(2) no more than three years in any other case.

Part C - Imprisonment

§5C1.1. IMPOSITION OF A TERM OF IMPRISONMENT

(a) A sentence conforms with the guidelines for imprisonment if it is within the minimum and maximum terms of the applicable guideline range.

(b) If the applicable guideline range is in Zone A of the Sentencing Table, a sentence of imprisonment is not required, unless the applicable guideline in Chapter Two expressly requires such a term.

(c) If the applicable guideline range is in Zone B of the Sentencing Table, the minimum term may be satisfied by—

(1) a sentence of imprisonment; or

(2) a sentence of imprisonment that includes a term of supervised release with a condition that substitutes community confinement or home detention according to the schedule in subsection (e), provided that at least one month is satisfied by imprisonment; or

(3) a sentence of probation that includes a condition or combination of conditions that substitute intermittent confinement, community confinement, or home detention for imprisonment according to the schedule in subsection (e).

(d) If the applicable guideline range is in Zone C of the Sentencing Table, the minimum term may be satisfied by—

(1) a sentence of imprisonment; or

(2) a sentence of imprisonment that includes a term of supervised release with a condition that substitutes community confinement or home detention according to the schedule in subsection (e), provided that at least one-half of the minimum term is satisfied by imprisonment.

(e) Schedule of Substitute Punishments:

(1) One day of intermittent confinement in prison or jail for one day of imprisonment (each 24 hours of confinement is credited as one day of intermittent confinement, provided, however, that one day shall be credited for any calendar day during which the defendant is employed in the community and confined during all remaining hours);

(2) One day of community confinement (residence in a community treatment center, halfway house, or similar residential facility) for one day of imprisonment;

(3) One day of home detention for one day of imprisonment.

(f) If the applicable guideline range is in Zone D of the Sentencing Table, the minimum term shall be satisfied by a sentence of imprisonment.

Part D - Supervised Release

§5D1.1. IMPOSITION OF A TERM OF SUPERVISED RELEASE

(a) The court shall order a term of supervised release to follow imprisonment when a sentence of imprisonment of more than one year is imposed, or when required by statute.

(b) The court may order a term of supervised release to follow imprisonment in any other case.

§5D1.2. TERM OF SUPERVISED RELEASE

(a) Subject to subsection (b), if a term of supervised release is ordered, the length of the term shall be:

(1) at least three years but not more than five years for a defendant convicted of a Class A or B felony;

(2) at least two years but not more than three years for a defendant convicted of a Class C or D felony;

(3) one year for a defendant convicted of a Class E felony or a Class A misdemeanor.

Notwithstanding subdivisions (1) through (3), the length of the term of supervised release for any offense listed in 18 U.S.C. § 2332b(g)(5)(B) the commission of which resulted in, or created a foreseeable risk of, death or serious bodily injury to another person (A) shall be not less than the minimum term of years specified for that class of offense under subdivisions (1) through (3); and (B) may be up to life.

(b) Except as otherwise provided, the term of supervised release imposed shall not be less than any statutorily required term of supervised release.

(c) (Policy Statement) If the instant offense of conviction is a sex offense, the statutory maximum term of supervised release is recommended.

Part E - Restitution, Fines, Assessments, Forfeitures

§5E1.2. FINES FOR INDIVIDUAL DEFENDANTS

(a) The court shall impose a fine in all cases, except where the defendant establishes that he is unable to pay and is not likely to become able to pay any fine.

(b) The applicable fine guideline range is that specified in subsection (c) below. If, however, the guideline for the offense in Chapter Two provides a specific rule for imposing a fine, that rule takes precedence over subsection (c) of this section.

(c)(1) The minimum of the fine guideline range is the amount shown in column A of the table below.

(2) Except as specified in (4) below, the maximum of the fine guideline range is the amount shown in column B of the table below.

(3) Fine Table:

Offense Level	A Minimum	B Maximum
3 and below	$100	$5,000
4-5	$250	$5,000
6-7	$500	$5,000
8-9	$1,000	$10,000
10-11	$2,000	$20,000
12-13	$3,000	$30,000
14-15	$4,000	$40,000
16-17	$5,000	$50,000
18-19	$6,000	$60,000
20-22	$7,500	$75,000
23-25	$10,000	$100,000
26-28	$12,500	$125,000
29-31	$15,000	$150,000
32-34	$17,500	$175,000
35-37	$20,000	$200,000
38 and above	$25,000	$250,000

(4) Subsection (c)(2), limiting the maximum fine, does not apply if the defendant is convicted under a statute authorizing (A) a maximum fine greater than $250,000, or (B) a fine for each day of violation. In such cases, the court may impose a fine up to the maximum authorized by the statute.

(d) In determining the amount of the fine, the court shall consider:

(1) the need for the combined sentence to reflect the seriousness of the offense (including the harm or loss to the victim and the gain to the defendant), to promote respect for the law, to provide just punishment and to afford adequate deterrence;

(2) any evidence presented as to the defendant's ability to pay the fine (including the ability to pay over a period of time) in light of his earning capacity and financial resources;

(3) the burden that the fine places on the defendant and his dependents relative to alternative punishments;

(4) any restitution or reparation that the defendant has made or is obligated to make;

(5) any collateral consequences of conviction, including civil obligations arising from the defendant's conduct;

(6) whether the defendant previously has been fined for a similar offense;

(7) the expected costs to the government of any term of probation, or term of imprisonment and term of supervised release imposed; and

(8) any other pertinent equitable considerations.

The amount of the fine should always be sufficient to ensure that the fine, taken together with other sanctions imposed, is punitive.

(e) If the defendant establishes that

(1) he is not able and, even with the use of a reasonable installment schedule, is not likely to become able to pay all or part of the fine required by the preceding provisions, or

(2) imposition of a fine would unduly burden the defendant's dependents, the court may impose a lesser fine or waive the fine. In these circumstances, the court shall consider alternative sanctions in lieu of all or a portion of the fine, and must still

impose a total combined sanction that is punitive. Although any additional sanction not proscribed by the guidelines is permissible, community service is the generally preferable alternative in such instances.

(f) If the defendant establishes that payment of the fine in a lump sum would have an unduly severe impact on him or his dependents, the court should establish an installment schedule for payment of the fine. The length of the installment schedule generally should not exceed twelve months, and shall not exceed the maximum term of probation authorized for the offense. The defendant should be required to pay a substantial installment at the time of sentencing. If the court authorizes a defendant sentenced to probation or supervised release to pay a fine on an installment schedule, the court shall require as a condition of probation or supervised release that the defendant pay the fine according to the schedule. The court also may impose a condition prohibiting the defendant from incurring new credit charges or opening additional lines of credit unless he is in compliance with the payment schedule.

(g) If the defendant knowingly fails to pay a delinquent fine, the court shall resentence him in accordance with 18 U.S.C. § 3614.

Part F - Sentencing Options

§5F1.5. OCCUPATIONAL RESTRICTIONS

(a) The court may impose a condition of probation or supervised release prohibiting the defendant from engaging in a specified occupation, business, or profession, or limiting the terms on which the defendant may do so, only if it determines that:

(1) a reasonably direct relationship existed between the defendant's occupation, business, or profession and the conduct relevant to the offense of conviction; and

(2) imposition of such a restriction is reasonably necessary to protect the public because there is reason to believe that, absent such restriction, the defendant will continue to engage in unlawful conduct similar to that for which the defendant was convicted.

(b) If the court decides to impose a condition of probation or supervised release restricting a defendant's engagement in a specified occupation, business, or profession, the court shall impose the condition for the minimum time and to the minimum extent necessary to protect the public.

Part H - Specific Offender Characteristics

§5H1.2. EDUCATION AND VOCATIONAL SKILLS (POLICY STATEMENT)

Education and vocational skills are not ordinarily relevant in determining whether a departure is warranted, but the extent to which a defendant may have misused special training or education to facilitate criminal activity is an express guideline factor. See §3B1.3 (Abuse of Position of Trust or Use of Special Skill).

Education and vocational skills may be relevant in determining the conditions of probation or supervised release for rehabilitative purposes, for public protection by restricting activities that allow for the utilization of a certain skill, or in determining the appropriate type of community service.

§5H1.4. PHYSICAL CONDITION, INCLUDING DRUG OR ALCOHOL DEPENDENCE OR ABUSE; GAMBLING ADDICTION (POLICY STATEMENT)

Physical condition or appearance, including physique, may be relevant in determining whether a departure is warranted, if the condition or appearance, individually or in combination with other offender characteristics, is present to an unusual degree and distinguishes the case from the typical cases covered by the guidelines. An extraordinary physical impairment may be a reason to depart downward; e.g., in the case of a seriously infirm defendant, home detention may be as efficient as, and less costly than, imprisonment.

Drug or alcohol dependence or abuse ordinarily is not a reason for a downward departure. Substance abuse is highly correlated to an increased propensity to commit crime. Due to this increased risk, it is highly recommended that a defendant who is incarcerated also be sentenced to supervised release with a requirement that the defendant participate in an appropriate substance abuse program (see §5D1.3(d)(4)). If participation in a substance abuse program is required, the length of supervised release should take into account the length of time necessary for the probation office to judge the success of the program.

In certain cases a downward departure may be appropriate to accomplish a specific treatment purpose. See §5C1.1, Application Note 6.

In a case in which a defendant who is a substance abuser is sentenced to probation, it is strongly recommended that the conditions of probation contain a requirement that the defendant participate in an appropriate substance abuse program (see §5B1.3(d)(4)).

Addiction to gambling is not a reason for a downward departure.

§5H1.10. RACE, SEX, NATIONAL ORIGIN, CREED, RELIGION, AND SOCIO-ECONOMIC STATUS (POLICY STATEMENT)

These factors are not relevant in the determination of a sentence.

§5H1.11. MILITARY, CIVIC, CHARITABLE, OR PUBLIC SERVICE; EMPLOYMENT-RELATED CONTRIBUTIONS; RECORD OF PRIOR GOOD WORKS (POLICY STATEMENT)

Military service may be relevant in determining whether a departure is warranted, if the military service, individually or in combination with other offender characteristics, is present to an unusual degree and distinguishes the case from the typical cases covered by the guidelines.

Civic charitable, or public service; employment-related contributions; and similar prior good works are not ordinarily relevant in determining whether a departure is warranted.

Part K - Departures

§5K2.0. GROUNDS FOR DEPARTURE (POLICY STATEMENT)

(a) Upward Departures in General and Downward Departures in Criminal Cases Other Than Child Crimes and Sexual Offenses.—

(1) In General.—The sentencing court may depart from the applicable guideline range if—

(A) in the case of offenses other than child crimes and sexual offenses, the court finds, pursuant to 18 U.S.C. § 3553(b)(1), that there exists an aggravating or mitigating circumstance; or

(B) in the case of child crimes and sexual offenses, the court finds, pursuant to 18 U.S.C. § 3553(b)(2)(A)(i), that there exists an aggravating circumstance, of a kind, or to a degree, not adequately taken into consideration by the Sentencing Commission in formulating the guidelines that, in order to advance the objectives set forth in 18 U.S.C. § 3553(a)(2), should result in a sentence different from that described.

(2) Departures Based on Circumstances of a Kind not Adequately Taken into Consideration.—

(A) Identified Circumstances.—This subpart (Chapter Five, Part K, Subpart 2 (Other Grounds for Departure)) identifies some of the circumstances that the Commission may have not adequately taken into consideration in determining the applicable guideline range (e.g., as a specific offense characteristic or other adjustment). If any such circumstance is present in the case and has not adequately been taken into consideration in determining the applicable guideline range, a departure consistent with 18 U.S.C. § 3553(b) and the provisions of this subpart may be warranted.

(B) Unidentified Circumstances.—A departure may be warranted in the exceptional case in which there is present a circumstance that the Commission has not identified in the guidelines but that nevertheless is relevant to determining the appropriate sentence.

(3) Departures Based on Circumstances Present to a Degree not Adequately Taken into Consideration.—A departure may be warranted in an exceptional case, even though the circumstance that forms the basis for the departure is taken into consideration in determining the guideline range, if the court determines that such circumstance is present in the offense to a degree substantially in excess of, or substantially below, that which ordinarily is involved in that kind of offense.

(4) Departures Based on not Ordinarily Relevant Offender Characteristics and Other Circumstances.—An offender characteristic or other circumstance identified in Chapter Five, Part H (Offender Characteristics) or elsewhere in the guidelines as not ordinarily relevant in determining whether a departure is warranted may be relevant to this determination only if such offender characteristic or other circumstance is present to an exceptional degree.

(b) Downward Departures in Child Crimes and Sexual Offenses.—Under 18 U.S.C. § 3553(b)(2)(A)(ii), the sentencing court may impose a sentence below the range established by the applicable guidelines only if the court finds that there exists a mitigating circumstance of a kind, or to a degree, that—

(1) Has been affirmatively and specifically identified as a permissible ground of downward departure in the sentencing guidelines or policy statements issued under section 994(a) of title 28, United States Code, taking account of any amendments to such sentencing guidelines or policy statements by act of Congress;

(2) Has not adequately been taken into consideration by the Sentencing Commission in formulating the guidelines; and

(3) Should result in a sentence different from that described. The grounds enumerated in this Part K of Chapter Five are the sole grounds that have been affirmatively and specifically identified as a permissible ground of downward departure in these sentencing guidelines and policy statements. Thus, notwithstanding any other

reference to authority to depart downward elsewhere in this Sentencing Manual, a ground of downward departure has not been affirmatively and specifically identified as a permissible ground of downward departure within the meaning of section 3553(b)(2) unless it is expressly enumerated in this Part K as a ground upon which a downward departure may be granted.

(c) Limitation on Departures Based on Multiple Circumstances.—The court may depart from the applicable guideline range based on a combination of two or more offender characteristics or other circumstances, none of which independently is sufficient to provide a basis for departure, only if—

(1) Such offender characteristics or other circumstances, taken together, make the case an exceptional one; and

(2) Each such offender characteristic or other circumstance is—

(A) present to a substantial degree; and

(B) identified in the guidelines as a permissible ground for departure, even if such offender characteristic or other circumstance is not ordinarily relevant to a determination of whether a departure is warranted.

(d) Prohibited Departures.—Notwithstanding subsections (a) and (b) of this policy statement, or any other provision in the guidelines, the court may not depart from the applicable guideline range based on any of the following circumstances:

(1) Any circumstance specifically prohibited as a ground for departure in §§5H1.10 (Race, Sex, National Origin, Creed, Religion, and Socio-Economic Status), 5H1.12 (Lack of Guidance as a Youth and Similar Circumstances), the last sentence of 5H1.4 (Physical Condition, Including Drug or Alcohol Dependence or Abuse; Gambling Addiction), the last sentence of 5K2.12 (Coercion and Duress), and 5K2.19 (Post-Sentencing Rehabilitative Efforts).

(2) The defendant's acceptance of responsibility for the offense, which may be taken into account only under 3E1.1 (Acceptance of Responsibility).

(3) The defendant's aggravating or mitigating role in the offense, which may be taken into account only under §3B1.1 (Aggravating Role) or §3B1.2 (Mitigating Role), respectively.

(4) The defendant's decision, in and of itself, to plead guilty to the offense or to enter a plea agreement with respect to the offense (i.e., a departure may not be based merely on the fact that the defendant decided to plead guilty or to enter into a plea agreement, but a departure may be based on justifiable, non-prohibited reasons as part of a sentence that is recommended, or agreed to, in the plea agreement and accepted by the court. See §6B1.2 (Standards for Acceptance of Plea Agreement).

(5) The defendant's fulfillment of restitution obligations only to the extent required by law including the guidelines (i.e., a departure may not be based on unexceptional efforts to remedy the harm caused by the offense).

(6) Any other circumstance specifically prohibited as a ground for departure in the guidelines.

(e) Requirement of Specific Written Reasons for Departure.--If the court departs from the applicable guideline range, it shall state, pursuant to 18 U.S.C. § 3553(c), its specific reasons for departure in open court at the time of sentencing and, with limited exception in the case of statements received in camera, shall state those reasons with specificity in the written judgment and commitment order.

CHAPTER 8 - SENTENCING OF ORGANIZATIONS

Part C - Fines

§8C1.1. DETERMINING THE FINE—CRIMINAL PURPOSE ORGANIZATIONS

If, upon consideration of the nature and circumstances of the offense and the history and characteristics of the organization, the court determines that the organization operated primarily for a criminal purpose or primarily by criminal means, the fine shall be set at an amount (subject to the statutory maximum) sufficient to divest the organization of all its net assets. When this section applies, Subpart 2 (Determining the Fine--Other Organizations) and §8C3.4 (Fines Paid by Owners of Closely Held Organizations) do not apply.

§8C2.4. BASE FINE

(a) The base fine is the greatest of:

(1) the amount from the table in subsection (d) below corresponding to the offense level determined under §8C2.3 (Offense Level); or

(2) the pecuniary gain to the organization from the offense; or

(3) the pecuniary loss from the offense caused by the organization, to the extent the loss was caused intentionally, knowingly, or recklessly.

(b) *Provided*, that if the applicable offense guideline in Chapter Two includes a special instruction for organizational fines, that special instruction shall be applied, as appropriate.

(c) *Provided, further*, that to the extent the calculation of either pecuniary gain or pecuniary loss would unduly complicate or prolong the sentencing process, that amount, i.e., gain or loss as appropriate, shall not be used for the determination of the base fine.

(d)   **Offense Level Fine Table**

Offense Level	Amount
6 or less	$5,000
7	$7,500
8	$10,000
9	$15,000
10	$20,000
11	$30,000
12	$40,000
13	$60,000
14	$85,000
15	$125,000
16	$175,000
17	$250,000
18	$350,000
19	$500,000
20	$650,000
21	$910,000
22	$1,200,000
23	$1,600,000
24	$2,100,000
25	$2,800,000
26	$3,700,000
27	$4,800,000
28	$6,300,000
29	$8,100,000
30	$10,500,000
31	$13,500,000
32	$17,500,000
33	$22,000,000
34	$28,500,000
35	$36,000,000
36	$45,500,000
37	$57,500,000
38 or more	$72,500,000

§8C2.5. CULPABILITY SCORE

(a) Start with 5 points and apply subsections (b) through (g) below.

(b) Involvement in or Tolerance of Criminal Activity.—If more than one applies, use the greatest:

> (1) If—
>> (A) the organization had 5,000 or more employees and
>>> (i) an individual within high-level personnel of the organization participated in, condoned, or was willfully ignorant of the offense; or
>>> (ii) tolerance of the offense by substantial authority personnel was pervasive throughout the organization; or
>> (B) the unit of the organization within which the offense was committed had 5,000 or more employees and
>>> (i) an individual within high-level personnel of the unit participated in, condoned, or was willfully ignorant of the offense; or
>>> (ii) tolerance of the offense by substantial authority personnel was pervasive throughout such unit,
>> add 5 points; or
> (2) If—
>> (A) the organization had 1,000 or more employees and
>>> (i) an individual within high-level personnel of the organization participated in, condoned, or was willfully ignorant of the offense; or
>>> (ii) tolerance of the offense by substantial authority personnel was pervasive throughout the organization; or
>> (B) the unit of the organization within which the offense was committed had 1,000 or more employees and
>>> (i) an individual within high-level personnel of the unit participated in, condoned, or was willfully ignorant of the offense; or
>>> (ii) tolerance of the offense by substantial authority personnel was pervasive throughout such unit,
>> add 4 points; or

(3) If—

    (A) the organization had 200 or more employees and

        (i) an individual within high-level personnel of the organization participated in, condoned, or was willfully ignorant of the offense; or

        (ii) tolerance of the offense by substantial authority personnel was pervasive throughout the organization; or

    (B) the unit of the organization within which the offense was committed had 200 or more employees and

        (i) an individual within high-level personnel of the unit participated in, condoned, or was willfully ignorant of the offense; or

        (ii) tolerance of the offense by substantial authority personnel was pervasive throughout such unit,

    add 3 points; or

(4) If the organization had 50 or more employees and an individual within substantial authority personnel participated in, condoned, or was willfully ignorant of the offense, add 2 points; or

(5) If the organization had 10 or more employees and an individual within substantial authority personnel participated in, condoned, or was willfully ignorant of the offense, add 1 point.

(c) Prior History.—If more than one applies, use the greater:

(1) If the organization (or separately managed line of business) committed any part of the instant offense less than 10 years after

    (A) a criminal adjudication based on similar misconduct; or

    (B) civil or administrative adjudication(s) based on two or more separate instances of similar misconduct, add 1 point; or

(2) If the organization (or separately managed line of business) committed any part of the instant offense less than 5 years after

    (A) a criminal adjudication based on similar misconduct; or

    (B) civil or administrative adjudication(s) based on two or more separate instances of similar misconduct, add 2 points.

(d) Violation of an Order.—If more than one applies, use the greater:

(1)(A) If the commission of the instant offense violated a judicial order or injunction, other than a violation of a condition of probation; or

(B) if the organization (or separately-managed line of business) violated a condition of probation by engaging in similar misconduct, i.e., misconduct similar to that for which it was placed on probation, add 2 points; or

(2) If the commission of the instant offense violated a condition of probation, add 1 point.

(e) Obstruction of Justice.—If the organization willfully obstructed or impeded, attempted to obstruct or impede, or aided, abetted, or encouraged obstruction of justice during the investigation, prosecution, or sentencing of the instant offense, or, with knowledge thereof, failed to take reasonable steps to prevent such obstruction or impedance or attempted obstruction or impedance, add 3 points.

(f) Effective Compliance and Ethics Program

(1) If the offense occurred even though the organization had in place at the time of the offense an effective compliance and ethics program, as provided in §8B2.1 (Effective Compliance and Ethics Program), subtract 3 points.

(2) Subsection (f)(1) shall not apply if, after becoming aware of an offense, the organization unreasonably delayed reporting the offense to appropriate governmental authorities.

(3)(A) Except as provided in subparagraphs (B) and (C), subsection (f)(1) shall not apply if an individual within high-level personnel of the organization, a person within high-level personnel of the unit of the organization within which the offense was committed where the unit had 200 or more employees, or an individual described in §8B2.1(b)(2)(B) or (C), participated in, condoned, or was willfully ignorant of the offense.

(B) There is a rebuttable presumption, for purposes of subsection (f)(1), that the organization did not have an effective compliance and ethics program if an individual —

(i) within high-level personnel of a small organization; or

(ii) within substantial authority personnel, but not within high-level personnel, of any organization, participated in, condoned, or was willfully ignorant of, the offense.

(C) Subparagraphs (A) and (B) shall not apply if—

(i) the individual or individuals with operational responsibility for the compliance and ethics program (see §8B2.1(b)(2)(C)) have direct reporting obligations to the governing authority or an appropriate subgroup thereof (e.g., an audit committee of the board of directors);

(ii) the compliance and ethics program detected the offense before discovery outside the organization or before such discovery was reasonably likely;

(iii) the organization promptly reported the offense to appropriate governmental authorities; and

(iv) no individual with operational responsibility for the compliance and ethics program participated in, condoned, or was willfully ignorant of the offense.

(g) Self-Reporting, Cooperation, and Acceptance of Responsibility.—If more than one applies, use the greatest:

(1) If the organization

(A) prior to an imminent threat of disclosure or government investigation; and

(B) within a reasonably prompt time after becoming aware of the offense, reported the offense to appropriate governmental authorities, fully cooperated in the investigation, and clearly demonstrated recognition and affirmative acceptance of responsibility for its criminal conduct, subtract 5 points; or

(2) If the organization fully cooperated in the investigation and clearly demonstrated recognition and affirmative acceptance of responsibility for its criminal conduct, subtract 2 points; or

(3) If the organization clearly demonstrated recognition and affirmative acceptance of responsibility for its criminal conduct, subtract 1 point.

§8C2.6. MINIMUM AND MAXIMUM MULTIPLIERS

Using the culpability score from §8C2.5 (Culpability Score) and applying any applicable special instruction for fines in Chapter Two, determine the applicable minimum and maximum fine multipliers from the table below.

Minimum and Maximum Fine Multipliers

Culpability Score	Minimum Multiplier	Maximum Multiplier
10 or more	2.00	4.00
9	1.80	3.60
8	1.60	3.20
7	1.40	2.80
6	1.20	2.40
5	1.00	2.00
4	0.80	1.60
3	0.60	1.20
2	0.40	0.80
1	0.20	0.40
0 or less	0.05	0.20

§8C2.7. GUIDELINE FINE RANGE—ORGANIZATIONS

(a) The minimum of the guideline fine range is determined by multiplying the base fine determined under §8C2.4 (Base Fine) by the applicable minimum multiplier determined under §8C2.6 (Minimum and Maximum Multipliers).

(b) The maximum of the guideline fine range is determined by multiplying the base fine determined under §8C2.4 (Base Fine) by the applicable maximum multiplier determined under §8C2.6 (Minimum and Maximum Multipliers).

§8C2.8. DETERMINING THE FINE WITHIN THE RANGE (POLICY STATEMENT)

(a) In determining the amount of the fine within the applicable guideline range, the court should consider:

(1) the need for the sentence to reflect the seriousness of the offense, promote respect for the law, provide just punishment,

afford adequate deterrence, and protect the public from further crimes of the organization;

(2) the organization's role in the offense;

(3) any collateral consequences of conviction, including civil obligations arising from the organization's conduct;

(4) any nonpecuniary loss caused or threatened by the offense;

(5) whether the offense involved a vulnerable victim;

(6) any prior criminal record of an individual within high-level personnel of the organization or high-level personnel of a unit of the organization who participated in, condoned, or was willfully ignorant of the criminal conduct;

(7) any prior civil or criminal misconduct by the organization other than that counted under §8C2.5(c);

(8) any culpability score under §8C2.5 (Culpability Score) higher than 10 or lower than 0;

(9) partial but incomplete satisfaction of the conditions for one or more of the mitigating or aggravating factors set forth in §8C2.5 (Culpability Score);

(10) any factor listed in 18 U.S.C. § 3572(a); and

(11) whether the organization failed to have, at the time of the instant offense, an effective compliance and ethics program within the meaning of §8B2.1 (Effective Compliance and Ethics Program).

(b) In addition, the court may consider the relative importance of any factor used to determine the range, including the pecuniary loss caused by the offense, the pecuniary gain from the offense, any specific offense characteristic used to determine the offense level, and any aggravating or mitigating factor used to determine the culpability score.

§8C3.3. REDUCTION OF FINE BASED ON INABILITY TO PAY

(a) The court shall reduce the fine below that otherwise required by §8C1.1 (Determining the Fine—Criminal Purpose Organizations), or §8C2.7 (Guideline Fine Range—Organizations) and §8C2.9

(Disgorgement), to the extent that imposition of such fine would impair its ability to make restitution to victims.

(b) The court may impose a fine below that otherwise required by §8C2.7 (Guideline Fine Range—Organizations) and §8C2.9 (Disgorgement) if the court finds that the organization is not able and, even with the use of a reasonable installment schedule, is not likely to become able to pay the minimum fine required by §8C2.7 (Guideline Fine Range—§8C2.9 (Disgorgement).

Provided, that the reduction under this subsection shall not be more than necessary to avoid substantially jeopardizing the continued viability of the organization.

§8C3.4. FINES PAID BY OWNERS OF CLOSELY-HELD ORGANIZATIONS

The court may offset the fine imposed upon a closely held organization when one or more individuals, each of whom owns at least a 5 percent interest in the organization, has been fined in a federal criminal proceeding for the same offense conduct for which the organization is being sentenced. The amount of such offset shall not exceed the amount resulting from multiplying the total fines imposed on those individuals by those individuals' total percentage interest in the organization.

Part D - Organizational Probation

§8D1.1. IMPOSITION OF PROBATION— ORGANIZATIONS

(a) The court shall order a term of probation:

(1) if such sentence is necessary to secure payment of restitution (§8B1.1), enforce a remedial order (§8B1.2), or ensure completion of community service (§8B1.3);

(2) if the organization is sentenced to pay a monetary penalty (e.g., restitution, fine, or special assessment), the penalty is not paid in full at the time of sentencing, and restrictions are necessary to safeguard the organization's ability to make payments;

(3) if, at the time of sentencing,
    (A) the organization
        (i) has 50 or more employees, or
        (ii) was otherwise required under law to have an effective compliance and ethics program; and
    (B) the organization does not have such a program;

(4) if the organization within five years prior to sentencing engaged in similar misconduct, as determined by a prior criminal adjudication, and any part of the misconduct underlying the instant offense occurred after that adjudication;

(5) if an individual within high-level personnel of the organization or the unit of the organization within which the instant offense was committed participated in the misconduct underlying the instant offense and that individual within five years prior to sentencing engaged in similar misconduct, as determined by a prior criminal adjudication, and any part of the misconduct underlying the instant offense occurred after that adjudication;

(6) if such sentence is necessary to ensure that changes are made within the organization to reduce the likelihood of future criminal conduct;

(7) if the sentence imposed upon the organization does not include a fine; or

(8) if necessary to accomplish one or more of the purposes of sentencing set forth in 18 U.S.C. § 3553(a)(2).

§8D1.2. TERM OF PROBATION—ORGANIZATIONS

(a) When a sentence of probation is imposed—

(1) In the case of a felony, the term of probation shall be at least one year but not more than five years.

(2) In any other case, the term of probation shall be not more than five years.

§8D1.4. RECOMMENDED CONDITIONS OF PROBATION—ORGANIZATIONS (POLICY STATEMENT)

(a) The court may order the organization, at its expense and in the format and media specified by the court, to publicize the nature of the offense committed, the fact of conviction, the nature of the punishment imposed, and the steps that will be taken to prevent the recurrence of similar offenses.

(b) If probation is imposed under §8D1.1(a)(2), the following conditions may be appropriate to the extent they appear necessary to safeguard the organization's ability to pay any deferred portion of an order of restitution, fine, or assessment:

(1) The organization shall make periodic submissions to the court or probation officer, at intervals specified by the court, reporting on the organization's financial condition and results of business operations, and accounting for the disposition of all funds received.

(2) The organization shall submit to:

(A) A reasonable number of regular or unannounced examinations of its books and records at appropriate business premises by the probation officer or experts engaged by the court; and

(B) interrogation of knowledgeable individuals within the organization. Compensation to and costs of any experts engaged by the court shall be paid by the organization.

(3) The organization shall be required to notify the court or probation officer immediately upon learning of

(A) any material adverse change in its business or financial condition or prospects, or

(B) the commencement of any bankruptcy proceeding, major civil litigation, criminal prosecution, or administrative proceeding against the organization, or any investigation or formal inquiry by governmental authorities regarding the organization.

(4) The organization shall be required to make periodic payments, as specified by the court, in the following priority:

(A) restitution;

(B) fine; and

(C) any other monetary sanction.

(c) If probation is ordered under §8D1.1(a)(3), (4), (5), or (6), the following conditions may be appropriate:

(1) The organization shall develop and submit to the court an effective compliance and ethics program consistent with §8B2.1 (Effective Compliance and Ethics Program). The organization shall include in its submission a schedule for implementation of the compliance and ethics program.

(2) Upon approval by the court of a program referred to in subdivision (1), the organization shall notify its employees and shareholders of its criminal behavior and its program to prevent and detect violations of law. Such notice shall be in a form prescribed by the court.

(3) The organization shall make periodic reports to the court or probation officer, at intervals and in a form specified by the court, regarding the organization's progress in implementing the program referred to in subdivision (1). Among other things, such reports shall disclose any criminal prosecution, civil litigation, or administrative proceeding commenced against the organization, or any investigation or formal inquiry by governmental authorities of which the organization learned since its last report.

(4) In order to monitor whether the organization is following the program referred to in subdivision (1), the organization shall submit to:

(A) A reasonable number of regular or unannounced examinations of its books and records at appropriate business premises by the probation officer or experts engaged by the court; and

(B) interrogation of knowledgeable individuals within the organization. Compensation to and costs of any experts engaged by the court shall be paid by the organization.

II

Documents

Deferred Prosecution Agreements

BRISTOL-MYERS SQUIBB

UNITED STATES

v.

BRISTOL-MYERS SQUIBB

Deferred Prosecution Agreement

1. Bristol-Myers Squibb Company ("BMS" or the "Company") by its undersigned attorneys, pursuant to authority granted by its Board of Directors, and the United States Attorney's Office for the District of New Jersey (the "Office"), enter into this Deferred Prosecution Agreement (the "Agreement"). Except as specifically provided below, the Agreement shall be in effect for a period of two years from the date it is fully executed.

2. The Office has informed BMS that it will file, on or shortly after the date this Agreement is fully executed, a criminal complaint in the United States District Court for the District of New Jersey charging BMS with conspiracy to commit securities fraud, contrary to Title 15, United States Code, Sections 78j(b) & 78ff and Title 17, Code of Federal Regulations, Section 240.10b-5, in violation of Title

18, United States Code, Section 371, during the period of 2000 through 2001.

3. BMS and the Office agree that, upon filing of the criminal complaint in accordance with the preceding paragraph, this Agreement shall be publicly filed in the United States District Court for the District of New Jersey, and BMS agrees to post the Agreement prominently on its website.

4. In light of BMS's remedial actions to date and its willingness to (a) undertake additional remediation; (b) acknowledge responsibility for its behavior; (c) continue its cooperation with the Office and other governmental regulatory agencies; (d) demonstrate its future good conduct and full compliance with the securities laws and Generally Accepted Accounting Principles; and (e) consent to payment of additional restitution as set forth in paragraph 21, the Office shall recommend to the Court that prosecution of BMS on the criminal complaint filed pursuant to paragraph 2 be deferred for a period of twenty-four (24) months from the filing date of the criminal complaint. If the Court declines to defer prosecution for any reason, this Agreement shall be null and void, and the parties will revert to their pre-Agreement positions.

5. BMS has undertaken extensive reforms and remedial actions in response to the conduct at BMS that is and has been the subject of the investigation by the Office. These reforms and remedial actions have included:

(a)   Retaining the Honorable Frederick B. Lacey as Independent Advisor, to conduct a comprehensive review of the implementation and effectiveness of the internal controls, financial reporting, disclosure, planning, budget and projection processes and related compliance functions of the Company, as well as to serve additional supervisory and monitoring functions described herein;

(b) Entering a Consent filed in the United States District Court for the District of New Jersey in United States Securities Exchange Commission v. Bristol-Myers Squibb Company, Civ. Action No. 04-3680 (FSH) (the "D.N.J. Action") providing for, among other things, the payment of a $100 million Civil Penalty and an additional $50 million Shareholder Fund payment, both of which amounts are to be distributed pursuant to the Fair Fund provisions of Section 308(a) of the Sarbanes-Oxley Act of 2002, as well as incorporating an array of remedial measures to be undertaken by BMS together with extensive supervisory and monitoring responsibilities to be carried out by the Independent Advisor during a review period extending through the filing of the Company's Form 10-K for the year ended 2005;

(c) Making a payment of an additional $300 million to compensate present and former BMS shareholders in connection with lawsuits filed and consolidated in In re Bristol-Myers Squibb Securities Litigation, Master File No. 02-CV-2251 (LAP) (S.D.N.Y.) (the "Consolidated Shareholder Litigation");

(d) Making significant personnel changes after April 2002 and after the Office commenced its investigation including:

(i) replacing the former Chief Financial Officer (CFO);

(ii) replacing the former President of the Worldwide Medicines Group;

(iii) replacing the former Controller;

(iv) establishing the position of Assistant Controller for Financial Compliance and Control;

(v) establishing the position of Chief Compliance Officer;

(vi) establishing a position for an experienced securities regulation and disclosure lawyer who has a significant role in all BMS disclosure responsibilities;

(e) Changing its budget process, to assure that appropriate consideration is given to input and analysis from the bottom to top, and not exclusively from top to bottom, and adequately documenting that process;

(f) Forming a business risk and disclosure group that includes senior management, the Independent Advisor and counsel to the Independent Advisor;

(g) Identifying and implementing actions to improve the effectiveness of its disclosure controls and procedures and internal controls, including enhancing its resources and training with respect to financial reporting and disclosure responsibilities, and reviewing such actions with its Audit Committee and independent auditors;

(h) Implementing a formal review and certification process of its annual and quarterly reports filed with the Securities and Exchange Commission (SEC); and

(i) Providing an effective mechanism in the form of a confidential hotline and e-mail address, of which BMS employees are informed and can use to notify BMS of any concerns about wholesaler inventory levels or the integrity of the financial disclosures, books and records of BMS.

6. BMS shall maintain and continue to implement any remedial measures already undertaken or mandated as part of agreements BMS has reached in the following matters: In re Bristol-Myers Squibb Derivative Litigation, Master File No. 02-CV-8571 (LAP) (S.D.N.Y.) (the "Shareholder Derivative Action"); the "D.N.J. Action"; and the "Consolidated Shareholder Litigation."

7. In addition to the extensive remedial actions that it has taken to date, BMS agrees to undertake additional remedial actions and corporate reforms as set forth herein.

8. BMS shall establish the position of non-executive Chairman of the BMS Board of Directors (the "Non-Executive Chairman"), to advance and underscore the Company's commitment to exemplary corporate citizenship, to best practices of effective corporate governance and the highest principles of integrity and professionalism, and to fostering a culture of openness, accountability and compliance throughout the Company. BMS shall retain the position of Non-Executive Chairman at least throughout the term of this Agreement.

9. BMS agrees to appoint an additional non-executive Director acceptable to the Office to the BMS Board of Directors within sixty (60) days of the execution of this Agreement.

10. The Company's CFO, General Counsel, and Chief Compliance Officer regularly shall brief and provide information to the Non-Executive Chairman, in a manner to be determined by the Non-Executive Chairman. In addition, the Non-Executive Chairman shall have the authority to meet with, and require reports on any subject from, any officer or employee of the Company.

11. BMS agrees that until at least the date of the filing of the Company's Form 10-K for the year ended 2006, it will retain an outside, independent individual or entity (the "Monitor"), selected by BMS and approved by the Office. BMS may employ as the Monitor

the Honorable Frederick B. Lacey. It shall be a condition of the Monitor's retention that the Monitor is independent of BMS and that no attorney-client relationship shall be formed between the Monitor and BMS.

12. The Monitor shall:

(a) Monitor BMS's compliance with this Agreement, and have authority to require BMS to take any steps he believes are necessary to comply with the terms of this Agreement;

(b) Continue the review, reforms and other functions undertaken as the Independent Advisor;

(c) Report to the Office, on at least a quarterly basis and between thirty and forty- five calendar days after the filing of the Company's Form 10-K for the year ended 2006, as to BMS's compliance with this Agreement and the implementation and effectiveness of the internal controls, financial reporting, disclosure processes and related compliance functions of the Company. The first report to the Office shall be due within forty-five (45) days after the close of the second quarter 2005, and subsequent quarterly reports (other than the final report) shall be due by the close of the quarter. The reporting function of the Monitor shall extend until forty-five (45) days subsequent to the filing of the Company's Form 10-K for the year ended 2006 in order to facilitate the submission of the Monitor's final report to the Office;

(d) Cooperate with the SEC and provide information about BMS as requested by that agency;

(e) Monitor BMS's compliance with applicable federal securities laws, and in his quarterly reports make recommendations necessary to ensure that the Company complies with applicable federal securities laws;

(f) Monitor BMS's compliance with agreements BMS has reached in the Shareholder Derivative Action, the D.N.J. Action, and the Consolidated Shareholder Litigation; and

(g) Monitor the information received by the confidential hotline and e-mail address described in paragraph 5(i).

13. BMS agrees that the Chief Executive Officer (CEO), Non-Executive Chairman, and General Counsel will meet quarterly with

the Office and the Monitor, in conjunction with the Monitor's quarterly reports.

14. BMS shall adopt all recommendations contained in each report submitted by the Monitor to the Office unless BMS objects to the recommendation and the Office agrees that adoption of the recommendation should not be required. The Monitor's reports to the Office shall not be received or reviewed by BMS prior to submission to the Office; such reports will be preliminary until senior management of BMS is given the opportunity, within ten (10) days after the submission of the report to the Office, to comment to the Monitor and the Office in writing upon such reports, and the Monitor has reviewed and provided to the Office responses to such comments, upon which such reports shall be considered final.

15. BMS agrees that the Monitor may also disclose his reports, as directed by the Office, to any other federal, state or foreign law enforcement or regulatory agency in furtherance of an investigation of any other matters discovered by, or brought to the attention of, the Office in connection with the Office's investigation of BMS or the implementation of this Agreement.

16. BMS agrees that if the Monitor resigns or is unable to serve the balance of his term, a successor shall be selected by BMS and approved by the Office within forty-five (45) days. BMS agrees that all provisions in this Agreement that apply to the Monitor shall apply to any successor Monitor.

17. The Non-Executive Chairman and the Compensation Committee of the Board of Directors shall set goals and objectives relevant to compensation of the CEO, evaluate the CEO's performance in light of those goals and objectives, and recommend to the Board of Directors compensation based on this evaluation.

18. BMS agrees that it will establish and maintain a training and education program, which shall be reviewed and approved by the Board of Directors, designed to advance and underscore the Company's commitment to exemplary corporate citizenship, to best practices of effective corporate governance and the highest principles of integrity and professionalism, and to fostering a culture of openness, accountability and compliance throughout the Company. Completion of such training shall be mandatory for (a) all BMS

officers, executives and employees who are involved in accounting and financial reporting functions, or the oversight thereof, whether at the corporate or the division level, including but not limited to each officer or employee responsible for closing the books within his or her area of responsibility at the end of a quarterly or annual reporting period; (b) all employees of the BMS legal division with responsibility for finance, business risk or disclosure issues; and (c) other senior officers and executives at BMS, at both the corporate and operating levels, as proposed by BMS and approved by the Office (collectively the "Mandatory Participants"). Such training and education program will cover, at a minimum, the following subjects: (a) the obligations imposed by the federal securities laws, including disclosure obligations; (b) proper internal accounting controls and procedures; (c) discovering and recognizing accounting practices that do not conform to Generally Accepted Accounting Principles or that are otherwise improper; and (d) the obligations assumed by, and responses expected of, the Mandatory Participants upon learning of improper, illegal or potentially illegal acts relating to BMS's accounting and financial reporting. The Board of Directors shall communicate to the Mandatory Participants, in writing or by video, its review and endorsement of the training and education program.

19. BMS shall commence providing the training mandated by paragraph 18 within ninety (90) days after the date of the execution of this Agreement and shall, at that time, submit to the Office a written description of the content and planned implementation of the training and education program. BMS shall thereafter provide such training and education on an annual basis for all those who become Mandatory Participants during the preceding twelve months.

20. BMS shall endow a chair at Seton Hall University School of Law dedicated to the teaching of business ethics and corporate governance, which position shall include conducting one or more seminars per year on business ethics and corporate governance at Seton Hall University School of Law that members of BMS's executive and management staff, along with representatives of the executive and management staffs of other companies in the New Jersey area, may attend.

21. BMS shall make an additional payment of $300 million into the shareholder compensation fund established pursuant to the consent judgment in the D.N.J. Action. This payment shall be administered according to the terms of such fund. Together with this payment, BMS will have paid a total of $839 million in compensation to its shareholders and former shareholders. This sum includes payments already made by BMS of $300 million in the Consolidated Shareholder Litigation, $150 million in the D.N.J. Action, and $89 million in actions by shareholders who requested to be excluded from the settlement in the Consolidated Shareholder Litigation, as well as the additional $300 million that BMS shall pay pursuant to this Agreement. BMS may make the additional payment of $300 million in a single payment at or before the close of the third quarter of 2005, or in four approximately equal quarterly installments, with the first installment due at the close of the third quarter of 2005. None of the proceeds of the payment required by this Agreement shall be payable as attorney's fees. Any costs of administering the distribution of the additional payment called for by this agreement shall be borne by BMS. To the extent that any money paid into the D.N.J. shareholder compensation fund pursuant to this Agreement is not claimed by shareholders or former shareholders within three years, the remaining amount shall be paid to the United States Treasury.

22. Within thirty (30) days of the execution of this Agreement, BMS agrees to call a meeting, on a date mutually agreed upon by BMS and the Office, of its senior executives and any senior financial personnel, and any other BMS employees who the Company desires to attend, such meeting to be attended by the United States Attorney and other representatives of the Office for the purpose of communicating the goals and expected effect of this Agreement.

23. For a period of one year from the execution of this Agreement, the Non-Executive Chairman, CEO, and General Counsel shall contemporaneously monitor either in person or telephonically BMS's quarterly conference calls for analysts ("analyst calls"), and the Non-Executive Chairman shall attend and participate in any preparatory meetings held among the CEO, the CFO, the General Counsel and other members of BMS senior management in anticipation of the analyst calls. The General Counsel

shall ensure that representatives of the BMS legal division are informed and consulted regarding, at a minimum, issues relating to disclosure or securities law that may arise in the course of preparing for the analyst calls.

24. The CEO and CFO shall prepare and submit to the Non-Executive Chairman, Chief Compliance Officer and the Monitor described in paragraph 11 written reports on the following subjects:

(a) all non-standard transactions with major U.S. wholesalers, such written report to be submitted within fifteen (15) days of such transaction;

(b) an overview and analysis of BMS's annual budget process for its major business units, including description of significant instances of any top-down changes to business unit submissions, such written report to be submitted together with the proposed budget submitted for approval to the Board of Directors;

(c) sales and earnings forecasts or projections at the corporate or major business unit level which indicate a quarterly target will not be met, together with a description of steps subsequently taken, if any, to achieve the budget target, such written report to be submitted quarterly and at least ten (10) business days prior to the Company's scheduled quarterly analyst call;

(d) description of significant instances in which the preliminary quarterly closing of the books of any major business unit indicated that the business unit would not meet its budget target for any sales or earnings measure.

25. BMS agrees that it shall include in its quarterly and annual public filings with the SEC and its annual report to shareholders financial disclosures concerning the following: (a)(i) for the Company's U.S. Pharmaceuticals business, estimated wholesaler/direct-customer inventory levels of the top fifteen (15) products sold by such business and (ii) for major non-U.S. countries, estimated aggregate wholesaler/direct-customer inventory levels of the top fifteen (15) pharmaceutical products sold in such countries taken as a whole measured by aggregate annual sales in such countries; (b) arrangements with and policies concerning wholesalers/direct customers and other distributors of such products,

including but not limited to efforts by BMS to control and monitor wholesaler/distributor inventory levels; (c) data concerning prescriptions or other measures of end-user demand for such top fifteen (15) BMS pharmaceutical products sold within the U.S. and in major non-U.S. countries; (d) acquisition, divestiture, and restructuring reserve policies and activity; and (e) rebate accrual policies and activity. The CEO shall, at the annual BMS shareholder meeting, report to the shareholders on these topics.

26. BMS agrees that it will continue to review and improve, where necessary, the content of its public financial and non-financial public disclosures, including periodic SEC filings, annual and other shareholder reports, press releases, and disclosures during analyst conference calls, as well as during meetings with investors and credit ratings agencies. BMS agrees that it will at all times strive for openness and transparency in its public reporting and disclosures.

27. BMS shall encourage the free flow of information between its employees and its external auditor, and encourage its CFO and senior finance personnel to seek advice from the external auditor. The CEO, CFO, General Counsel, and Chief Compliance Officer shall meet quarterly with the Company's external auditors, such meeting to occur following the closing of the Company's books for the quarter and prior to the Company's scheduled quarterly analyst call. At the quarterly meeting, the BMS attendees shall discuss business and financial reporting developments, issues and trends with the external auditor, as well as provide information to the external auditor concerning the subjects described in paragraph 24 above, and shall respond to inquiries from the external auditor.

28. BMS accepts and acknowledges responsibility for the facts set forth in the Statement of Facts attached as Appendix A (the "Statement of Facts") and incorporated by reference herein by entering into this Agreement and by, among other things, (a) the extensive remedial actions that it has taken to date, (b) its continuing commitment to full cooperation with the Office and other governmental agencies, and (c) and the other undertakings it has made as set forth in this Agreement.

29. BMS agrees that in the event that future criminal proceedings are brought by the Office in accordance with paragraphs 4 and 36

through 39 of this Agreement, BMS will not contest the admissibility of the Statement of Facts in any such proceedings. Nothing in this Agreement shall be construed as an acknowledgment by BMS that the Agreement, including the Statement of Facts, is admissible or may be used in any proceeding other than in a proceeding brought by the Office.

30. BMS expressly agrees that it shall not, through its present or future attorneys, Board of Directors, agents, officers or employees, make any public statement contradicting any statement of fact contained in the Statement of Facts. Any such contradictory public statement by BMS, its present or future attorneys, Board of Directors, agents, officers or employees, shall constitute a breach of this Agreement as governed by paragraphs 36 and 37 of this Agreement, and BMS would thereafter be subject to prosecution pursuant to the terms of this Agreement. The decision of whether any public statement by any such person contradicting a fact contained in the Statement of Facts will be imputed to BMS for the purpose of determining whether BMS has committed a knowing and material breach of this Agreement shall be at the sole discretion of the Office. Should the Office notify BMS of a public statement by any such person that in whole or in part contradicts a statement of fact contained in the Statement of Facts, BMS may avoid breach of this Agreement by publicly repudiating such statement within forty-eight (48) hours after such notification. This paragraph is not intended to apply to any statement by any former BMS employee, officer or director, or any BMS employee, officer or director testifying in any proceeding in an individual capacity and not on behalf of BMS

31. BMS agrees that its continuing cooperation during the term of this Agreement shall include, but shall not be not limited to, the following:

    (a) Not engaging in or attempting to engage in any criminal conduct as defined in paragraph 34.

    (b) Completely, truthfully and promptly disclosing all information concerning all matters about which the Office and other government agencies designated by the Office may inquire, and continuing to provide the Office, upon request, all documents and other materials relating to matters about which the Office inquires, and analysis or other work product as may be requested by the Office, as promptly as is practicable. Cooperation under this paragraph shall include identification of documents that may be relevant to the matters under investigation.

(c) Consenting to any order sought by the Office permitting disclosure of any materials that constitute "matters occurring before the grand jury" within the meaning of Rule 6(e) of the Federal Rules of Criminal Procedure.

(d) Not asserting, in relation to any request of the Office, any claims of attorney-client privilege or attorney work-product doctrine as to any documents, records, information or testimony requested by the Office related to: (i) factual internal investigations undertaken by the Company or its counsel relating to the matters under investigation by the Office; (ii) legal advice given contemporaneously with, and related to, such matters. Such materials are referred to hereinafter as the "Confidential Materials." By producing the Confidential Materials pursuant to this Agreement, BMS does not intend to waive the protection of the attorney-client privilege or the attorney work-product doctrine, or any other applicable privilege, as to third parties. The Office will maintain the confidentiality of the Confidential Materials pursuant to this Agreement and will not disclose them to any third party, except to the extent that the Office determines, in its sole discretion, that disclosure is otherwise required by law or would be in furtherance of the discharge of the duties and responsibilities of the Office.

(e) Making available BMS officers, directors, and employees and using its best efforts to make available former BMS officers, directors, and employees to provide information and/or testimony at all reasonable times as requested by the Office, including sworn testimony before a federal grand jury or in federal trials, as well as interviews with federal law enforcement authorities. Cooperation under this paragraph shall include identification of witnesses who, to BMS's knowledge, may have material information regarding the matters under investigation.

(f) Providing testimony, certifications, and other information deemed necessary by the Office or a court to identify or establish the original location, authenticity, or other evidentiary foundation necessary to admit into evidence documents in any criminal or other proceeding as requested by the Office.

32. BMS has provided extensive cooperation to the Office in connection with its investigation. BMS acknowledges and understands that its prior, ongoing and future cooperation are important factors in the decision of the Office to enter into this Agreement, and BMS agrees to continue to cooperate fully with the Office, and with any other governmental agency designated by the Office, regarding any issue about which BMS has knowledge or information.

33. BMS authorizes the Office and the SEC to share information from and about BMS with each other and hereby waives any confidentiality accorded to that information by law, agreement or otherwise that would, absent authorization by BMS, prohibit or limit such sharing. No other waivers of confidentiality shall be required in that regard.

34. BMS will inform the Office of any credible evidence of criminal conduct at BMS occurring after the date of the Agreement, including making available internal audit reports, letters threatening litigation, "whistleblower" complaints, civil complaints, and documents produced in civil litigation so evidencing such criminal conduct. For purposes of this Agreement, "criminal conduct" is defined as (a) any crime related to BMS's business activities committed by one or more BMS executive officers or directors; (b) securities fraud, accounting fraud, financial fraud or other business fraud materially affecting the books, records or publicly-filed reports of BMS; and (c) obstruction of justice.

35. The Office may continue to investigate current and former BMS employees. Nothing in this Agreement restricts in any way the ability of the Office to investigate and prosecute any BMS employee or former BMS employee.

36. Should the Office determine during the term of this Agreement that BMS has committed any criminal conduct as defined in paragraph 34 commenced subsequent to the date of this Agreement, or otherwise in any other respect knowingly and materially breached this Agreement, BMS shall, in the discretion of the Office, thereafter be subject to prosecution for any federal crimes of which the Office has knowledge, including crimes relating to the matters set forth in the Statement of Facts. Except in the event of a

breach of this Agreement, it is the intention of the parties to this Agreement that all investigations of BMS relating to the matters set forth in the Statement of Facts that have been, or could have been, conducted by the Office prior to the date of this Agreement shall not be pursued further as to BMS.

37. Should the Office determine that BMS has knowingly and materially breached any provision of this Agreement, the Office shall provide written notice to BMS of the alleged breach and provide BMS with a two-week period in which to make a presentation to the Office to demonstrate that no breach occurred, or, to the extent applicable, that the breach was not material or knowingly committed or has been cured. The parties understand and agree that should BMS fail to make a presentation to the Office within a two-week period after receiving written notice of an alleged breach, it shall be conclusively presumed that BMS is in breach of this Agreement. The parties further understand and agree that the determination whether BMS has breached this Agreement rests solely in the discretion of the Office, and the exercise of discretion by the Office under this paragraph is not subject to review in any court or tribunal outside the Department of Justice. In the event of a breach of this Agreement that results in a prosecution of BMS, such prosecution may be premised upon any information provided by or on behalf of BMS to the Office at any time, unless otherwise agreed when the information was provided.

38. BMS shall expressly waive all rights to a speedy trial pursuant to the Sixth Amendment of the United States Constitution, Title 18, United States Code, Section 3161, Federal Rule of Criminal Procedure 48(b), and any applicable Local Rules of the United States District Court for the District of New Jersey, for the period that this Agreement is in effect.

39. In case of a knowing material breach of this Agreement, any prosecution of BMS relating to the facts set forth in Appendix A that are not time-barred by the applicable statute of limitations as of the execution of this Agreement may be commenced against BMS notwithstanding the expiration of any applicable statute of limitations during the deferred prosecution period. BMS agrees to waive the statute of limitations with respect to any crime that would otherwise

expire during the two- year term of this Agreement, and this waiver is knowing and voluntary and in express reliance on the advice of counsel.

40. This agreement expires twenty-four (24) months after the date of its execution, except that, in the event that the Office is conducting an ongoing investigation, prosecution or proceeding related to the facts set forth in the Statement of Facts, the provisions of paragraph 31(b)-(f) regarding the Company's cooperation shall remain in effect until such investigation, prosecution or proceeding is concluded.

41. The Office agrees that if BMS is in full compliance with all of its obligations under this Agreement, the Office, within ten (10) days of the expiration of twenty-four (24) months from the execution of this Agreement, will seek dismissal with prejudice of the criminal complaint filed pursuant to paragraph 2. Except as otherwise provided herein, during and upon the conclusion of the term of this Agreement, the Office agrees that it will not prosecute BMS further for the matters that have been the subject of the Office's investigation relating to this Agreement.

42. BMS agrees that, if it sells or merges all or substantially all of its business operations as they exist as of the date of this Agreement to or into a single purchaser or group of affiliated purchasers during the term of this Agreement, it shall include in any contract for sale or merger a provision binding the purchaser/successor to the obligations described in this Agreement.

43. It is understood that this Agreement is limited to BMS and the Office on behalf of the U.S. Department of Justice and cannot bind other federal, state or local authorities. However, the Office will bring this Agreement and the cooperation of BMS and its compliance with its other obligations under this Agreement to the attention of other prosecuting offices, if requested to do so.

44. This Agreement constitutes the full and complete agreement between BMS and the Office and supersedes any previous agreement between them. No additional promises, agreements, or conditions have been entered into other than those set forth in this Agreement, and none will be entered into unless in writing and signed by the Office, BMS's counsel, and a duly authorized representative of BMS

It is understood that the Office may permit exceptions to or excuse particular requirements set forth in this Agreement at the written request of BMS or the Monitor, but any such permission shall be in writing.

AGREED TO:

_____   _____
Bristol-Myers Squibb Company   Christopher J. Christie
                                      United States Attorney
                                      District of New Jersey

Date: June 15, 2005   Date: June 15, 2005

APPENDIX A — STATEMENT OF FACTS

Bristol-Myers Squibb Company ("B.M.S." or the "Company") is a Delaware corporation with offices in New Jersey and one of the world's leading producers of pharmaceuticals and health care products. For 2000, B.M.S. reported sales of $18.216 billion and net earnings of $4.711 billion. For 2001, B.M.S. reported sales of $19.423 billion and net earnings of $5.245 billion. The great majority of BMS's sales and earnings in 2000 and 2001 were from sales of pharmaceutical products.

B.M.S. is a publicly traded corporation, the common stock of which is listed on the New York Stock Exchange. BMS's shareholders are located throughout the United States, including in the District of New Jersey.

Wholesaler Sales & Channel Stuffing

B.M.S. manufactures pharmaceutical products and distributes those products through wholesalers. In 2000 to 2001, four U.S. wholesalers handled the distribution of approximately 85% of BMS's U.S. pharmaceutical products. These wholesalers delivered B.M.S. pharmaceutical products to thousands of independent pharmacies, retail chains, hospitals and other health care providers across the country. Wholesalers generally purchased product at least sufficient to meet the demand of these retail businesses.

In 2000 to 2001, B.M.S. regularly used financial incentives to spur wholesalers to buy product in excess of prescription demand, so that B.M.S. could report higher sales and earnings. This practice, which is commonly known as "channel stuffing," was also referred to as "sales acceleration" or "trade loading."

B.M.S. used a variety of financial incentives to spur wholesalers to buy and hold additional product in excess of prescription demand. The financial incentives included:

(a) pre-price increase buy-ins — allowing wholesalers to purchase product in advance of a B.M.S. price increase for the product;

(b) "extended datings" of invoices — extending the due date for the wholesaler's payment beyond the usual thirty days;

(c) additional early payment discounts — discounts beyond those customarily offered to wholesalers for paying early for product; and

(d) "future file" purchases — allowing wholesalers to buy at an old, lower price, even after a price increase had become effective.

Growth of Excess Inventory

Channel stuffing in 2000 to 2001 resulted in "excess inventory" at the wholesalers, because the wholesalers took on more inventory than the amount needed to meet anticipated demand. In the absence of sales incentives or investment purchases, a wholesaler's "normal" inventory level was generally in the approximate range of three weeks' to one month's supply or a mature prescription drug.

The process of reducing excess inventory to levels closer to normal was often called a "workdown," and generally involved selling less than demand during the workdown period. High levels of excess inventory were therefore likely to have an adverse effect on future sales.

Double-Double, Mega-Double and "Top Down" Budgeting

In 1994, B.M.S. announced what became known as the "Double-Double" goal: to double BMS's sales, earnings and earnings per share ("EPS") in a seven year period. The Double-Double required average compound annual growth of approximately 10%. The last year of the Double-Double was 2000, and at the end of the year B.M.S. announced that it had achieved the doubling of earnings and EPS, and that it "virtually" doubled its sales since 1993.

In September 2000 B.M.S. announced the "Strategy for Growth," which incorporated what became known as the "Mega-Double" goal, a plan to double year-end 2000 sales and earnings by the end of 2005, a five-year period. Achievement of the Mega-Double required average compound annual growth of nearly 15%.

The Double-Double and Mega-Double goals were accompanied by what was known as a "top-down" budget process. B.M.S. set aggressive sales and earnings budget targets for the Company and its business units, consistent with the Double-Double and Mega-Double goals.

Earnings Guidance and Estimates

The management of many public companies, including B.M.S., provided "guidance" to the investing public regarding the expected performance of the business, including EPS, for upcoming quarters and years. In 2000 and at least until December 13, 2001, B.M.S. advised the investing public through its guidance that it expected performance consistent with the Double-Double and Mega-Double.

Relying in part on a company's guidance, professional securities analysts then made public their own estimates of the company's expected performance. These "earnings estimates" or "analyst expectations" — which when averaged were referred to as the "consensus estimates" — were closely followed by investors.

By 2000, B.M.S. had met or exceeded analysts' consensus estimates for at least twenty-four (24) straight quarters, and this consistency was part of the company's public image. B.M.S. understood that its failure to meet or exceed the consensus estimates for a quarter likely would result in a decrease in the company's stock price.

SEC Reporting

As a public company, B.M.S. was required to comply with the rules and regulations of the United States Securities and Exchange Commission (SEC). The SEC is an independent agency of the United States government which was charged by law with maintaining honest and efficient markets in securities. The SEC's rules and regulations were designed to protect members of the investing public by, among other things, ensuring that a company's financial information was accurately disclosed to the investing public.

Under the SEC's rules and regulations, B.M.S. and its officers were required to submit quarterly reports on Form 10-Q and annual reports on Form 10-K which included financial statements that accurately presented BMS's financial condition and the results of its business operations. Federal law further required the data in these reports to be truthful and consistent with the underlying facts and required the accounting treatments employed in these reports to be consistent with generally accepted accounting principles ("GAAP").

Federal law also required that the Forms 10-Q and 10-K include a section entitled Management's Discussion and Analysis ("MD&A") containing additional information about the company's financial condition and operations. MD&A must contain any material information necessary to make the accompanying financial statements not misleading. The purpose of MD&A was to give investors an opportunity to look at the company through the eyes of management, and understand the company's prospects for the future. MD&A is required to focus on material events and uncertainties known to management that would cause reported financial information not to be necessarily indicative of future operating results or of future financial condition.

Press Releases and Conference Calls

After the end of each quarter, B.M.S. made public announcements about its sales, earnings and business operations generally. The company issued press releases which described sales performance, overall and by product, and held conference calls for analysts regarding the performance of the business. In preparation for the conference calls, senior B.M.S. executives met and discussed issues expected to arise and how to respond to those issues.

The Scheme to Defraud

"Making the Numbers"

B.M.S. promoted a corporate culture in which meeting or exceeding company budget targets and the consensus estimates was considered mandatory. Achieving these goals was known as "making the numbers" or "hitting the numbers." Meeting internal B.M.S.

budget targets generally also resulted in sales and earnings that met or exceeded the consensus estimates.

To this end, B.M.S. set aggressive internal sales and earnings targets for 2000, 2001 and earlier periods that would enable the company to hit the widely-touted Double-Double and Mega-Double goals. Every quarter, and at year-end, B.M.S. pressured lower-level employees to meet their budget targets. Certain employees who suggested that the company's budget targets were too aggressive or expressed doubts that they could make the numbers were transferred or demoted.

In the late 1990s, BMS's use of channel stuffing and the accompanying build-up of excess inventory at the wholesalers caused concern among several B.M.S. executives, and during 1999 the Company made some effort to reduce or slow the growth of excess inventory. At the end of 1999, however, senior management refused to accept a proposed B.M.S. budget that would have missed the Double-Double goal, and reassigned the senior executive responsible for the budget proposal. No serious or systematic effort to work down inventory was adopted or undertaken by B.M.S. during the period 2000 to 2001.

Throughout 2000 and 2001, B.M.S. used channel stuffing to boost its sales and artificially inflate its earnings, which enabled B.M.S. to make its numbers and report results consistent with the Double-Double and Mega-Double. This use of channel stuffing to boost sales and earnings, and the resulting steadily increasing levels of excess inventory at the wholesalers, was concealed from the investing public, and was not disclosed to BMS's external auditors and Board of Directors. Without channel stuffing, B.M.S. would have missed its budget targets and the consensus estimates.

Manipulation of Corporate Reserves

B.M.S. regularly set aside funds in "reserve" accounts, to be used for costs related to events such as corporate acquisitions, divestitures or restructuring. Under GAAP, reserves were to be based on good-faith estimates of costs that were reasonably likely to occur. B.M.S. was not permitted to establish reserves that were not based on good-faith estimates of reasonably likely future costs, or to carry excess amounts in its reserve accounts for future use. B.M.S. was not permitted to use reserves to increase revenue in the future or for expenses not related to the purpose for which the funds were originally set aside.

B.M.S. maintained a "reserve schedule" showing available funds from B.M.S.'s improperly-established reserves, as well as excess amounts from other reserves. B.M.S. used funds from the reserve schedule for improper purposes, in particular to boost B.M.S. revenue when the company needed additional income to hit the consensus estimates.

Deliberate Rebate Under-Accrual

B.M.S. expected, at the time it sold its products, that at a later time it would have to pay rebates in connection with a portion of those sales. These rebates included Medicaid, "prime vendor" and "managed health care" rebates. Because B.M.S. sold its products to wholesalers, there was a period of time — a "lag" — between the time of sale and when B.M.S. received and paid the rebate claims. In keeping with GAAP, B.M.S. was required to set aside funds to pay for expected rebates at the time it booked revenue from its sales.

As BMS's excess inventory at the wholesalers grew in 2000 and 2001, B.M.S. imposed accounting policies and procedures which caused B.M.S. not to accrue for the rebate liabilities for excess inventory. These policies were inconsistent with GAAP and resulted in an under-accrual in BMS's rebate accounts.

Throughout 2000 and 2001 B.M.S. finance staff used an artificially low lag period of six months to estimate accrual balances, even as the excess inventory at the wholesalers grew steadily. By deviating from GAAP and intentionally under-accruing in the Medicaid rebate account, B.M.S. hid the growth of excess inventory and made B.M.S.'s sales figures look stronger than they actually were.

Closing Budget Gaps Through Channel Stuffing and Improper Accounting

In 2000 and 2001, B.M.S. often approached the end of a quarter with a gap between actual sales and earnings and the level of sales necessary to hit the company's budget targets. B.M.S. used channel stuffing to make up the company's sales and earnings shortfalls and close the gap. This practice led to a steady increase in excess inventory at the wholesalers.

At various times during a quarter or at quarter-end, in order to supplement the revenue from channel stuffing activity, B.M.S. used funds from improperly-established reserves to bolster income and enable B.M.S. to hit its earnings targets and the consensus estimates.

In every quarter in 2000 and 2001, B.M.S. publicly announced that it had met or exceeded the consensus estimates. B.M.S. would not have been able to make its numbers without channel stuffing and improper accounting measures. B.M.S. did not disclose to the investing public that its success in makings its numbers was due to channel stuffing and improper accounting measures.

False and Misleading Disclosure

In 2000 and 2001, B.M.S. did not disclose the nature or extent of the company's channel stuffing in its 10Ks and 10Qs or in its quarterly press releases and analyst conference calls. For example, B.M.S. did not disclose:

(a) the use of financial incentives to the wholesalers to generate sales in excess of demand;
(b) the use of sales in excess of demand to close budget gaps and hit budget targets;
(c) the level of excess inventory at the wholesalers; and
(d) the amount that excess inventory increased each quarter in 2000 and 2001.

Items (a) through (d) above constituted information reasonably likely to have a material effect on BMS's financial condition or results of its business operations. Failure to disclose this information deprived the investing public of information regarding B.M.S.'s past performance and future prospects. Further, in addition to omitting material information, B.M.S. made or caused others to make or permitted false and misleading statements of material fact on the quarterly analyst conference calls and in the company's SEC filings.

DIRECTOR'S CERTIFICATE

I have read this agreement and carefully reviewed every part of it with counsel for Bristol- Myers Squibb Company ("B.M.S."). I understand the terms of this Agreement and voluntarily agree, on behalf of B.M.S., to each of the terms. Before signing this Agreement, I consulted with the attorney for B.M.S. The attorney fully advised me of BMS's rights, of possible defenses, of the Sentencing Guidelines' provisions, and of the consequences of entering into this Agreement. No promises or inducements have been made other than those contained in this Agreement. Furthermore, no one has threatened or forced me, or to my knowledge any person authorizing this Agreement on behalf of B.M.S., in any way to enter into this Agreement. I am also satisfied with the attorney's representation in this matter. I certify that I am a director of B.M.S., and that I have been duly authorized by the Board of Directors of B.M.S. to execute this certificate on behalf of B.M.S.

6/13/05
Date   Bristol-Myers Squibb Company

CERTIFICATE OF COUNSEL

I am counsel for Bristol-Myers Squibb Company ("B.M.S."). In connection with such representation, I have examined relevant B.M.S. documents, and have discussed this Agreement with the authorized representative of B.M.S. Based on my review of the foregoing materials and discussions, I am of the opinion that:

1. The undersigned counsel is duly authorized to enter into this Agreement on behalf of B.M.S.

2. This Agreement has been duly and validly authorized, executed and delivered on behalf of B.M.S., and is a valid and binding obligation of B.M.S.

Further, I have carefully reviewed every part of this Agreement with directors of B.M.S. I have fully advised these directors of BMS's rights, of possible defenses, of the Sentencing Guidelines' provisions, and of the consequences of entering into this Agreement. To my knowledge, BMS's decision to enter into this Agreement is an informed and voluntary one.

_____   6/15/05   Date

_____   6/15/05   Date

Attorneys for Bristol-Myers Squibb Company

CERTIFIED COPY OF RESOLUTION

Upon motion duly made, seconded, and unanimously carried by the affirmative vote of all the Directors present, the following resolutions were adopted:

WHEREAS, Bristol-Myers Squibb Company ("B.M.S.") has been engaged in discussions with the United States Attorney's Office for the District of New Jersey (the "Office") in connection with an investigation being conducted by the Office into activities of B.M.S. relating to wholesaler inventory and certain accounting issues;

WHEREAS, the Board of Directors of B.M.S. consents to resolution of these discussions by entering into a deferred prosecution agreement that the Board of Directors has reviewed with outside counsel representing B.M.S., relating to a criminal complaint to be filed in the U.S. District Court for the District of New Jersey charging B.M.S. with conspiracy to commit securities fraud,

NOW THEREFORE, BE IT RESOLVED that outside counsel representing B.M.S. from Debevoise & Plimpton LLP be, and they hereby are authorized to execute the Deferred Prosecution Agreement on behalf of B.M.S. substantially in the same form as reviewed by the Board of Directors at this meeting and as attached hereto as Exhibit A, and that a Director of the Company is authorized to execute the Director's Certificate attached thereto.

SECRETARY'S CERTIFICATION

I, Sandra Leung, the duly elected Secretary of Bristol-Myers Squibb Company (the "Company") a corporation duly organized under the laws of the State of Delaware, hereby certify that the following is a true and exact copy of a resolution approved by the Board of Directors of the Company at a meeting held at New York, New York on June 12, 2005;

WHEREAS, Bristol-Myers Squibb Company ("B.M.S.") has been engaged in discussions with the United States Attorney's Office for the District of New Jersey (the "Office") in connection with an investigation being conducted by the Office into activities of B.M.S. relating to wholesaler inventory and certain accounting issues;

WHEREAS, the Board of Directors of BMS consents to resolution of these discussions by entering into a deferred prosecution agreement that the Board of Directors has reviewed with outside counsel representing B.M.S., relating to a criminal complaint to be filed in the U.S. District Court for the District of New Jersey charging B.M.S. with conspiracy to commit securities fraud,

NOW THEREFORE, BE IT RESOLVED that outside counsel representing B.M.S. from Debevoise & Plimpton LLP be, and they hereby are authorized to execute the Deferred Prosecution Agreement on behalf of B.M.S. substantially in the same form as reviewed by the Board of Directors at this meeting and as attached hereto as Exhibit A, and that a Director of the Company is authorized to execute the Director's Certificate attached thereto.

IN WITNESS WHEREOF, I have hereunto signed my name as Secretary and affixed the Seal of said Corporation this 13th day of June, 2005.

———————————————
                                              Secretary

CORPORATE SEAL

KPMG

U.S. Department of Justice

United States Attorney
Southern District of New York

The Silvio J. Mollo Building
One Saint Andrew's Plaza
New York, New York 10007

August 26, 2005

Robert S. Bennett, Esq.
Skadden, Arps, Slate, Meagher & Flom LLP
1440 New York Avenue, N.W.
Washington, D.C. 20005-2111

Re: KPMG — Deferred Prosecution Agreement

Dear Mr. Bennett:

Pursuant to our discussions and written exchanges, the United States Attorney's Office for the Southern District of New York (the "Office") and the defendant KPMG LLP ("KPMG"), by its undersigned attorneys, pursuant to authority granted by its Board of Directors in the form of a Board Resolution (a copy of which is attached hereto as Exhibit A), hereby enter into this Deferred Prosecution Agreement (the "Agreement").

The Criminal Information

1. KPMG will consent to the filing of a one-count Information (the "Information") in the United States District Court for the Southern District of New York (the "Court") charging KPMG with participating in a conspiracy in violation of 18 U.S.C. § 371 to (i)

defraud the United States and its agency the Internal Revenue Service (hereinafter "IRS"); (ii) commit tax evasion in violation of 26 U.S.C. § 7201; and (iii) make and subscribe false and fraudulent tax returns, and aid and assist in the preparation and filing of said tax returns in violation of 26 U.S.C. § 7206. A copy of the Information is attached hereto as Exhibit B.

Acceptance of Responsibility for Violation of Law

2. KPMG admits and accepts that, as set forth in detail in the Statement of Facts, attached hereto as Exhibit C, through the conduct of certain KPMG tax leaders, partners, and employees, during the period from 1996 through 2002, KPMG:

> Assisted high net worth United States citizens to evade United States individual income taxes on billions of dollars in capital gain and ordinary income by developing, promoting and implementing unregistered and fraudulent tax shelters. A number of KPMG tax partners engaged in conduct that was unlawful and fraudulent, including: (i) preparing false and fraudulent tax returns for shelter clients; (ii) drafting false and fraudulent proposed factual recitations and representations as part of the documentation underlying the shelters; (iii) issuing opinions that contained those false and fraudulent statements and that purported to rely upon those representations, although the KPMG tax partners and the high net worth individual clients knew they were not true; (iv) actively taking steps to conceal from the IRS these shelters and the true facts regarding them; and (v) impeding the IRS by knowingly failing to locate and produce all documents called for by IRS summonses and misrepresenting to the IRS the nature and extent of KPMG's role with respect to certain tax shelters.

3. KPMG agrees that it will pay a total of $456,000,000 to the United States as part of this Agreement, which payments are attributable to the following: a fine consisting of disgorgement of $128,000,000 of fees received by KPMG from the activities described in the Statement of Facts; restitution to the IRS of $228,000,000 for actual losses suffered as a result of, among other

things, the running of statutes of limitations because of among other things, KPMG's failure to register its tax shelters, KPMG's failure to disclose its participation in certain fraudulent shelter transactions to the IRS in response to summonses, and KPMG's misrepresentation to the IRS of its involvement in those transactions, as detailed in the Statement of Facts; and an IRS penalty of $100,000,000 to settle the IRS's promoter penalty examination of KPMG pursuant to the closing agreement described in paragraph 19, below. KPMG agrees that it will satisfy this obligation with an initial payment of $256,000,000 to be paid on or before September 1, 2005, a second payment of $100,000,000 to be paid on or before June 30, 2006, and the remaining balance of $100,000,000 to be paid on or before December 21, 2006. In the event that KPMG fails to make these payments on a timely basis, the Office, in its sole discretion, can treat the failure to pay as a violation of the terms of the Agreement or require KPMG to extend the length of the Deferred Prosecution for a period of up to an additional eighteen (18) months.

4. KPMG agrees that no portion of the $456,000,000 that KPMG has agreed to pay to the United States under the terms of this Agreement is deductible on any Federal or State tax or information return.

5. KPMG has represented to the United States that no portion of the $456,000,000 that it has agreed to pay to the United States under the terms of this Agreement will be covered by any insurance policy in existence at the time of the conduct alleged in the Information or at the time any notice of claim was made to its insurer(s), which representation was material to the United States in determining KPMG's ability to make full restitution and pay penalties to the United States, which amounts, in the Government's view, were far in excess of the $456,000,000 agreed to herein. KPMG agrees that, in the event that any portion of KPMG's $456,000,000 obligation to the United States is ultimately covered by insurance, 50 percent of any insurance funds received by KPMG shall be remitted to the United States. The payment to the United States of a portion of the amounts received from insurance shall be over and above the $456,000,000 that KPMG has agreed to pay, but in no event shall the total payments made by KPMG to the United States (which total

payments includes both the underlying $456,000,000 and insurance proceeds) exceed $600,000,000. In addition, KPMG agrees that it will not enter into any agreement or understanding with its insurance carrier(s) to receive insurance coverage for any portion of that $456,000,000 in exchange for increased insurance premium payments made by KPMG in the future.

Permanent Restrictions On And Elevated Standards
For KPMG's Tax Practice

6. KPMG agrees to the following permanent restrictions and elevated standards for its tax practice:

(a). KPMG will cease its private client tax practice by February 28, 2006, and will take on no new clients or engagements in its private client tax practice after the signing of this Agreement (provided, however, that it will not be a violation of this provision for KPMG, during the 30 days following the signing of this Agreement, inadvertently to take on a new client or engagement, provided that the engagement is promptly terminated upon discovery of the error);

(b). KPMG will cease its compensation and benefits tax practice (exclusive of technical expertise maintained within its Washington National Tax practice) by February 28, 2006, or by such other later date as is reasonably determined by the Monitor, and promptly after the signing of this Agreement will commence a process to transition out of this practice;

(c). KPMG will not develop or assist in developing, market or assist in marketing, sell or assist in selling, or implement or assist in implementing, any pre-packaged tax product;

(d). KPMG will not participate in marketing, implementing, or issuing any "covered opinion" (as defined below in subparagraph (i)(I)) with respect to any "listed transaction" (as defined below in subparagraph (i)(III));

(e). KPMG will not provide any tax services under any conditions of confidentiality (as defined in 26 C.F.R. § 1.6011-4(b)(3)(ii));

(f). KPMG will not charge or accept fees subject to contractual protection (as defined in 26 C.F.R. § 1.6011-4(b)(4)) or any fees that are not based exclusively on the number of hours worked at set hourly rates, which rates may not exceed twice KPMG's standard rates, provided that (I) KPMG may charge or accept fees described in 31 C.F.R. § 10.27(b) in the case of reverse sales and use tax audits, (II) KPMG may enter into arrangements to limit the total fees in any matter to a maximum amount or to limit fees to a specified amount per return, in each case where the fees to be charged under such arrangement would not exceed the amount that would be charged if the fees were instead based on the number of hours worked at hourly rates not more than twice KPMG's standard rates, and (III) this subparagraph (f) does not apply with respect to engagements involving a claim for refund or application for other tax incentives where the claim or application has been filed prior to the date of this Agreement;

(g). KPMG will comply with the ethics and independence rules concerning independence, tax services, and contingent fees as adopted by the Public Company Accounting Oversight Board on July 26, 2005, or as thereafter amended, as of the effective date of those rules;

(h). Except as provided in subparagraphs (a) or (k), KPMG will not prepare tax returns, or provide tax advice of any kind to any individual clients except that KPMG will be permitted to provide: (I) individual tax planning and compliance services to individuals who are owners or senior executives of privately held business clients of KPMG, (II) individual tax services as part of its international executive services practice, which provides advice regarding the tax obligations of personnel of public company or private entity clients of KPMG who are stationed outside of their home country, and (III) bank trust outsourcing services where KPMG prepares trust tax returns for trust departments of large financial institutions;

(i). KPMG will comply with the minimum opinion thresholds set forth in the following table for opinions issued after September 28, 2005, and will comply with the minimum return position thresholds set forth in the following tables for tax returns that are filed after October 17, 2005:

	Standard for: **Covered Opinion on Principal Purpose Transaction**	Standard for: **Tax Return Preparation on Principal Purpose or Listed Transactions**	Standard for: **Covered Opinion on Other Transactions**	Standard for: **Tax Return Preparation on Other Transactions**
CLIENT TYPE				
Individuals	Should	Should	Should	More likely than not
Other private entities	Should	Should	Should	More likely than not
Large private entities	Should	Should	More likely than not	Realistic possibility of success
Public companies	Should	Should	More likely than not	Realistic possibility of success

For purposes of this subparagraph (i):

(I) The term "covered opinion" has the meaning set forth in 31 C.F.R. § 10.35(b)(2), and for purposes of this Agreement it is not interpreted to include: (A) any advice rendered to any entity for purposes of permitting that entity or its auditors (including KPMG, when KPMG acts as auditor of the entity) to determine whether a previously booked tax benefit is required to be reversed pursuant to FAS 109 (taking into account the provisions of the proposed interpretation thereof released by the Financial Accounting Standards Board on July 14, 2005 and any subsequent interpretations) or any similar provisions of international accounting standards, or (B) any advice rendered within KPMG for purposes of determining whether the firm, when acting as auditor of any entity, can attest to the manner in which the entity's financial statements reflect any tax benefit or contingent liability for unpaid taxes pursuant to FAS 109 (taking into account the provisions of the proposed interpretation thereof released by the Financial Accounting Standards Board on July 14, 2005 and any subsequent interpretations) or any similar provisions of international accounting standards;

(II) The term "principal purpose transaction" has the meaning set forth in 31 C.F.R. §§ 10.35(b)(2)(i)(B) and 10.35(b)(10);

(III) The term "listed transaction" has the meaning set forth in 31 C.F.R. § 10.35(b)(2)(i)(A);

(IV) The term "large private entity" means any privately held entity with prior year gross revenues of $300,000,000 or more, but only if the audited financial statements of the entity are prepared (1) in a manner that is comparable in all material respects to FAS 109 (including the proposed interpretation thereof released by the Financial Accounting Standards Board on July 14, 2005 and any subsequent interpretations), and (2) are either prepared in accordance with U.S. GAAP or are prepared in accordance with international/foreign country financial reporting standards;

(V) In the event the Treasury Department promulgates regulations or rules of practice establishing higher standards than those set forth in the table above, the above table will be deemed amended to incorporate such higher standards;

(VI) KPMG will collect in a central location all covered opinions issued during the 30 days following the date of this Agreement in order to facilitate review of those opinions by KPMG's compliance office and by the Monitor; and

(VII) In order to provide a limited exception to the standards set forth in the above table for "tax returns preparation on other transactions" for "individuals" and for "other private entities," for situations that are difficult to foresee and that (A) are identified shortly before the due date of the return, and (B) do not meet the elevated standards set forth in the above table, the parties agree that if, despite the exercise of reasonable due diligence, KPMG discovers within sixty days of the date on which a tax return is required to be filed (taking into account applicable extensions) that a position taken on the return does not meet the applicable standard set forth above for "other transactions," then KPMG will recommend to the client the adoption of an alternative return position that does meet the applicable standard, and if such alternative position is rejected by the client, KPMG will resign from its engagement to prepare or review the tax return unless (A) the taxpayer agrees to include a disclosure statement with the tax return on Form 8275-R (or any similar form prescribed by the IRS that includes a detailed description of the transaction and the position taken on the tax return), and (B) the completion of the engagement is approved by KPMG's tax compliance personnel. KPMG will compile in a central location, available for review by the IRS and the Monitor, copies of all Forms 8275-R (or similar form described above) prepared by KPMG pursuant to this paragraph of the Agreement. The Monitor may review the application of this exception and recommend changes as appropriate.

(j).   KPMG will not rely on an opinion issued by other professional firms to determine whether it complies with the minimum standards set forth in subparagraph (i) above unless KPMG concurs with the conclusions of such opinion; and

(k).   With respect to KPMG's federal, state and local tax controversy representation, (I) KPMG will not represent persons or entities other than public companies, private entities, or persons for whom KPMG is permitted to prepare tax returns under subparagraph (h); (II) KPMG will not defend any transaction that is or becomes a "listed transaction," and (III) after February 28, 2006, KPMG will not defend any transaction with respect to which the firm could not render an opinion or prepare a return in compliance with the standards set forth in subparagraph (i).

Cooperation

7.   KPMG acknowledges and understands that its cooperation with the criminal investigation by the Office is an important and material factor underlying the Office's decision to enter into this Agreement, and, therefore, KPMG agrees to cooperate fully and actively with the Office, the IRS, and with any other agency of the government designated by the Office ("Designated Agencies") regarding any matter relating to the Office's investigation about which KPMG has knowledge or information.

8. KPMG agrees that its continuing cooperation with the Office's investigation shall include, but not be limited to, the following:

(a).   Completely and truthfully disclosing all information in its possession to the Office and the IRS about which the Office and the IRS may inquire, including but not limited to all information about activities of KPMG, present and former partners, employees, and agents of KPMG;

(b). Providing to the Office, by December 31, 2005, a complete and truthful analysis and complete and detailed description of the design, marketing and implementation by KPMG of all the transactions listed on Exhibit A to the IRS Closing Agreement described below in paragraph 19, including where necessary and appropriate a detailed description of representative client transactions;

(c). Volunteering and providing to the Office any information and documents that come to KPMG's attention that may be relevant to the Office's investigation;

(d). Assembling, organizing, and providing, in responsive and prompt fashion, and, upon request, expedited fashion, all documents, records, information, and other evidence in KPMG's possession, custody, or control as may be requested by the Office or the IRS;

(e). Not asserting, in relation to the Office, any claim of privilege (including but not limited to the attorney-client privilege and the work product protection) as to any documents, records, information, or testimony requested by the Office related to its investigation, provided that:

(I) notwithstanding the provisions of this subparagraph (e), KPMG may assert the attorney-client privilege, work product protection, or other privileges with respect to (A) privileged communications between KPMG and its counsel that post-date February 1, 2004 and that concern the Office's investigation, (B) privileged communications between KPMG and Skadden, Arps, Slate, Meagher & Flom LLP, concerning the IRS's promoter penalty audit, or (C) any private civil litigation; and

(II) by producing privileged materials pursuant to this subparagraph (e), KPMG does not intend to waive the protection of the attorney-client privilege, work product protection, or any other applicable privilege as to third parties.

(f). Using its reasonable best efforts to make available its present and former partners and employees to provide information and/or testimony as requested by the Office and the IRS, including sworn testimony before a grand jury or in court proceedings, as well as interviews with law enforcement authorities, and to identify witnesses who, to KPMG's knowledge and information, may have material information concerning the Office's investigation, including but not limited to the conduct set forth in the Information and the Statement of Facts;

(g). Providing testimony or information necessary to identify or establish the original location, authenticity, or other basis for admission into evidence of documents or physical evidence in any criminal or other proceeding as requested by the Office or the IRS, including information and testimony concerning the Office's investigation, including but not limited to the conduct set forth in the Information and the Statement of Facts; and

(h). With respect to any information, testimony, documents, records or physical evidence provided by KPMG to the Office or a grand jury, KPMG consents to any and all disclosures of such materials to such Designated Agencies as the Office, in its sole discretion, deems appropriate. With respect to any such materials that constitute "matters occurring before the grand jury" within the meaning of Rule 6(e) of the Federal Rules of Criminal Procedure, KPMG further consents to: (I) any order sought by the Office permitting such disclosures; and (II) the Office's ex parte or in camera application for such orders.

9. KPMG agrees that its obligations to cooperate will continue even after the dismissal of the Information, and KPMG will continue to fulfill the cooperation obligations set forth in this Agreement in connection with any investigation, criminal prosecution or civil proceeding brought by the Office or by or against the IRS or the United States relating to or arising out of the conduct set forth in the Information and the Statement of Facts and relating in any way to the Office's investigation. KPMG's obligation to cooperate is not intended to apply in the event that a prosecution against KPMG by this Office is pursued and not deferred.

Deferral of Prosecution

10. In consideration of KPMG's entry into this Agreement and its commitment to: (a) accept and acknowledge responsibility for its conduct; (b) cooperate with the Office and the IRS; (c) make the payments specified in this Agreement; (d) comply with Federal criminal laws, including Federal tax laws; and (e) otherwise comply with all of the terms of this Agreement, the Office shall recommend to the Court that prosecution of KPMG on the Information be deferred for the period through December 31, 2006. KPMG shall expressly waive indictment and all rights to a speedy trial pursuant to the Sixth Amendment of the United States Constitution, Title 18, United States Code, Section 3161, Federal Rule of Criminal Procedure 48(b), and any applicable Local Rules of the United States District Court for the Southern District of New York for the period during which this Agreement is in effect.

11. The Office agrees that, if KPMG is in compliance with all of its obligations under this Agreement, the Office will, at the expiration of the period of deferral (including any extensions thereof), seek dismissal without prejudice as to KPMG of the Information filed against KPMG pursuant to paragraphs 1 and 10 of this Agreement. Except in the event of a violation by KPMG of any term of this Agreement, the Office will bring no additional charges against KPMG relating to its: (1) development, marketing, and implementation of FLIP, OPIS, BLIPS, and SOS and their variants, as described in the Statement of Facts, or any of the transactions described in Exhibit A to the Closing Agreement described below in paragraph 19; and (2) efforts to impair and impede the IRS and Senate investigations by concealing such transactions, as described in the Statement of Facts and Information. This Agreement does not provide any protection against prosecution for any crimes except as set forth above and does not apply to any individual or entity other than KPMG. KPMG and the Office understand that the Agreement to defer prosecution of KPMG must be approved by the Court, in accordance with 18 U.S.C. § 3161(h)(2). Should the Court decline to approve the Agreement to defer prosecution for any reason, both the

Office and KPMG are released from any obligation imposed upon them by this Agreement, and this Agreement shall be null and void.

12. It is further understood that should the Office in its sole discretion determine that KPMG has, after the date of the execution of this Agreement: (a) given false, incomplete or misleading information, (b) committed any crime other than a minor state violation, or (c) otherwise violated any provision of this Agreement, KPMG shall, in this Office's sole discretion, thereafter be subject to prosecution for any federal criminal violation of which the Office has knowledge, including but not limited to a prosecution based on the Information or the conduct described therein. Any such prosecution may be premised on any information provided by or on behalf of KPMG to the Office or the IRS at any time. Any such prosecutions that are not time-barred by the applicable statute of limitations on the date of this Agreement may be commenced against KPMG within the applicable period governing the statute of limitations. In addition, KPMG agrees to toll, and exclude from any calculation of time, the running of the criminal statute of limitations for a period of 5 years from the date of the execution of this Agreement. By this Agreement, KPMG expressly intends to and hereby does waive its rights in the foregoing respects, including any right to make a claim premised on the statute of limitations, as well as any constitutional, statutory, or other claim concerning pre-indictment delay. Such waivers are knowing, voluntary, and in express reliance on the advice of KPMG's counsel.

13. It is further agreed that in the event that the Office, in its sole discretion, determines that KPMG has violated any provision of this Agreement, including KPMG's failure to meet its obligations under this Agreement: (a) all statements made by or on behalf of KPMG to the Office and the IRS, including but not limited to the Statement of Facts, or any testimony given by KPMG or by any agent of KPMG before a grand jury, or elsewhere, whether before or after the date of this Agreement, or any leads from such statements or testimony, shall be admissible in evidence in any and all criminal proceedings hereinafter brought by the Office against KPMG; and (b) KPMG shall not assert any claim under the United States Constitution, Rule 11(f) of the Federal Rules of Criminal Procedure, Rule 410 of the

Federal Rules of Evidence, or any other federal rule, that statements made by or on behalf of KPMG before or after the date of this Agreement, or any leads derived therefrom, should be suppressed or otherwise excluded from evidence. It is the intent of this Agreement to waive any and all rights in the foregoing respects.

14. KPMG agrees that, in the event that the Office determines during the period of deferral of prosecution described in paragraph 10 above (or any extensions thereof) that KPMG has violated any provision of this Agreement, a one-year extension of the period of deferral of prosecution may be imposed in the sole discretion of the Office, and, in the event of additional violations, such additional one-year extensions as appropriate, but in no event shall the total term of the deferral-of-prosecution period of this Agreement exceed five years.

15. KPMG agrees that it shall not, through its attorneys, agents, partners, or employees, make any statement, in litigation or otherwise, contradicting the Statement of Facts or its representations in this Agreement. Consistent with this provision, KPMG may raise defenses and/or assert affirmative claims in any civil proceedings brought by private parties as long as doing so does not contradict the Statement of Facts or such representations. Any such contradictory statement by KPMG, its present or future attorneys, agents, partners, or employees shall constitute a breach of this Agreement and KPMG thereafter shall be subject to prosecution as specified in paragraphs 10 through 13, above, or the deferral-of-prosecution period shall be extended pursuant to paragraph 14, above. The decision as to whether any such contradictory statement will be imputed to KPMG for the purpose of determining whether KPMG has breached this Agreement shall be at the sole discretion of the Office. Upon the Office's notifying KPMG of any such contradictory statement, KPMG may avoid a finding of breach of this Agreement by repudiating such statement both to the recipient of such statement and to the Office within 48 hours after receipt of notice by the Office. KPMG consents to the public release by the Office, in its sole discretion, of any such repudiation.

The Compliance & Ethics Program

16. In addition to the remedial actions that KPMG has taken to date, KPMG shall implement and maintain an effective compliance and ethics program that fully comports with the criteria set forth in Section 8B2.1 of the United States Sentencing Guidelines (the "Compliance & Ethics Program"). As part of the Compliance & Ethics Program, KPMG shall maintain a permanent compliance office and a permanent educational and training program relating to the laws and ethics governing the work of KPMG's partners and employees, paying particular attention to practice areas that pose high risks, including the determination whether transactions in which KPMG and its clients are involved constitute "reportable transactions" within the meaning of 26 C.F.R. § 1.6011-4(b), and the determination of whether the appropriate level for opinions and advice set forth in paragraph 6(i) of this Agreement and all applicable laws have been satisfied. KPMG agrees that all KPMG professionals and any employees of KPMG shall receive appropriate training pursuant to the Compliance & Ethics Program within one year of the execution of this Agreement, and shall be given such training on a regular basis but in any event no less than annually for the tax practice and no less than every two years for other practices at KPMG. Also as part of the Compliance & Ethics Program, KPMG shall (I) ensure that an effective program be maintained to punish violators of laws, policies, and standards, and reward those who report such violators; (II) ensure that no partner, employee, agent, or consultant of KPMG is penalized in any way for providing information relating to KPMG's compliance or noncompliance with laws, policies, and standards to any KPMG official, government agency, compliance officer, or the Monitor appointed pursuant to paragraph 18; and (III) ensure that all KPMG partners and employees have access to a hot-line or other means to provide information to KPMG's compliance office relating to KPMG's compliance or noncompliance with laws, policies, and standards. KPMG shall take steps to audit the Compliance & Ethics Program to ensure it is carrying out the duties and responsibilities set out in this Agreement.

17. KPMG shall take such additional personnel actions for wrongdoing as are warranted.

Independent Monitor

18. KPMG agrees to oversight and monitoring by a monitor appointed by the Office as described below (hereinafter the "Monitor"), whose powers, rights and responsibilities shall be as set forth below.

  (a). Jurisdiction, Powers, and Oversight Authority. The Monitor shall:

  (I). review and monitor KPMG's compliance with this Agreement and make such recommendations as the Monitor believes are necessary to comply with this Agreement;

  (II). review and monitor KPMG's maintenance and execution of the Compliance & Ethics Program and recommend such changes as are necessary to ensure conformity with the Sentencing Guidelines and this Agreement, and that are necessary to ensure that the Program is effective;

  (III). review and monitor the implementation and execution of personnel decisions regarding individuals who engaged in or were responsible (either by act or omission) for the illegal conduct described in the Information and may require any personnel action, including termination, regarding any such individuals;

  (IV). review and monitor KPMG's compliance with the restrictions on the tax practice outlined in paragraph 6 above, and recommend such changes as are necessary to comply with those restrictions; and

  (V). review and monitor the operations and decisions of any practice area involving "reportable" or "listed" transactions to ensure that those practices are complying with the restrictions outlined in paragraph 6 above and all applicable laws.

It is the intent of this Agreement that the provisions regarding the Monitor's jurisdiction, powers and oversight authority and duties be broadly construed. KPMG shall adopt all recommendations submitted by the Monitor unless KPMG objects to any recommendation and the

Office agrees that adoption of such recommendation should not be required.

       (b). <u>Access to Information</u>. The Monitor shall have the authority to take such reasonable steps, in the Monitor's view, as necessary to be fully informed about those operations of KPMG within or relating to his or her jurisdiction. To that end, the Monitor shall have:

> (I). access to, and the right to make copies of, any and all books, records, accounts, correspondence, files, and any and all other documents or electronic records, including e-mails, of KPMG and its partners, agents and employees, within or relating to his or her jurisdiction.
> (II). the right to interview any partner, employee, agent, or consultant of KPMG and to participate in any meeting concerning any matter within or relating to his or her jurisdiction.

The Monitor shall take appropriate steps to maintain the confidentiality of any non-public information entrusted to him or her and shall share such information only with the Office, the IRS, or any Designated Agency. The Office and KPMG agree that the Monitor's performance of his or her duties pursuant to this Agreement constitutes a "quality review" pursuant to 26 C.F.R. § 301.7216-2(O). In addition, to further facilitate the Monitor's performance of his duties and to effectuate the intent of this Agreement, KPMG consents to the entry of an order pursuant to 26 U.S.C. § 7216(b)(1)(B) permitting disclosures by KPMG to the Monitor (and any agents of the Monitor), and by the Monitor to the Office. A proposed order is attached hereto as Exhibit D. It is the intent of the parties to this Agreement that this proposed Order be issued by the Court contemporaneous with the Court's acceptance of this Agreement.

       (c). <u>Hiring Authority</u>. The Monitor shall have the authority to employ legal counsel, consultants, investigators, experts, and any other personnel necessary to assist in the proper discharge of the Monitor's duties.

(d). <u>Implementing Authority</u>. The Monitor shall have the authority to take any other actions that are necessary to effectuate his or her oversight and monitoring responsibilities.

(e). <u>Miscellaneous Provisions</u>.

(I). <u>Term</u>. The Monitor's authority set forth herein shall extend for a period of three years from the Monitor's entry on duty, except that in the event the Office determines during the period of the Monitorship (or any extensions thereof), that KPMG has violated any provision of this Agreement, a one-year extension of the period of the Monitorship may be imposed in the sole discretion of the Office, and, in the event of additional violations, an additional one-year extension, but in no event shall the total term of the Monitorship exceed five years.

(II). <u>Selection of the Monitor</u>. The Office shall consult with KPMG using its best efforts to select and appoint a mutually acceptable Monitor (and any replacement Monitors, if required) as promptly as possible. In the event that the Office is unable to select a Monitor acceptable to KPMG, the Office shall have the sole right to select a Monitor (and any replacement Monitors, if required).

(III). <u>Notice regarding the Monitor: Monitor's Authority to Act on Information received from Employees: No Penalty for Reporting</u>. KPMG shall establish an independent, toll-free answering service to facilitate communication anonymously or otherwise with the Monitor. Within 10 days of the commencement of the Monitor's duties, KPMG shall advise each of its partners and employees in writing of the appointment of the Monitor, the Monitor's powers and duties as set forth in this Agreement, the toll-free number established for contacting the Monitor, and email and mail addresses designated by the Monitor. Such notice shall inform employees that they may communicate with the Monitor anonymously or otherwise, and that no partner, agent, consultant, or employee of KPMG shall be penalized in any way for providing information to the Monitor. In addition, such notice shall direct that, if a partner or employee is aware of any violation of any law or any unethical conduct that has not been reported to an appropriate federal, state or municipal agency, the partner and employee is obligated to report such violation or conduct to KPMG's compliance office or the Monitor.

(IV). <u>Reports to the Office</u>. The Monitor shall keep records of his or her activities, including copies of all correspondence and telephone logs, as well as records relating to actions taken in response to correspondence or telephone calls. If potentially illegal or unethical conduct is reported to the Monitor, the Monitor may, at his or her option, conduct an investigation, and/or refer the matter to KPMG's compliance office, the Office, the IRS, or a Designated Agency. The Monitor may report to the Office whenever the Monitor deems fit but, in any event, shall file a written report not less often than every four months regarding: the Monitor's activities; whether KPMG is complying with the terms of this Agreement; and any changes that are necessary to foster KPMG's compliance with any applicable laws and standards. Such periodic written reports are to be provided to KPMG and the Office. The Office may, in its sole discretion, provide all or part of any such periodic written report, or other information provided to the Office by the Monitor, to the IRS or any Designated Agency. Should the Monitor determine that it appears that KPMG has violated any law, has violated any provision of this Agreement, or has engaged in any conduct that could warrant the modification of his or her jurisdiction, the Monitor shall promptly notify the Office, and when appropriate, KPMG.

(V). <u>Cooperation with the Monitor</u>. KPMG and all of its partners, employees, agents, and consultants shall have an affirmative duty to cooperate with and assist the Monitor in the execution of his or her duties and shall inform the Monitor of any information that may relate to the Monitor's duties or lead to information that relates to his or her duties. Failure of any KPMG partner, employee, or agent to cooperate with the Monitor may, in the sole discretion of the Monitor, serve as a basis for the Monitor to recommend dismissal or other disciplinary action.

(VI). <u>Compensation and Expenses</u>. The compensation and expenses of the Monitor, and of the persons hired under his or her authority, shall be paid by KPMG. The Monitor, and any persons hired by the Monitor, shall be compensated in accordance with their respective typical hourly rates. KPMG shall pay bills for compensation and expenses promptly, and in any event within 30 days. In addition, within one week after the selection of the Monitor, KPMG shall make available office space, telephone service and clerical assistance sufficient for the Monitor to carry out his or her duties.

(VII). Indemnification. KPMG shall provide an appropriate indemnification agreement to the Monitor with respect to any claims arising out of the performance of the Monitor's duties.

(VIII). No Affiliation. The Monitor is not, and shall not be treated for any purpose, as an officer, employee, agent, or affiliate of KPMG.

Closing Agreement With The IRS

19. Contemporaneously with the execution of this Agreement, KPMG and the IRS will enter into a closing agreement pursuant to 26 U.S.C. § 7121 providing for enhanced oversight and regulatory compliance and resolving the examination of KPMG under 26 U.S.C. §§ 6694, 6700, 6701, 6707, 6708, 7407, and 7408, and pursuant to which KPMG will pay the $100,000,000 promoter penalty described in paragraph 3 above. The closing agreement provides, among other things, that following termination of the three-year term of the Monitor (and any extensions thereof), the IRS will monitor KPMG's compliance with the restrictions and elevated standards established by paragraph 6 of this Agreement for a period of two years, provided however that in no event shall the period of IRS monitoring extend beyond the five-year anniversary of the Monitor's entry on duty. KPMG's failure to comply with any provision of the closing agreement shall constitute a violation of this Agreement.

The Office's Discretion

20. KPMG agrees that it is within the Office's sole discretion to choose, in the event of a violation, the remedies contained in paragraphs 10 through 13 above, or instead to choose to extend the period of deferral of prosecution pursuant to paragraph 14 and/or to extend the period of the Monitorship pursuant to paragraph 18. KPMG understands and agrees that the exercise of the Office's discretion under this Agreement is unreviewable by any court. Should the Office determine that KPMG has violated this Agreement, the Office shall provide notice to KPMG of that determination and

provide KPMG with an opportunity to make a presentation to the Office to demonstrate that no violation occurred, or, to the extent applicable, that the violation should not result in the exercise of those remedies or in an extension of the period of deferral of prosecution or the period of the Monitorship.

No Department Of Justice Debarment

21. KPMG has been involved in an engagement to audit the Department of Justice's financial statements. The Department of Justice's debarring official has determined that KPMG is currently a responsible contractor. The debarring official has determined that suspension or debarment of KPMG is not warranted because KPMG has agreed to the terms of this Deferred Prosecution Agreement, in which, among other things, KPMG has admitted its involvement in unlawful conduct and has agreed to take steps to ensure that KPMG, its leadership, partners, personnel, and clients will adhere to the highest standards of ethics and compliance with the United States tax laws.

Limits Of This Agreement

22. It is understood that this Agreement is binding on the Office and the Department of Justice but specifically does not bind any other Federal agencies, any state or local law enforcement agencies, any licensing authorities, or any regulatory authorities. However, if requested by KPMG or its attorneys, the Office will bring to the attention of any such agencies, including but not limited to any licensing authorities, the Agreement, the cooperation of KPMG and its compliance with its obligations under this Agreement.

Public Filing

23. KPMG and the Office agree that, upon filing of the Information in accordance with paragraph 1 and 10 hereof, this Agreement (including the Statement of Facts and the other

attachments hereto) shall be filed publicly in the proceedings in the United States District Court for the Southern District of New York.

Integration Clause

24. This Agreement sets forth all the terms of the Deferred Prosecution Agreement between KPMG and the Office. No modifications or additions to this Agreement shall be valid unless they are in writing and signed by the Office, KPMG's attorneys, and a duly authorized representative of KPMG.

DAVID N. KELLEY
United States Attorney
Southern District of New York

By: _____
Justin S. Weddle
Kevin M. Downing
Stanley J. Okula, Jr.
Assistant United States Attorneys

_____
Shirah Neiman
Chief Counsel to the U.S. Attorney

_____
Celeste Koeleveld
Chief, Criminal Division

Accepted agreed to:

_____

Skadden, Arps, Slate, Meagher & Flom LLP
Robert S. Bennett, Esq.
Carl S. Rauh, Esq.
Armando Gomez, Esq.
Joseph L. Barloon, Esq.
Matthew D. Michael, Esq.
Attorneys for KPMG LLP

_____

KPMG LLP

Indictments

ENRON

UNITED STATES DISTRICT COURT
SOUTHERN DISTRICT OF TEXAS

---X   I N D I C T M E N T

UNITED STATES OF AMERICA,   Cr. No. _____
                             (T. 18, U.S.C., §§
-against-   1512(b) (2) and 3551
                             et seq.)

ARTHUR ANDERSEN, LLP,

       Defendant.
---X

    THE GRAND JURY CHARGES:

I. ANDERSEN AND ENRON

    1.   ARTHUR ANDERSEN, LLP ("ANDERSEN"), is a partnership that performs, among other things, accounting and consulting services for clients that operate businesses throughout the United States and the world. ANDERSEN is one of the so-called "Big Five" accounting firms in the United States. ANDERSEN has

its headquarters in Chicago, Illinois, and maintains offices throughout the world, including in Houston, Texas.

2. Enron Corp. ("Enron") was an Oregon corporation with its principal place of business in Houston, Texas. For most of 2001, Enron was considered the seventh largest corporation in the United States based on its reported revenues. In the previous ten years, Enron had evolved from a regional natural gas provider to, among other things, a trader of natural gas, electricity and other commodities, with retail operations in energy and other products.

3. For the past 16 years, up until it filed for bankruptcy in December 2001, Enron retained ANDERSEN to be its auditor. Enron was one of ANDERSEN's largest clients worldwide, and became ANDERSEN's largest client in ANDERSEN's Gulf Coast region. ANDERSEN earned tens of millions of dollars from Enron in annual auditing and other fees.

4. ANDERSEN performed both internal and external auditing work for Enron mainly in Houston, Texas. ANDERSEN established within Enron's offices in Houston a work space for the ANDERSEN team that had primary responsibility for performing audit work for Enron. In addition to Houston, ANDERSEN personnel performed work for Enron in, among other locations, Chicago, Illinois, Portland, Oregon, and London, England.

II. THE ANTICIPATION OF LITIGATION AGAINST ENRON AND ANDERSEN

5. In the summer and fall of 2001, a series of significant developments led to ANDERSEN's foreseeing imminent civil litigation against, and government investigations of, Enron and ANDERSEN.

6. On or about October 16, 2001, Enron issued a press release announcing a $618 million net loss for the third quarter of 2001. That same day, but not as part of the press release, Enron announced to analysts that it would reduce shareholder equity by approximately $1.2 billion. The market reacted immediately and the stock price of Enron shares plummeted.

7. The Securities and Exchange Commission ("SEC"), which investigates possible violations of the federal securities laws, opened an inquiry into Enron the very next day, requesting in writing information from Enron.

8. In addition to the negative financial information disclosed by Enron to the public and to analysts on October 16, 2001, ANDERSEN was aware by this time of additional significant facts unknown to the public.

- The approximately $1.2 billion reduction in shareholder equity disclosed to analysts on October 16, 2001, was necessitated by ANDERSEN and Enron having previously improperly categorized hundreds of millions of dollars as an increase, rather than a decrease, to Enron shareholder equity.
- The Enron October 16, 2001, press release characterized numerous charges against income for the third quarter as "non-recurring" even though ANDERSEN believed the company did not have a basis for concluding that the charges would in fact be non-recurring. Indeed, ANDERSEN advised Enron against using that term, and documented its objections internally in the event of litigation, but did not report its objections or otherwise take steps to cure the public statement.
- ANDERSEN was put on direct notice of the allegations of Sherron Watkins, a current Enron employee and former ANDERSEN employee, regarding possible fraud and other improprieties at Enron, and in particular, Enron's use of off-balance-sheet "special purpose entities" that enabled the company to camouflage the true financial condition of the company. Watkins had reported her concerns to a partner at ANDERSEN, who thereafter disseminated them within ANDERSEN, including to the team working on the Enron audit. In addition, the team had received warnings about possible undisclosed side-agreements at Enron.
- The ANDERSEN team handling the Enron audit directly contravened the accounting methodology approved by ANDERSEN's own specialists working in its Professional Standards Group. In opposition to the views of its own

experts, the ANDERSEN auditors had advised Enron in the spring of 2001 that it could use a favorable accounting method for its "special purpose entities."

- In 2000, an internal review conducted by senior management within ANDERSEN evaluated the ANDERSEN team assigned to audit Enron and rated the team as only a "2" on a scale of one to five, with five being the highest rating.

- On or about October 9, 2001, correctly anticipating litigation and government investigations, ANDERSEN, which had an internal department of lawyers for routine legal matters, retained an experienced New York law firm to handle future Enron-related litigation.

III.   THE WHOLESALE DESTRUCTION OF DOCUMENTS BY ANDERSEN

9.   By Friday, October 19, 2001, Enron alerted the ANDERSEN audit team that the SEC had begun an inquiry regarding the Enron "special purpose entities" and the involvement of Enron's Chief Financial Officer. The next morning, an emergency conference call among high-level ANDERSEN management was convened to address the SEC inquiry. During the call, it was decided that documentation that could assist Enron in responding to the SEC was to be assembled by the ANDERSEN auditors.

10. After spending Monday, October 22, 2001 at Enron, ANDERSEN partners assigned to the Enron engagement team launched on October 23, 2001, a wholesale destruction of documents at ANDERSEN's offices in Houston, Texas. ANDERSEN personnel were called to urgent and mandatory meetings. Instead of being advised to preserve documentation so as to assist Enron and the SEC, ANDERSEN employees on the Enron engagement team were instructed by ANDERSEN partners and others to destroy immediately documentation relating to Enron, and told to work overtime if necessary to accomplish the destruction. During the next few weeks, an unparalleled initiative was undertaken to shred physical documentation and delete computer files. Tons of paper relating to the Enron audit were promptly shredded as part of the

orchestrated document destruction. The shredder at the ANDERSEN office at the Enron building was used virtually constantly and, to handle the overload, dozens of large trunks filled with Enron documents were sent to ANDERSEN's main Houston office to be shredded. A systematic effort was also undertaken and carried out to purge the computer hard-drives and E-mail system of Enron-related files.

11. In addition to shredding and deleting documents in Houston, Texas, instructions were given to ANDERSEN personnel working on Enron audit matters in Portland, Oregon, Chicago, Illinois, and London, England, to make sure that Enron documents were destroyed there as well. Indeed, in London a coordinated effort by ANDERSEN partners and others, similar to the initiative undertaken in Houston, was put into place to destroy Enron-related documents within days of notice of the SEC inquiry. Enron-related documents also were destroyed by ANDERSEN partners in Chicago.

12. On or about November 8, 2001, the SEC served ANDERSEN with the anticipated subpoena relating to its work for Enron. In response, members of the ANDERSEN team on the Enron audit were alerted finally that there could be "no more shredding" because the firm had been "officially served" for documents.

THE CHARGE: OBSTRUCTION OF JUSTICE

13. On or about and between October 10, 2001, and November 9, 2001, within the Southern District of Texas and elsewhere, including Chicago, Illinois, Portland, Oregon, and London, England, ANDERSEN, through its partners and others, did knowingly, intentionally and corruptly persuade and attempt to persuade other persons, to wit: ANDERSEN employees, with intent to cause and induce such persons to (a) withhold records, documents and other objects from official proceedings, namely: regulatory and criminal proceedings and investigations, and (b) alter, destroy, mutilate and conceal objects with intent to impair the objects' integrity and availability for use in such official proceedings.

(Title 18, United States Code, Sections 1512(b) (2) and 3551 et seq.)

A TRUE BILL

_____

FOREPERSON

JOSHUA R. HOCHBERG
ACTING UNITED STATES ATTORNEY
SOUTHERN DISTRICT OF TEXAS

LESLIE R. CALDWELL
DIRECTOR, ENRON TASK FORCE

By:

    Samuel W. Buell
    Andrew Weissmann
    Special Attorneys
    Department of Justice

IMCLONE

UNITED STATES DISTRICT COURT
SOUTHERN DISTRICT OF NEW YORK

- x

UNITED STATES OF AMERICA	:	SUPERSEDING
- v. -	:	INDICTMENT
MARTHA STEWART and	:	S1 03 Cr. 717 (MGC)
PETER BACANOVIC,	:	
Defendants.	:	

- x

COUNT ONE

(Conspiracy to Obstruct Justice,
Make False Statements, and Commit Perjury)

The Grand Jury charges:

Background

1. At all times relevant to this Indictment, MARTHA STEWART, the defendant, was chairman of the board of directors and chief executive officer of Martha Stewart Living Omnimedia, Inc. ("MSLO"). MSLO was a corporation organized under the laws of Delaware with its principal executive and administrative offices located at 11 West 42nd Street, New York, New York. MSLO was engaged in businesses spanning four major areas: publishing of magazines and books; television production; merchandising; and internet and catalog sales. MSLO's products bear the "Martha Stewart" brand name. MSLO's common stock was listed and traded on the New York Stock Exchange ("NYSE"), a national securities exchange located in New York, New York, under the symbol "MSO."

209

2. Prior to forming MSLO, MARTHA STEWART had been licensed by NASD, a national securities association, to sell securities and was employed as a securities broker from in or about 1968 through in or about 1973. On March 22, 2002, STEWART was nominated to serve on the board of directors of the NYSE. On June 6, 2002, STEWART was elected to the NYSE board of directors, a position which she held until she resigned on October 3, 2002.

3. At all times relevant to this Indictment, PETER BACANOVIC, the defendant, was licensed by NASD to sell securities. BACANOVIC was employed as a securities broker with the title "Financial Advisor" at Merrill Lynch & Co., Inc. ("Merrill Lynch"), a broker-dealer headquartered in New York, New York, at a branch office located at 1251 Avenue of the Americas, New York, New York.

4. At all times relevant to this Indictment, MARTHA STEWART maintained securities brokerage accounts at Merrill Lynch. PETER BACANOVIC was the registered representative for STEWART's Merrill Lynch accounts and had a close personal relationship with STEWART. Because of commissions generated from her accounts and accounts that BACANOVIC obtained as a result of his relationship with STEWART, as well as her high public profile, STEWART was one of BACANOVIC's most important brokerage clients.

5. At all times relevant to this Indictment, Douglas Faneuil, a co-conspirator not named as a defendant herein, was employed by Merrill Lynch as an assistant to PETER BACANOVIC.

<u>Merrill Lynch's Policies on Safeguarding</u>
<u>Client Information and Insider Trading</u>

6. At all times relevant to this Indictment, Merrill Lynch established and distributed to its employees, including to PETER BACANOVIC, policies regarding employees' duties to maintain in strict confidence information concerning Merrill Lynch's clients. The policies stated, in relevant part:

Confidentiality of Client Information

You may not discuss the business affairs of any client with anyone, including other employees except on a need-to-know basis. Information or records concerning the business of the Firm and/or its clients may not be released except to persons legally entitled to receive them.

Client Information Privacy Policy

Merrill Lynch protects the confidentiality and security of client information. Employees must understand the need for careful handling of this information. Merrill Lynch's client information privacy policy provides that —

. . .

• Employees may not discuss the business affairs of any client with any other employee, except on a strict need-to-know basis.

• We do not release client information, except upon a client's authorization or when permitted or required by law.

7. At all times relevant to this Indictment, Merrill Lynch specifically warned its employees, including PETER BACANOVIC, of the impropriety of so-called "piggybacking" — buying or selling a security after a client bought or sold the same security in order to take advantage of that client's perceived knowledge or expertise. The directive stated, in pertinent part:

You should not "piggyback," that is, enter transactions after a client's trades to take advantage of perceived expertise or knowledge on the part of the client. If the client's successful trading pattern arose from an improper element such as inside information, you (and the Firm) could be subject to a regulatory or criminal investigation or proceeding.

8. At all times relevant to this Indictment, Merrill Lynch also distributed policies advising its employees, including PETER BACANOVIC, of their responsibilities under the federal securities laws, which stated in part:

Inside Information
Background and Definition
U.S. Federal and State securities laws and laws of certain other
countries make it unlawful for anyone in possession of non-public
material information to take advantage of such information in
connection with purchasing or selling securities or recommending
to others the purchase or sale of securities. Such information must
not be disclosed to others who may, thereafter, take advantage of
it in purchasing or selling securities.

Information is material if a reasonable person would want to
consider it in determining whether to engage in a securities
transaction or if it could reasonably be expected to affect the
market price of a security if it becomes generally known.
Information should be considered non-public if it has not been
disclosed in the news media, research reports, corporate public
filings or reports, or in some other similar public manner. Nonpublic information should generally be regarded as material unless
it is clearly unimportant to investors.

BACANOVIC's Acquisition of Confidential, Nonpublic Information

9. At all times relevant to this Indictment, ImClone Systems
Incorporated ("ImClone") was a corporation organized under the
laws of the State of Delaware with its principal place of business in
New York, New York. ImClone was engaged in the business of
developing biologic medicines, including Erbitux, a biologic
treatment for irinotecan-refractory colorectal cancer. ImClone
publicly described Erbitux as its lead product candidate. ImClone's
common stock was listed and traded on the NASDAQ National
Market System, an electronic securities market system administered
by NASD, under the symbol "IMCL."

10. At all times relevant to this Indictment, Samuel Waksal was
the president, chief executive officer, and a director of ImClone.
Waksal and several members of his family were clients of PETER
BACANOVIC.

11. At all times relevant to this Indictment, MARTHA
STEWART and Samuel Waksal were personal friends.

12. On or about October 31, 2001, ImClone submitted to the United States Food and Drug Administration (the "FDA") a Biologics Licensing Application ("BLA") for approval of Erbitux (the "Erbitux BLA"). Pursuant to FDA regulations, within 60 days following the submission of a BLA, the FDA must decide whether the BLA is administratively and scientifically complete to be accepted for FDA review. Only if a BLA is accepted for filing does the FDA review the application to determine whether the proposed treatment will be approved. It had been publicly reported that the FDA's decision whether to accept the Erbitux BLA for filing was expected by the end of December 2001.

13. On the morning of December 27, 2001, between 9:00 a.m. and 10:00 a.m. (EST), Douglas Faneuil informed PETER BACANOVIC that Samuel Waksal and a member of his family (the "Waksal Family Member") were seeking to sell all the ImClone shares they held at Merrill Lynch, then worth over $7.3 million (collectively referred to as the "Waksal Shares"). Faneuil advised BACANOVIC that the Waksal Family Member had placed an order to sell all of the Waksal Family Member's ImClone stock. By approximately 9:48 a.m., the Waksal Family Member's approximately 39,472 shares had been sold for approximately $2,472,837. Faneuil further advised BACANOVIC that Samuel Waksal had requested that all of the ImClone stock in Samuel Waksal's Merrill Lynch account, approximately 79,797 shares, then worth approximately $4.9 million, be transferred to the Waksal Family Member and then sold. Samuel Waksal's written direction to Merrill Lynch stated that the transfer request was "URGENT — IMMEDIATE ACTION REQUIRED" and that it was "imperative" that the transfer take place during the morning of December 27, 2001.

14. On December 27, 2001, information regarding efforts by ImClone's CEO, Samuel Waksal, to sell all of the ImClone shares that he held at Merrill Lynch constituted confidential, nonpublic information.

STEWART's Sale of ImClone Stock

15. In breach of the duties PETER BACANOVIC owed to Merrill Lynch and its clients to keep client information confidential, on or about December 27, 2001, BACANOVIC directed his assistant, Douglas Faneuil, to disclose to MARTHA STEWART information regarding the sale and attempted sale of the Waksal Shares — information that BACANOVIC had misappropriated and stolen from Merrill Lynch and its clients.

16. On December 27, 2001, at approximately 10:04 a.m. (EST), within minutes after being informed of the sale and attempted sale of the Waksal Shares, PETER BACANOVIC called MARTHA STEWART. After being told that STEWART was in transit and unavailable, BACANOVIC left a message, memorialized by STEWART's assistant, that "Peter Bacanovic thinks ImClone is going to start trading downward." At approximately 10:04 a.m., the price of ImClone stock was approximately $61.53 per share. BACANOVIC, who was on vacation, directed Douglas Faneuil to inform STEWART about the Waksal transactions when she returned the call.

17. On December 27, 2001, at approximately 1:39 p.m. (EST), MARTHA STEWART telephoned the office of PETER BACANOVIC and spoke to Douglas Faneuil, who informed her that Samuel Waksal was trying to sell all of the ImClone stock that Waksal held at Merrill Lynch. Upon hearing this news, STEWART directed Faneuil to sell all of her ImClone stock — October 18, 2006 3,928 shares. All 3,928 ImClone shares owned by STEWART were sold that day at approximately 1:52 p.m. (EST) at an average price of $58.43 per share, yielding proceeds of approximately $228,000.

18. As a client of Merrill Lynch and as a former securities broker, MARTHA STEWART knew that information regarding the sale and attempted sale of the Waksal Shares had been communicated to her in violation of the duties of trust and confidence owed to Merrill Lynch and its clients.

Public Announcement of the FDA Decision

19. After the close of business on December 28, 2001, ImClone issued a press release announcing that the FDA had refused to accept the Erbitux BLA for filing.

20. On December 28, 2001, prior to the public announcement of the FDA decision, the price of ImClone stock closed at $55.25 per share. On December 31, 2001, the first day that ImClone stock traded after the FDA's decision was publicly announced, the price of ImClone stock opened at $45.39, representing a decline of approximately 18%.

21. By selling a total of 3,928 shares of ImClone stock on the same day as the sale and attempted sale of the Waksal Shares, MARTHA STEWART avoided significant trading losses. If STEWART had sold at the price at which ImClone stock opened on December 31, 2001, STEWART would have lost $51,222. If STEWART had sold at the price at which ImClone stock closed on December 31, 2001, STEWART would have lost $45,673.

The Scheme to Obstruct Justice

22. In or about January 2002, the Northeast Regional Office of the United States Securities and Exchange Commission ("SEC"), an agency of the United States, the Federal Bureau of Investigation (the "FBI"), and the United States Attorney's Office for the Southern District of New York commenced investigations into trading in ImClone securities in advance of the public announcement of the FDA's negative decision, including into the trades conducted by Samuel Waksal and MARTHA STEWART. The investigations focused on whether such trades were made in violation of federal securities laws and regulations that prohibit trading on the basis of material, nonpublic information. It was material to the investigations to determine, among other things, what was communicated to STEWART about ImClone on December 27, 2001 and the reasons for STEWART's December 27, 2001 sale of ImClone stock.

23. As described more fully below, after learning of the investigations, MARTHA STEWART and PETER BACANOVIC,

and others known and unknown, entered into an unlawful conspiracy to obstruct the investigations; to make false statements and provide false and misleading information regarding STEWART's sale of ImClone stock; and to commit perjury, all to conceal and cover up that BACANOVIC had breached his duties of trust and confidence to Merrill Lynch and its clients and caused STEWART to be provided information regarding the sale and attempted sale of the Waksal Shares, and that STEWART had sold her ImClone stock while in possession of that information. Specifically, and among other things, STEWART and BACANOVIC agreed that rather than tell the truth about the communications with STEWART on December 27, 2001 and the reasons for STEWART's sale of ImClone stock on December 27, 2001, they would instead fabricate and attempt to deceive investigators with a fictitious explanation for her sale — that STEWART sold her ImClone stock on December 27, 2001 because she and BACANOVIC had a pre-existing agreement to sell the stock if and when the price dropped to $60 per share.

BACANOVIC's False Statements on January 7, 2002

24. On or about January 7, 2002, in New York, New York, SEC staff attorneys interviewed PETER BACANOVIC by telephone. During the interview, the SEC staff attorneys questioned BACANOVIC regarding, among other things, the sale of ImClone stock on December 27, 2001 by MARTHA STEWART. In furtherance of the conspiracy, and with the intent and purpose to conceal and cover up that BACANOVIC had caused STEWART to be provided information regarding the sale and attempted sale of the Waksal Shares and that STEWART had sold her ImClone stock while in possession of that information, BACANOVIC made the following false statements, in substance and in part, and concealed and covered up the following facts that were material to the SEC's investigation, among others:

a. BACANOVIC stated that in a conversation with STEWART on December 20, 2001, STEWART said that she had decided to sell her ImClone shares if ImClone's market price fell to $60 per share. This statement was false in that, as BACANOVIC well knew, STEWART did not inform him of such a decision to sell her shares.

b. BACANOVIC stated that on December 27, 2001, STEWART had spoken to BACANOVIC, that he told STEWART that ImClone's price had dropped below $60 per share, and that STEWART placed her order to sell her ImClone stock with him. This statement was false in that, as BACANOVIC well knew, STEWART did not speak to BACANOVIC when she placed her order to sell ImClone stock, but rather spoke to Douglas Faneuil, and concealed and covered up that Faneuil conveyed information to STEWART regarding the sale and attempted sale of the Waksal Shares.

STEWART's Alteration of BACANOVIC's December 27, 2001 Message

25. On or about January 25, 2002, the FBI and the U.S. Attorney's Office contacted the office of MARTHA STEWART and requested to interview STEWART. The interview was scheduled to occur on February 4, 2002.

26. On or about January 31, 2002, after learning that the FBI and the U.S. Attorney's Office had requested an interview with her, and immediately following a lengthy conversation with her attorney, MARTHA STEWART accessed the phone message log maintained on computer by her assistant and reviewed the phone message that PETER BACANOVIC had left for her on December 27, 2001. In furtherance of the conspiracy, and knowing that BACANOVIC's message for STEWART was based on information regarding the sale and attempted sale of the Waksal Shares that BACANOVIC subsequently caused to be conveyed to her, STEWART deleted the substance of BACANOVIC's phone message, changing the message from "Peter Bacanovic thinks ImClone is going to start trading downward," to "Peter Bacanovic re imclone." After altering the message, STEWART directed her assistant to return the message to its original wording.

STEWART's False Statements on February 4, 2002

27. On or about February 4, 2002, MARTHA STEWART, accompanied by her lawyers, was interviewed in New York, New York by the SEC, the FBI, and the U.S. Attorney's Office. In furtherance of the conspiracy, and with the intent and purpose to conceal and cover up that BACANOVIC had caused STEWART to be provided information regarding the sale and attempted sale of the Waksal Shares and that STEWART had sold her ImClone stock while in possession of that information, STEWART made the following false statements of facts, in substance and in part, and concealed and covered up the following material facts, among others:

a. STEWART stated that at a time when ImClone was trading at approximately $74 per share (which prior to December 27, 2001, had last occurred on December 6, 2001), STEWART and PETER BACANOVIC both decided that STEWART would sell her ImClone shares when ImClone started trading at $60 per share. This statement was false and misleading in that, as STEWART well knew, no such decision had been made.

b. STEWART stated that she did not know whether the phone message BACANOVIC left for STEWART on December 27, 2001 was recorded in the phone message log maintained by her assistant. This statement was false and misleading in that, as STEWART well knew but concealed and covered up, the message was recorded in the phone message log, the substance of which — "Peter Bacanovic thinks ImClone is going to start trading downward" — STEWART had reviewed when she temporarily altered the message just four days before the interview.

c. STEWART stated that on December 27, 2001, STEWART spoke to BACANOVIC, who told her that ImClone was trading a little below $60 per share and asked STEWART if she wanted to sell. STEWART stated that after being informed of ImClone's stock price, she directed BACANOVIC to sell her ImClone shares that day because she did not want to be bothered over her vacation. These statements were false and misleading in that, as STEWART well knew but concealed and covered up, STEWART spoke to Faneuil, not BACANOVIC, on December 27, 2001, and

STEWART sold her ImClone shares that day after Douglas Faneuil conveyed to her information regarding the sale and attempted sale of the Waksal Shares.

    d. STEWART stated that before concluding their telephone conversation on December 27, 2001, BACANOVIC and STEWART discussed "how MSLO stock was doing" and Kmart. This statement was false and misleading in that, as STEWART well knew, STEWART spoke to Douglas Faneuil, not BACANOVIC, and had no such discussions that day with either BACANOVIC or Faneuil regarding MSLO or Kmart. STEWART provided these false details of her purported conversation with BACANOVIC to conceal and cover up the fact that STEWART spoke on December 27, 2001 to Douglas Faneuil, who conveyed to her information regarding the sale and attempted sale of the Waksal Shares.

    e. STEWART stated that, during the period from December 28, 2001 to the date of the interview, February 4, 2002, STEWART had only one conversation with BACANOVIC regarding ImClone, in which only publicly disclosed matters in the "public arena" were discussed. STEWART further stated that although BACANOVIC mentioned that Merrill Lynch had been questioned by the SEC regarding trading in ImClone generally, BACANOVIC did not inform STEWART that he had been questioned by the SEC or that he had been questioned regarding STEWART's account. These statements were false and misleading in that, as STEWART well knew, during the period from December 28, 2001 through February 4, 2002, STEWART had conversations with BACANOVIC regarding STEWART's sale of ImClone shares and the investigation of that sale, and BACANOVIC had informed STEWART that he had been questioned by the SEC regarding her sale of ImClone. STEWART made these false statements to conceal and cover up that she and BACANOVIC had agreed to provide false information to the SEC, the FBI, and the U.S. Attorney's Office regarding STEWART's sale of ImClone stock and conceal and cover up that BACANOVIC had caused STEWART to be provided information regarding the sale and attempted sale of the Waksal Shares and that STEWART had sold her ImClone stock while in possession of that information.

BACANOVIC's Alteration of His "Worksheet"

28. On or about January 28, 2002, the SEC issued an Order Directing Private Investigations and Designating Officers to Take Testimony. On or about the same date, the SEC served upon Merrill Lynch a request for production of documents, requesting, among other things, documents relating to brokerage accounts maintained by MARTHA STEWART. On or about January 29, 2002, the SEC's request was communicated to PETER BACANOVIC by representatives of Merrill Lynch.

29. As described more fully below, in furtherance of the scheme to obstruct justice, PETER BACANOVIC altered a document in order to fabricate evidence that would purportedly corroborate BACANOVIC's and MARTHA STEWART's claims that STEWART had decided to sell her ImClone stock if the market price fell to $60 per share.

30. In or about December 2001, PETER BACANOVIC had discussions with MARTHA STEWART regarding engaging in "tax loss selling," i.e., selling stocks that had declined below the price at which they had been purchased in order to recognize losses from those sales to offset taxable gains realized during the same year from profitable sales of other securities. On December 21 and 24, 2001, BACANOVIC executed sales at a loss of stock in twenty-two companies that STEWART held in her Merrill Lynch portfolio.

31. On or about December 21, 2001, PETER BACANOVIC printed a "worksheet" that listed each of the stocks held by MARTHA STEWART at Merrill Lynch, including ImClone, as well as, among other things, the market value of each of the holdings as of the close of business on December 20, 2001, and STEWART's unrealized profit or loss in each stock as of the close of business on December 20, 2001 (the "Worksheet"). On or about December 21, 2001, BACANOVIC made handwritten notes in blue ballpoint ink on the Worksheet concerning transactions and planned transactions in STEWART's account. On or about December 21, 2001, BACANOVIC made no notes on the Worksheet regarding any purported decision to sell STEWART's ImClone shares at $60 per share.

32. In furtherance of the conspiracy, after learning of the SEC's investigation of STEWART's sale of ImClone stock and with the intent and purpose to mislead the SEC and others into believing that there existed documentary evidence corroborating BACANOVIC's and STEWART's false claim that they had an agreement to sell STEWART's ImClone shares if the market price fell to $60 per share, PETER BACANOVIC altered the Worksheet, using ink that was blue ballpoint, but was scientifically distinguishable from the ink used elsewhere on the Worksheet. BACANOVIC added the notation "@ 60" near the entry for ImClone.

33. In furtherance of the conspiracy, on or about January 30, 2002, PETER BACANOVIC gave the altered Worksheet to a Merrill Lynch manager with the intent that the altered Worksheet be produced to the SEC in response to the SEC's request for documents. BACANOVIC falsely represented to the Merrill Lynch manager that the altered Worksheet was used in a "selling discussion" he had with MARTHA STEWART. On or about February 14, 2002, Merrill Lynch produced the altered Worksheet to the SEC pursuant to the SEC's request for production of documents.

BACANOVIC's Perjured Testimony Before the SEC

34. On or about February 4, 2002, the SEC issued a subpoena to PETER BACANOVIC directing BACANOVIC to provide testimony under oath.

35. On February 13, 2002, PETER BACANOVIC appeared before the SEC in New York, New York, pursuant to subpoena, and gave testimony under oath. In furtherance of the conspiracy, and with the intent and purpose to conceal and cover up that BACANOVIC had caused STEWART to be provided information regarding the sale and attempted sale of the Waksal Shares and that STEWART had sold her ImClone stock while in possession of that information, BACANOVIC falsely testified, in substance and in part, about the following matters, among others:

a. BACANOVIC testified that on December 20, 2001, after the close of business, BACANOVIC and MARTHA STEWART had a telephone conversation in which they decided that STEWART would sell her ImClone shares if ImClone fell to $60 per share. This testimony was false in that, as BACANOVIC well knew, they had made no such decision.

b. BACANOVIC testified that he had notes of his conversation with STEWART on December 20, 2001, that reflected their discussion regarding a decision to sell ImClone at $60 per share. This testimony was false in that, as BACANOVIC well knew, he had no notes that reflected any actual discussion on or about December 20, 2001 about a decision to sell ImClone at $60 per share. BACANOVIC also well knew that he had falsely added the notation "@ 60" to the Worksheet after STEWART's sale of ImClone stock and after he learned of the SEC's investigation, for the purpose of obstructing that investigation.

c. BACANOVIC testified that during the period from December 28, 2001 through the date of his testimony, February 13, 2002, BACANOVIC and STEWART did not discuss STEWART's December 27, 2001 sale of ImClone stock. BACANOVIC further testifed that he did not inform STEWART of any questions asked by anyone regarding that sale. This testimony was false in that, as BACANOVIC well knew, BACANOVIC had conversations with STEWART in January and February 2002 regarding, among other matters, the investigations of STEWART's sale of ImClone stock.

STEWART's False Statements on April 10, 2002

36. On or about April 10, 2002, MARTHA STEWART was interviewed by telephone by the SEC, the FBI, and the U.S. Attorney's Office, the representatives of which were in New York, New York. In furtherance of the conspiracy, and with the intent and purpose to conceal and cover up that PETER BACANOVIC had caused STEWART to be provided information regarding the sale and attempted sale of the Waksal Shares and that STEWART had sold her ImClone stock while in possession of that information, STEWART made the following false and misleading statements, in substance and in part, and concealed and covered up the following material facts, among others:

a. STEWART stated that she did not recall if she and BACANOVIC discussed Samuel Waksal on December 27, 2001, nor did she recall being informed on December 27, 2001 that any of the Waksals were selling their ImClone stock. This statement was false and misleading in that STEWART in fact recalled that she was informed on December 27, 2001 that Samuel Waksal was attempting to sell all of his ImClone shares at Merrill Lynch.

b. STEWART stated that the conversation with PETER BACANOVIC that she had previously described in her February 4, 2002 interview (referenced in ¶ 27 above) — the conversation in which BACANOVIC and STEWART purportedly decided that STEWART would sell her ImClone shares when ImClone started trading at $60 per share — occurred sometime in November or December 2001, after she sold all of her ImClone shares from the Martha Stewart Defined Pension Fund (which occurred on or about October 26, 2001). This statement was false and misleading in that, as STEWART well knew, STEWART and BACANOVIC had made no such decision.

c. STEWART stated that on December 27, 2001, STEWART spoke to BACANOVIC, who told her that ImClone was trading below $60 per share and suggested that STEWART sell her ImClone shares. These statements were false and misleading in that, as STEWART well knew but concealed and covered up, STEWART spoke to Faneuil, not BACANOVIC, on December 27, 2001, and STEWART sold her ImClone shares that day after Douglas Faneuil conveyed to her information regarding the sale and attempted sale of the Waksal Shares.

The Conspiracy

37. From in or about January 2002 until in or about April 2002, in the Southern District of New York and elsewhere, PETER BACANOVIC and MARTHA STEWART, and others known and unknown, unlawfully, willfully, and knowingly did combine, conspire, confederate and agree together and with each other to commit offenses against the United States, to wit: to obstruct justice, in violation of Section 1505 of Title 18, United States Code; to make

false statements, in violation of Section 1001 of Title 18, United States Code; and to commit perjury, in violation of Section 1621 of Title 18, United States Code.

Objects of the Conspiracy
Obstruction of Justice

38. It was a part and an object of the conspiracy that MARTHA STEWART and PETER BACANOVIC, and others known and unknown, unlawfully, willfully and knowingly, would and did corruptly influence, obstruct and impede, and endeavor to influence, obstruct and impede the due and proper administration of the law under which a pending proceeding was being had before a department and agency of the United States, namely, an investigation by the SEC, in violation of Title 18, United States Code, Section 1505.

False Statements

39. It was further a part and an object of the conspiracy that MARTHA STEWART and PETER BACANOVIC, and others known and unknown, unlawfully, willfully and knowingly, in a matter within the jurisdiction of the executive branch of the Government of the United States, would and did falsify, conceal, and cover up by trick, scheme, and device material facts, and make materially false, fictitious, and fraudulent statements and representations, and make and use false writings and documents knowing the same to contain materially false, fictitious, and fraudulent statements and entries, in violation of Title 18, United States Code, Section 1001.

Perjury

40. It was further a part and an object of the conspiracy that PETER BACANOVIC, having taken an oath before a competent tribunal, officer and person, in a case in which the law of the United States authorizes an oath to be administered, namely, in testimony

before the SEC, that he would testify, declare, depose and certify truly, and that any written testimony, declaration, deposition and certificate by him subscribed, would be true, unlawfully, willfully, knowingly, and contrary to such oath, would and did state and subscribe material matters which he did not believe to be true, in violation of Title 18, United States Code, Section 1621.

Overt Acts

41. In furtherance of the conspiracy and to effect the illegal objects thereof, the following overt acts, among others, were committed in the Southern District of New York and elsewhere:

a. On January 7, 2002, in New York, New York, PETER BACANOVIC provided false and misleading information to the SEC regarding the December 27, 2001 sale of ImClone stock by MARTHA STEWART.

b. In January 2002, PETER BACANOVIC in New York, New York, encouraged Douglas Faneuil to refrain from disclosing that Faneuil had informed MARTHA STEWART on December 27, 2001 of the sale and attempted sale of the Waksal Shares.

c. On January 25, 2002, after MARTHA STEWART learned that the FBI and the U.S. Attorney's Office requested to interview her, STEWART placed a call from her cellular telephone to PETER BACANOVIC's cellular telephone.

d. On or about January 30, 2002, in New York, New York, PETER BACANOVIC provided the altered Worksheet to a Merrill Lynch manager with the intent that the Worksheet be produced to the SEC.

e. At 7:09 a.m. on February 4, 2002, the morning of MARTHA STEWART's interview with the SEC, the FBI, and the U.S. Attorney's Office, PETER BACANOVIC placed a call from his cellular telephone to STEWART's cellular telephone.

f. On February 4, 2002, in New York, New York, MARTHA STEWART made false and misleading statements to the SEC, the FBI, and the U.S. Attorney's Office regarding her December 27, 2001 sale of ImClone stock.

g.   On February 13, 2002, in New York, New York, PETER BACANOVIC gave false and misleading testimony regarding MARTHA STEWART's December 27, 2001 sale of ImClone stock.

h. On April 10, 2002, in New York, New York, MARTHA STEWART made false and misleading statements to the SEC, the FBI, and the U.S. Attorney's Office regarding her December 27, 2001 sale of ImClone stock.

(Title 18, United States Code, Section 371).

COUNT TWO
(False Statements by Peter Bacanovic)

The Grand Jury further charges:

42. The allegations of paragraphs 1 through 36 are repeated and realleged as though fully set forth herein.

43. On or about January 7, 2002, in the Southern District of New York, PETER BACANOVIC unlawfully, willfully, and knowingly, in a matter within the jurisdiction of the executive branch of the Government of the United States, falsified, concealed, and covered up by trick, scheme, and device material facts, and made materially false, fictitious, and fraudulent statements and representations, to wit, BACANOVIC participated in an interview by telephone with SEC staff attorneys in New York, New York, in which he made the following false statements and concealed and covered up facts that were material to the SEC's investigation:

Specification One

BACANOVIC falsely stated that on December 20, 2001, he had a conversation with STEWART in which she decided to sell her ImClone stock at $60 per share.

Specification Two

BACANOVIC falsely stated that he had a conversation with MARTHA STEWART on December 27, 2001, in which he told

STEWART that ImClone's stock price had dropped and STEWART told him to sell her ImClone stock.

(Title 18, United States Code, Sections 1001(a)(1) and (2)).

COUNT THREE
(False Statements by Martha Stewart)

The Grand Jury further charges:

44. The allegations of paragraphs 1 through 36 and 41 are repeated and realleged as though fully set forth herein.

45. On or about February 4, 2002, in the Southern District of New York, MARTHA STEWART unlawfully, willfully, and knowingly, in a matter within the jurisdiction of the executive branch of the Government of the United States, falsified, concealed, and covered up by trick, scheme, and device material facts, and made materially false, fictitious, and fraudulent statements and representations, to wit, STEWART participated in an interview with the SEC, the FBI, and the U.S. Attorney's Office for the Southern District of New York in New York, New York, in which she made the following false statements and concealed and covered up facts that were material to the investigations:

Specification One

STEWART falsely stated that in a conversation that had occurred at a time when ImClone was trading at $74 per share, STEWART and BACANOVIC decided that STEWART would sell her shares when ImClone started trading at $60 per share.

Specification Two

STEWART falsely stated that on December 27, 2001, at approximately 1:30 p.m. (EST), STEWART spoke to BACANOVIC, who told STEWART that ImClone was trading a little below $60 per share and that he asked STEWART if she wanted to sell, and then STEWART told BACANOVIC to sell her shares.

Specification Three

STEWART falsely stated that she did not recall speaking to BACANOVIC's assistant on December 27, 2001.

Specification Four

STEWART falsely stated that before ending her call with BACANOVIC on December 27, 2001, STEWART and BACANOVIC had discussions regarding what MSLO stock was doing and regarding Kmart.

Specification Five

STEWART falsely stated that she decided to sell her ImClone stock on December 27, 2001 because she did not want to be bothered over her vacation.

Specification Six

STEWART falsely stated that she did not know if there was a phone message from BACANOVIC on December 27, 2001 in the log of telephone messages maintained by her assistant.

Specification Seven

STEWART falsely stated that since December 28, 2001, she had only one conversation with BACANOVIC regarding ImClone, in which they only discussed matters in the "public arena."

Specification Eight

STEWART falsely stated that since December 28, 2001, BACANOVIC mentioned to STEWART in a telephone conversation that Merrill Lynch had been questioned by the SEC regarding ImClone, but did not tell STEWART that he had been questioned by the SEC or that he had been questioned by the SEC regarding STEWART's account.

(Title 18, United States Code, Sections 1001(a)(1) and (2)).

COUNT FOUR
(False Statements by Martha Stewart)

The Grand Jury further charges:

46. The allegations of paragraphs 1 through 36 and 41 are repeated and realleged as though fully set forth herein.

47. On or about April 10, 2002, in the Southern District of New York, MARTHA STEWART unlawfully, willfully, and knowingly, in a matter within the jurisdiction of the executive branch of the Government of the United States, falsified, concealed, and covered up by trick, scheme, and device material facts, and made materially false, fictitious, and fraudulent statements and representations, to wit, STEWART participated in an interview with the SEC, the FBI, and the U.S. Attorney's Office for the Southern District of New York in New York, New York, in which she made the following false statements and concealed and covered up facts that were material to the investigations:

Specification One

STEWART falsely stated that she did not recall if she and BACANOVIC discussed Samuel Waksal on December 27, 2001, nor did she recall being informed on December 27, 2001 that any of the Waksals were selling their ImClone stock.

Specification Two

STEWART falsely stated that in a conversation that occurred sometime in November or December 2001, after she sold all of her ImClone shares from the Martha Stewart Defined Pension Fund, STEWART and BACANOVIC decided that STEWART would sell her shares when ImClone started trading at $60 per share.

Specification Three

STEWART falsely stated that on December 27, 2001, at approximately 1:30 p.m. (EST), STEWART spoke to BACANOVIC, who told her that ImClone was trading below $60 per share and suggested that STEWART sell her ImClone shares.
(Title 18, United States Code, Sections 1001(a)(1) and (2)).

COUNT FIVE
(Making and Using False Documents by Peter Bacanovic)

The Grand Jury further charges:
48. The allegations of paragraphs 1 through 36 and 41 are repeated and realleged as though fully set forth herein.
49. In or about January 2002, in the Southern District of New York and elsewhere, PETER BACANOVIC unlawfully, willfully, and knowingly, in a matter within the jurisdiction of the executive branch of the Government of the United States, made and used false writings and documents knowing the same to contain materially false, fictitious, and fraudulent statements and entries, to wit, BACANOVIC altered the Worksheet to add the notation "@ 60" and caused it to be produced to the SEC.
(Title 18, United States Code, Sections 1001(a)(3) and 2).

COUNT SIX
(Perjury by Peter Bacanovic)

The Grand Jury further charges:

50. The allegations of paragraphs 1 through 36 and 41 are repeated and realleged as though fully set forth herein.
51. On February 13, 2002, in the Southern District of New York, PETER BACANOVIC, having taken an oath before a competent tribunal, officer and person, in a case in which the law of the United States authorizes an oath to be administered, namely, in testimony before an officer of the SEC, that he would testify, declare, depose and certify truly, and that any written testimony, declaration,

deposition and certificate by him subscribed, would be true, unlawfully, willfully, knowingly, and contrary to such oath, stated and subscribed material matters which he did not believe to be true, namely, the testimony on or about February 13, 2002, the underlined portions of which he believed to be materially false:

Specification One
(Page 14, Line 11 – Page 16, Line 7)

Q: And she [MARTHA STEWART's assistant] told you that Ms. Stewart was in transit?

A: Ms. Stewart was in transit, that she didn't know when she would be speaking with her, and that she would try to give her the message.

Q: And what was the message?

A: The message was to please call us back, and also to please advise her that ImClone stock was at whatever the price was at that time.

. . .

Q: And you specifically told [MARTHA STEWART's assistant] that ImClone stock was dropping? A: No. We just gave her the price of the stock. . . .

Q: When you called [MARTHA STEWART's assistant], can you just try and think, to be as specific as possible, when you asked her to ask Ms. Stewart to please call you back, did you say, "It's urgent, call me back immediately"? Something like that?

A: No. I said, "I would like to speak with her, if possible, today and regarding ImClone and the current price of the stock is. Understanding that she is in transit and that she sometimes is very, very difficult to reach."

Specification Two
(Page 69, Line 2 – Page 72, Line 4)

Q: When was the last time you saw her?

A: In January.

Q: When in January?

A: I would be able to give you the exact date, it's in my office in my calendar. I saw her approximately in the middle of the month.

. . .

Q: Did ImClone come up in the meeting at all?

A: <u>She had asked me if I had spoken to Sam, and I said, no, I had not. And that was it.</u>

. . .

Q: Did her investment in ImClone come up at all?

A: <u>No</u>.

. . .

Q: In addition to that meeting, have you talked to her at all since December 28th? Besides that meeting?

A: Well, I spoke with her about the fact that I wanted to schedule the meeting. I spoke with her to confirm that I had received the second part of the transfer. And then she — and I spoke with her when she reconfirmed that these payments were going to be going out.

Q: And when you spoke with her in any of these conversations, did ImClone come up?

A: <u>Did not</u>.

Q: Did Sam Waksal come up?

A: No. Oh — I don't recall. Possibly. I don't recall if Sam Waksal — we might have made reference to a newspaper article.

Q: What newspaper article?

A: There have been so many, I don't really remember. One of the earlier ones that began to appear.

Q: Do you remember what it was about the article that you guys were discussing?

A: Just the publicity.

Q: The publicity involving her?

A: No. There was no publicity, this was not about her, this is about Sam.

Specification Three
(Page 77, Line 16 – Page 82, Line 21)

Q: Did there come a time when she wanted to sell the ImClone stock?

A: Well, it was at my solicitation.

Q: Tell me about that.

A: When we were doing her portfolio review for tax planning purposes that took place in the week prior to Christmas, it came to me as a great surprise, having felt that I had liquidated all ImClone shares from her accounts at that time, that the stock was still there.

Q: Let me just — you had a tax planning discussion with her?

A: Which was also a portfolio review — a comprehensive portfolio review with her.

Q: And this happened the week before Christmas?

A: Correct.

Q: So, approximately?

A: I believe the exact date was December 20th, I believe.

Q: And where did this take place?

A: On the telephone. And we reviewed each and every position in the account. And we discussed the fundamentals of all the positions. We discussed gains and losses for all the positions. We discussed the overall status of the portfolio, and included in that discussion was ImClone. And so we reviewed ImClone and discussed what her intentions were for ImClone at that time versus my recommendations.

Q: What were her desires for the ImClone stock?

A: She felt — that the time, the stock had already come off its highs a little bit. And she wanted to hold the stock, and I challenged that by saying, "The stock has [sic] clearly declining, why would you hold it? Why are you holding this, considering we sold 50,000 or 40,000 shares two months ago?" . . . And she goes — and at that point, we determined that if, in fact, it fell much further, then we would sell it.

. . .

Q: So, going back, she didn't really want to sell it, you recommended that she sell it. You can continue on from there.

A: So, we made a deal. I said, "Okay, if you would not like to sell the stock now, how long are you going to wait before you sell this stock?"

Q: I'm sorry, on December 20th, when you had this conversation, do you remember what the price of the stock was?

A: It was in the mid 60s. <u>And, at that point, we determined that $60 a share would be a suitable price, should it ever fall that low.</u> Of course, she never thought it would.

Specification Four
(Page 104, Line 15 – Page 105, Line 8)

Q: Did you ever tell Martha Stewart that the SEC had been speaking with Merrill Lynch about sales in ImClone at the end of the year?

A: <u>I said that we had had — we had been reviewing this internally. And that was all</u>.

Q: In other words, you didn't mention that the SEC was looking into this?

A: <u>No.</u>

Q: Tell me about the conversation you had with her when you said, "We've been reviewing this internally."

A: I said, you know, "In light of the news, the disclosures and news and following the stock price, Merrill Lynch has been reviewing, you know, all our transactions in ImClone."

Q: Did you tell her that anyone was asking questions about her transactions specifically?

A: <u>I did not.</u>

Q: Did she ask you that?

A: <u>She did not.</u>

(Page 124, Line 22 – Page 125, Line 13)

Q: At any time, did you and she discuss the investigation — any investigation by the Securities and Exchange Commission?

A: No.

Q: Did you and she discuss any investigation by any entity at all into trading in ImClone stock or —

A: I believe I said earlier that Merrill Lynch itself was investigating the situation with ImClone without making reference to any transaction or any person and obliquely just referring to the company.

Q: Other than the Merrill Lynch investigation, did you and she discuss any other investigation into ImClone? . . . Can you just say that out loud —

A: No.

Q: — for the record?

A: No, we did not.

Specification Five
(Page 106, Line 13 – Page 107, Line 6)

Q: Did you say anything that would give her cause for concern, the fact that she sold on December 27th?

A: No. Because she had no cause for concern. Because we had reviewed this position, I have notes of the conversation, it was completely typical, and she would have had no cause for concern. So, no.

Q: And you have notes of what conversation?

A: Well, I mean, I have a worksheet that I worked from that day, that we did on the 20th, where all of this stuff, which is a printout of a screen, with all sorts of markings on it. And so, I mean, all of this was discussed at the time, long prior. And so she had no reason for concern.

Q: And the information about her selling — her possibly selling ImClone at 60 would be reflected on that worksheet?

A: Yeah, I mean, reflected on the worksheet in a very loose way. I mean, things are highlighted, marked for sales. Some things are circled. I mean, it's scribbled on.

Specification Six
(Page 114, Line 10 – Page 115, Line 3)

Q: Who came up with the $60 price for ImClone? To sell?
A: We quibbled over it. And so we came to this price together.
Q: What was the price you recommended? Did you recommend a price —?
A: I recommended an immediate sale.
Q: So you wanted her to sell about —
A: Right away.
Q: And what price did she come to you and say, "I'll sell it at."
A: She didn't really have a price. I said, "Listen, what will you settle for? How low does this have to go before you're prepared to part with this?" She said, "I don't know." I said, "Well, how about $60 a share? Does that sound reasonable?" And the conversation was something like that. She said, "Yes, sure, $60."
  (Title 18, United States Code, Section 1621).

COUNT SEVEN
(Obstruction of Justice by Peter Bacanovic)

The Grand Jury further charges:

52. The allegations of paragraphs 1 through 36, 41 and 51 are repeated and realleged as though fully set forth herein.

53. From in or about January 2002 through in or about April 2002, in the Southern District of New York and elsewhere, PETER BACANOVIC unlawfully, willfully and knowingly, corruptly influenced, obstructed and impeded, and endeavored to influence, obstruct and impede the due and proper administration of the law under which a pending proceeding was being had before a department and agency of the United States, namely, the SEC, by providing and causing to be provided false and misleading

information and documents to the SEC relating to the sale of ImClone stock by MARTHA STEWART.

(Title 18, United States Code, Sections 1505 and 2).

COUNT EIGHT
(Obstruction of Justice by Martha Stewart)

The Grand Jury further charges:

54. The allegations of paragraphs 1 through 36, 41 and 51 are repeated and realleged as though fully set forth herein.

55. From in or about January 2002 through in or about April 2002, in the Southern District of New York and elsewhere, MARTHA STEWART unlawfully, willfully and knowingly, corruptly influenced, obstructed and impeded, and endeavored to influence, obstruct and impede the due and proper administration of the law under which a pending proceeding was being had before a department and agency of the United States, namely, the SEC, by providing and causing to be provided false and misleading information to the SEC relating to STEWART's sale of ImClone stock.

(Title 18, United States Code, Sections 1505 and 2).

COUNT NINE
(Securities Fraud by Martha Stewart)

The Grand Jury further charges:

56. The allegations of paragraphs 1 through 36 and 41 are repeated and realleged as though fully set forth herein.

57. At all times relevant to this Indictment, MARTHA STEWART's reputation, as well as the likelihood of any criminal or regulatory action against STEWART, were material to MSLO's shareholders because of the negative impact that any such action or damage to her reputation could have on the company which bears her name, as STEWART well knew. In MSLO's 1999 prospectus the company stated, "Our continued success and the value of our brand name therefore depends, to a large degree, on the reputation of Martha Stewart."

58. During the evening of June 6, 2002, the Associated Press reported that MARTHA STEWART sold ImClone shares prior to the news of the FDA's rejection of the Erbitux application, a fact which had not previously been publicly reported. On June 7, 2002, following the public announcement that STEWART had sold ImClone shares on the same day as members of the family of Samuel Waksal, MSLO's market price began steadily to fall, from a closing price of $19.01 on June 6, 2002 to a closing price of $11.47 on June 28, 2002.

59. As of June 6, 2002, MARTHA STEWART held 30,713,475 shares of MSLO Class A common stock, which constituted 62.6% of the outstanding Class A common stock of MSLO. STEWART also held 100% of the outstanding 30,619,375 shares of MSLO Class B common stock. Each share of the Class B common stock was convertible on a one-for-one basis into Class A common stock at STEWART's option. Combined, these shares gave STEWART control over 94.4% of shareholders' voting power.

60. As set forth more fully below, in an effort to stop or at least slow the steady erosion of MSLO's stock price caused by investor concerns, STEWART made or caused to be made a series of false and misleading public statements during June 2002 regarding her sale of ImClone stock on December 27, 2001 that concealed and omitted that STEWART had been provided information regarding the sale and attempted sale of the Waksal Shares and that STEWART had sold her ImClone stock while in possession of that information. STEWART made these false and misleading statements with the intent to defraud and deceive purchasers and sellers of MSLO common stock and to maintain the value of her own MSLO stock by preventing a decline in the market price of MSLO's stock. These false and misleading statements were contained in: (a) statements made on behalf of STEWART by STEWART's attorney to the Wall Street Journal, published on June 7, 2002; (b) written public statements issued by STEWART on June 12 and 18, 2002; and (c) statements made by STEWART at a conference for securities analysts and investors on June 19, 2002.

The June 7 Statement

61. On or about June 6, 2002, MARTHA STEWART was advised that the Wall Street Journal intended to publish an article stating that STEWART sold ImClone shares on December 27, 2001, a fact that had not yet been publicly reported. With the intent and knowledge that false and misleading information would be publicly disseminated, STEWART caused her attorney in New York, New York to provide to the Wall Street Journal the following false and misleading information regarding the reason for STEWART's December 27, 2001 sale of ImClone stock (the "June 7 Statement") that concealed that STEWART had been provided information regarding the sale and attempted sale of the Waksal Shares and that STEWART had sold her ImClone stock while in possession of that information:

> The sale was executed because Ms. Stewart had a predetermined price at which she planned to sell the stock. That determination, made more than a month before that trade, was to sell if the stock ever went less than $60.

This false and misleading information was published in an article in the Wall Street Journal on June 7, 2002.

The June 12 Statement

62. On June 12, 2002, the news media widely reported that Samuel Waksal had been arrested and charged in a criminal complaint with insider trading. Following this announcement, the stock price of MSLO fell approximately 5.6%, from an opening price of $15.90 to a closing price of $15.

63. On June 12, 2002, after the close of trading on the NYSE, MARTHA STEWART in New York, New York, prepared and caused to be issued a public statement (the "June 12 Statement"), in which STEWART made the following false and misleading statements that concealed that STEWART had been provided information regarding the sale and attempted sale of the Waksal

Shares and that STEWART had sold her ImClone stock while in possession of that information, among others:

   a.   STEWART falsely stated that she had agreed with her broker "several weeks" after a tender offer made by Bristol-Myers Squibb to ImClone shareholders in October 2001, at a time when the ImClone shares were trading at about $70, that "if the ImClone stock price were to fall below $60, we would sell my holdings";

   b.   STEWART falsely stated that on December 27, 2001, "I returned a call from my broker advising me that ImClone had fallen below $60 . . . and reiterated my instructions to sell the shares"; and

   c.   STEWART falsely stated that she "did not have any nonpublic information regarding ImClone when [she] sold [her] ImClone shares."

The June 18 Statement

64. As of June 18, 2002, MARTHA STEWART was scheduled to speak at a conference for securities analysts and investors (the "Conference"), at which she expected that questions could be asked about her sale of ImClone shares. In preparation for that Conference, STEWART prepared and approved another public statement about her ImClone sale. On June 18, 2002, after the close of trading on the NYSE, MARTHA STEWART in New York, New York, prepared and caused to be issued a public statement (the "June 18 Statement"), in which she made the following false and misleading statements that concealed that STEWART had been provided information regarding the sale and attempted sale of the Waksal Shares and that STEWART had sold her ImClone stock while in possession of that information, among others:

   a.   STEWART falsely stated that "[i]n my June 12, 2002 statement I explained what did happen";

   b.   STEWART falsely stated that her December 27, 2001 sale of ImClone stock "was based on information that was available to the public that day";

   c.   STEWART falsely stated that "[s]ince the stock had fallen below $60, I sold my shares, as I had previously agreed to do with my broker"; and

    d. STEWART falsely stated that she had cooperated with the SEC and U.S. Attorney's Office "fully and to the best of my ability."

    65. On the morning of June 19, 2002, MARTHA STEWART read the June 18 Statement at the Conference in New York, New York.

Statutory Allegations

    66. In or about June 2002, in the Southern District of New York and elsewhere, MARTHA STEWART unlawfully, willfully and knowingly, directly and indirectly, by use of the means and instrumentalities of interstate commerce, the mails and the facilities of national securities exchanges, did use and employ manipulative and deceptive devices and contrivances, in violation of Title 17, Code of Federal Regulations, Section 240.10b-5, by (a) employing devices, schemes and artifices to defraud; (b) making untrue statements of material facts and omitting to state material facts necessary in order to make the statements made, in the light of the circumstances under which they were made, not misleading; and (c) engaging in acts, practices and courses of business which operated and would operate as a fraud and deceit upon purchasers and sellers of MSLO common stock.

    (Title 15, United States Code, Sections 78j(b) and 78ff;
Title 17, Code of Federal Regulations, Section 240.10b-5;
and Title 18, United States Code, Section 2.)

_____   _____
FOREPERSON   DAVID N. KELLEY
                                   United States Attorney

WORLDCOM

UNITED STATES DISTRICT COURT
SOUTHERN DISTRICT OF NEW YORK

- -x

UNITED STATES OF AMERICA	:	INDICTMENT
-v-	:	S3 02 Cr. 1144 (BSJ)
BERNARD J. EBBERS,	:	
Defendant.	:	

- -x

COUNT ONE

(Conspiracy To Commit Securities Fraud)

The Grand Jury charges:

RELEVANT PERSONS AND ENTITIES

1. At all times relevant to this Indictment, WorldCom, Inc. ("WorldCom") was a corporation organized under the laws of the State of Georgia with its headquarters in Clinton, Mississippi.

2. At all times relevant to this Indictment, WorldCom's common stock was listed under the symbol "WCOM" on the NASDAQ National Market System, an electronic securities market system. As of May 31, 2002, WorldCom's largest institutional shareholders included Bernstein Investment Research and Management, Oppenheimer Capital, Merrill Lynch Investment Managers, and College Retirement Equities Fund, all of which maintained offices in New York, New York.

3.   At all times relevant to this Indictment, BERNARD J. EBBERS, the defendant, served as Chief Executive Officer, President, and a director of WorldCom. At all times relevant to this Indictment, EBBERS signed the Annual Reports on Form 10-K that WorldCom filed with the United States Securities and Exchange Commission (the "SEC"). At all times relevant to this Indictment, EBBERS owned millions of shares, and options to purchase shares, of WorldCom common stock.

4. At various times relevant to this Indictment, Scott D. Sullivan, a co-conspirator not named as a defendant herein, served as Chief Financial Officer, Treasurer, and Secretary of WorldCom. At all times relevant to this Indictment, Sullivan directed the preparation of and signed the Annual Reports on Form 10-K and Quarterly Reports on Form 10-Q that WorldCom filed with the SEC.

BACKGROUND
WorldCom's Business

5. At all times relevant to this Indictment, WorldCom provided to businesses and consumers around the world a broad range of communications services, including, among other things, data transmission services, Internet-related services, commercial voice services, international communication services, long distance service, and other telecommunication services. WorldCom owned and operated extensive global network facilities, which spanned six continents, reached every major city center in the world, and connected more than 60,000 buildings. WorldCom's global network included more than 90,000 route miles of terrestrial and undersea fiber-optic cable. This network was designed to support the largest array of data communication products and services in the world.

6. At all times relevant to this Indictment, to serve customers that were not directly connected to its network, WorldCom paid fees to use or lease facilities and connections from other telecommunication companies. These fees, known as "line costs," were WorldCom's largest expense.

WorldCom's Communications With The Investing Public

7.   At all times relevant to this Indictment, BERNARD J. EBBERS and Scott D. Sullivan, on behalf of WorldCom, provided members of the investing public with information concerning WorldCom's financial results and operating performance. EBBERS and Sullivan provided such information through various methods, including in WorldCom's public filings with the SEC, in periodic news releases and other corporate announcements, in statements made in conference calls with professional securities analysts and investors, and in meetings and conferences held with analysts and investors in New York, New York and elsewhere. Members of the investing public considered and relied upon the information provided by EBBERS and Sullivan in deciding whether to purchase, hold, or sell WorldCom securities.

8.   Part of the information routinely provided by BERNARD J. EBBERS and Scott D. Sullivan to members of the investing public was so-called "guidance" concerning WorldCom's operational and financial results for upcoming reporting periods. The "guidance" provided by EBBERS and Sullivan concerned various measures of WorldCom's operational and financial performance, including its expected cash earnings per share ("EPS"), "Earnings Before Interest, Taxes, Depreciation, and Amortization" ("EBITDA"), net income, expenses, revenue growth, and capital expenditures.

9.   At all times relevant to this Indictment, numerous securities analysts and investors relied on the "guidance" provided by BERNARD J. EBBERS and Scott D. Sullivan to gauge WorldCom's performance, to predict WorldCom's expected earnings, and to disseminate estimates of WorldCom's expected performance to the larger investing public. Members of the investing public closely followed such "earnings estimates" or "analysts' expectations" because, historically, when company earnings fail to meet such estimates, company stock prices typically decline, and when company earnings exceed such estimates, company stock prices typically rise.

WorldCom's Financial Reporting Process

10. At all times relevant to this Indictment, at the close of each month and each quarter of WorldCom's fiscal year, employees in WorldCom's financial and accounting departments collected and summarized information reflecting WorldCom's operating performance and financial results for the particular period in question. This information was reflected in various financial statements and reports.

11. At all times relevant to this Indictment, WorldCom tracked its revenue on a monthly basis through the use of a report referred to internally as "MonRev." BERNARD J. EBBERS designed MonRev to allow himself, Scott D. Sullivan, and other WorldCom officers to review the revenue generated by each of WorldCom's sales channels, including "Major Nationals," "Wholesale," "Global," "Mass Markets," "International," and "Specialized Sales." Revenue that was not generated through these sales channels was tracked separately and classified in MonRev as "Corporate Unallocated." Members of WorldCom's Revenue Accounting Department prepared MonRev each month and provided it to EBBERS, Sullivan, and others. EBBERS carefully scrutinized every MonRev report. Unlike all other recipients of MonRev, EBBERS demanded that his copy be printed on a special "green-bar" computer paper to facilitate his review. EBBERS and Sullivan regularly met to discuss the results reported in MonRev.

12. At all times relevant to this Indictment, WorldCom tracked its Selling, General, and Administrative expenses ("SG&A") on a monthly and quarterly basis through its "Management Budget Variance Report." Members of WorldCom's General Accounting Department prepared the Management Budget Variance Report each month and provided it to BERNARD J. EBBERS, Scott D. Sullivan, and others. EBBERS and Sullivan regularly met to discuss the results reported in the Management Budget Variance Report.

13. At all times relevant to this Indictment, WorldCom tracked expenses relating to its line costs on a quarterly basis through the preparation of a preliminary income statement. Members of WorldCom's General Accounting Department prepared a preliminary

income statement each quarter and provided it to Scott D. Sullivan and others. Sullivan, in turn, provided these preliminary income statements to BERNARD J. EBBERS. At the close of each financial reporting period, EBBERS and Sullivan met to discuss WorldCom's preliminary operating results, including WorldCom's line cost expenses.

14. At all times relevant to this Indictment, WorldCom's senior management participated in periodic meetings to discuss expectations regarding WorldCom's operating results for the upcoming months. In connection with these so-called "Outlook" meetings, BERNARD J. EBBERS and Scott D. Sullivan, among others, reviewed documents that summarized anticipated events that would affect WorldCom's revenues in the following months. EBBERS and Sullivan regularly met to discuss the financial results and projections reflected in the various documents presented during the "Outlook" meetings.

THE SCHEME TO DEFRAUD
Introduction

15. As set forth more fully below, from in or about September 2000 through in or about June 2002, BERNARD J. EBBERS, Scott D. Sullivan, and their co-conspirators engaged in an illegal scheme to deceive members of the investing public, WorldCom shareholders, securities analysts, the SEC, and others, concerning WorldCom's true operating performance and financial results.

16. As BERNARD J. EBBERS, Scott D. Sullivan, and their co-conspirators knew, by no later than in or about September 2000, WorldCom's true operating performance and financial results were in decline and had fallen materially below analysts' expectations. EBBERS nevertheless insisted that WorldCom publicly report financial results that met analysts' expectations. As a result, rather than disclosing WorldCom's true condition and suffer the ensuing decline in the price of WorldCom's common stock, Sullivan, with EBBERS's knowledge and approval, directed co-conspirators to make false and fraudulent adjustments to WorldCom's books and records.

17. Thereafter, from in or about September 2000 through in or about June 2002, for the purpose of disguising WorldCom's true operating performance and financial results, EBBERS, Sullivan, and their co-conspirators caused WorldCom's reported figures for revenue, SG&A and line cost expenses, EBITDA, depreciation expense, net income, and EPS to be falsely and fraudulently manipulated. As EBBERS, Sullivan, and their co-conspirators knew, the aggregate effect of these adjustments, which were made in round-dollar amounts and consistently totaled hundreds of millions of dollars per quarter, was to present a materially false and misleading picture of WorldCom's true operating performance and financial results.

18. From in or about September 2000 through in or about June 2002, in furtherance of the scheme, BERNARD J. EBBERS, Scott D. Sullivan, and their co-conspirators made repeated public statements in which they (a) falsely described WorldCom's operating performance and financial results, (b) omitted to disclose material facts necessary to make the statements that they made about WorldCom's operating performance and financial results complete, accurate, and not misleading, and (c) caused WorldCom to file financial statements with the SEC that presented a materially false and misleading description of WorldCom's operating performance and financial results. Through this scheme, EBBERS, Sullivan, and their co-conspirators inflated and maintained artificially the price of WorldCom common stock.

19. On or about June 25, 2002, WorldCom announced that, as a result of an internal investigation, it would have to issue restated financial statements. In the days following this announcement, the price of WorldCom's common stock plummeted more than 90%, resulting in an aggregate decline in shareholder value of more than $2 billion.

The Fraudulent Adjustments To WorldCom's Books And Records

20. In or about September 2000, after reviewing MonRev and other documents summarizing WorldCom's financial results and operating performance for July and August 2000, Scott D. Sullivan

advised BERNARD J. EBBERS that WorldCom's operating performance and financial results had deteriorated, and that WorldCom's earnings for the upcoming reporting period would not meet analysts' expectations. Sullivan further advised EBBERS that WorldCom should issue an "earnings warning" to alert the investing public about WorldCom's deteriorating financial performance. EBBERS refused to issue an earnings warning. Instead, EBBERS and Sullivan agreed to take steps to conceal WorldCom's true financial condition and operating performance from the investing public.

21. In or about October 2000, rather than disclosing WorldCom's true financial condition and operating performance, BERNARD J. EBBERS and Scott D. Sullivan instructed subordinates, in substance and in part, to falsely and fraudulently book certain entries in WorldCom's general ledger, which were designed to increase artificially WorldCom's reported revenue and to decrease artificially WorldCom's reported expenses, resulting in, among other things, artificially-inflated figures for WorldCom's EPS, EBITDA, and revenue growth rate. The adjustments included (a) reductions made to line cost expense accounts by debiting certain reserve and liability accounts, which reductions lacked any business justification or supporting documentation, and (b) increases to revenue, which in light of their departure from prior revenue recognition policies, and in light of their aggregate amount, made WorldCom's reported revenue materially misleading. EBBERS and Sullivan instructed others to make these adjustments solely in an effort to report results that would satisfy analysts' expectations, even though EBBERS and Sullivan knew that WorldCom's true results in fact failed to meet those expectations.

22. In or about January 2001, BERNARD J. EBBERS and Scott D. Sullivan again determined that WorldCom's financial results for the fourth quarter of 2000 would not meet analysts' expectations. Rather than disclose WorldCom's true financial condition and operating performance, in or about February 2001, EBBERS and Sullivan instructed subordinates, in substance and in part, to falsely and fraudulently book certain entries in WorldCom's general ledger, which were designed to increase artificially WorldCom's reported revenue and to decrease artificially WorldCom's reported expenses,

resulting in, among other things, artificially-inflated figures for WorldCom's EPS, EBITDA, and revenue growth rate. These adjustments included (a) reductions made to line cost expense accounts by debiting certain reserve and liability accounts, which lacked any business justification or supporting documentation, and (b) increases to revenue, which in light of their departure from prior revenue recognition policies, and in light of their aggregate amount, made WorldCom's reported revenue materially misleading. EBBERS and Sullivan instructed others to make these adjustments solely in an effort to report results that would satisfy analysts' expectations, even though EBBERS and Sullivan knew that WorldCom's true results in fact failed to meet those expectations.

23. In or about March 2001, BERNARD J. EBBERS and Scott D. Sullivan determined that WorldCom's financial results for the first quarter of 2001 would not meet analysts' expectations. Sullivan advised EBBERS, in substance and in part, that members of WorldCom's General Accounting Department could no longer reduce line cost expense accounts by debiting certain reserve and liability accounts, as they had done previously. Instead, Sullivan advised EBBERS, in substance and in part, that members of WorldCom's General Accounting Department would transfer line cost expenses to capital expenditure accounts. Sullivan advised EBBERS, in substance and in part, that these transfers were being made to keep WorldCom's expenses-to-revenue ratio in line with figures reported in previous periods and in an effort to meet analysts' expectations for WorldCom's net income, EPS, and EBITDA.

24. In or about March 2001, Scott D. Sullivan instructed members of the General Accounting Department to make journal entries in WorldCom's general ledger, which resulted in the transfer of hundreds of millions of dollars from line cost expense accounts to capital expenditure accounts. Sullivan's instructions were communicated, and the journal entries affecting the transfers were made, after WorldCom's field offices' books were closed for the quarter. EBBERS and Sullivan instructed others to make these adjustments solely in an effort to satisfy analysts' expectations, including those regarding WorldCom's net income, EPS, and EBITDA, even though EBBERS and Sullivan knew that WorldCom's

true results in fact failed to meet those expectations. As described more fully below, Sullivan directed similar line cost transfers in each of the quarters from March 2001 through March 2002, resulting in improper transfers totaling approximately $3.8 billion.

25. In or about June 2001, BERNARD J. EBBERS and Scott D. Sullivan determined that WorldCom's financial results for the second quarter of 2001 would not meet analysts' expectations. In or about July 2001, rather than disclose WorldCom's true operating performance and financial condition, EBBERS and Sullivan instructed subordinates, in substance and in part, to falsely and fraudulently book certain entries in WorldCom's general ledger, which were designed to increase artificially WorldCom's reported revenue and to decrease artificially WorldCom's reported expenses, resulting in, among other things, artificially inflated figures for WorldCom's EPS, EBITDA, and revenue growth rate. These adjustments included (a) the improper capitalization of line cost expenses, and (b) increases to revenue, which in light of their departure from prior revenue recognition policies, and in light of their aggregate amount, made WorldCom's reported revenue materially misleading. With respect to these revenue adjustments, WorldCom created a process, referred to internally as "Close the Gap," designed solely to identify adjustments that would increase reported revenue in an effort to satisfy analysts' expectations. EBBERS and Sullivan both participated extensively in the "Close the Gap" process. EBBERS and Sullivan instructed others to make these adjustments solely in an effort to report results that would satisfy analysts' expectations, even though EBBERS and Sullivan knew that WorldCom's true results in fact failed to meet those expectations.

26. In or about September 2001, BERNARD J. EBBERS and Scott D. Sullivan determined that WorldCom's financial results for the third quarter of 2001 would not meet analysts' expectations. Rather than disclose WorldCom's true operating performance and financial condition, in or about October 2001, EBBERS and Sullivan instructed subordinates, in substance and in part, to falsely and fraudulently book certain entries in WorldCom's general ledger, which were designed to increase artificially WorldCom's reported revenue and to decrease artificially WorldCom's reported expenses,

resulting in, among other things, artificially inflated figures for WorldCom's EPS, EBITDA, and revenue growth rate. The adjustments included (a) the improper capitalization of line cost expenses, and (b) increases to revenue, which in light of their departure from prior revenue recognition policies, and in light of their aggregate amount, made WorldCom's reported revenue materially misleading. With regard to the revenue adjustments, EBBERS and Sullivan, through the "Close the Gap" process, caused WorldCom to report publicly revenue growth of approximately 12 percent, even though WorldCom's true operating performance yielded revenue growth of approximately 6 percent. EBBERS and Sullivan instructed others to make these adjustments solely in an effort to report results that would satisfy analysts' expectations, even though EBBERS and Sullivan knew that WorldCom's true results in fact failed to meet those expectations.

27. In or about January 2002, BERNARD J. EBBERS and Scott D. Sullivan determined that WorldCom's financial results for the fourth quarter of 2001 would not meet analysts' expectations. Rather than disclose WorldCom's true operating performance and financial condition, in or about February 2002, EBBERS and Sullivan instructed subordinates, in substance and in part, to falsely and fraudulently book certain entries in WorldCom's general ledger, which were designed to increase artificially WorldCom's reported revenue and to decrease artificially WorldCom's reported expenses, resulting in, among other things, artificially inflated figures for WorldCom's EPS, EBITDA, and revenue growth rate. These adjustments included (a) the improper capitalization of line cost expenses, and (b) increases to revenue, which in light of their departure from prior revenue recognition policies, and in light of their aggregate amount, made WorldCom's reported revenue materially misleading. EBBERS and Sullivan instructed others to make these adjustments solely in an effort to report results that would satisfy analysts' expectations, even though EBBERS and Sullivan knew that WorldCom's true results in fact failed to meet those expectations.

28. In or about March 2002, BERNARD J. EBBERS and Scott D. Sullivan determined that WorldCom's financial results for the first quarter of 2002 would not meet analysts' expectations. Rather than

disclose WorldCom's true operating performance and financial condition, in or about April 2002, EBBERS and Sullivan instructed subordinates, in substance and in part, to falsely and fraudulently book certain entries in WorldCom's general ledger, which were designed to increase artificially WorldCom's reported revenue and to decrease artificially WorldCom's reported expenses, resulting in, among other things, artificially inflated figures for WorldCom's EPS, EBITDA, and revenue growth rate. These adjustments included (a) the improper capitalization of line cost expenses, and (b) increases to revenue, which in light of their departure from prior revenue recognition policies, and in light of their aggregate amount, made WorldCom's reported revenue materially misleading. EBBERS and Sullivan instructed others to make these adjustments solely in an effort to report results that would satisfy analysts' expectations, even though EBBERS and Sullivan knew that WorldCom's true results in fact failed to meet those expectations.

<u>False Statements And Misleading Omissions</u>
<u>In WorldCom's SEC Filings</u>

29. To sell securities to members of the public and maintain public trading of its securities in the United States, WorldCom was required to comply with provisions of the federal securities laws, including the Securities Exchange Act of 1934 and regulations promulgated thereunder, that were designed to ensure that the company's financial information was accurately recorded and disclosed to the public.

30. Under these securities laws and regulations, WorldCom was required to, among other things (a) file with the SEC annual financial statements audited by an independent accountant; (b) file with the SEC quarterly updates of its financial statements that disclosed its financial condition and the results of its business operations for each three-month period; (c) devise and maintain a system of internal accounting controls sufficient to provide reasonable assurances that the company's transactions were recorded as necessary to permit preparation of financial statements in conformity with Generally Accepted Accounting Principles and other applicable criteria; and (d)

make and keep books, records, and accounts that accurately and fairly reflected the company's business transactions.

31.   At all times relevant to this Indictment, WorldCom's quarterly and annual financial statements were transmitted to the New York, New York offices of Merrill Communications LLC ("Merrill"), a filing agent that assisted companies in electronically filing periodic reports with the SEC, and were thereafter transmitted electronically by Merrill or a Merrill subcontractor, located in New York, New York, to the SEC for filing.

32.   The quarterly and annual reports filed by WorldCom for the third quarter of 2000 through the first quarter of 2002 included financial statements that reflected the above-described fraudulent adjustments to WorldCom's expenses and revenue, which had been made solely in an effort to satisfy analysts' expectations.

33.   BERNARD J. EBBERS, Scott D. Sullivan, and their co-conspirators failed to disclose in WorldCom's SEC filings, or in any other public statement, the artificial adjustments to WorldCom's expenses and revenue. By directing these adjustments to be made, and falsely concealing the adjustments from the SEC and members of the investing public, EBBERS, Sullivan, and their co-conspirators disguised WorldCom's true operating performance and financial condition from the SEC and the investing public. As a result, EBBERS, Sullivan, and their co-conspirators caused WorldCom to report financial results, which, as EBBERS, Sullivan, and their co-conspirators knew, exceeded by material amounts WorldCom's actual financial results in each reporting period.

False Statements And Misleading Omissions In WorldCom's Public Statements

34.   In statements and presentations made on behalf of WorldCom to members of the investing public, securities analysts, and others, BERNARD J. EBBERS, Scott D. Sullivan, and their co-conspirators falsely described WorldCom's true operating performance and financial condition, and omitted to disclose facts necessary to make those statements complete, accurate, and not misleading. EBBERS and Sullivan (a) made statements about

WorldCom's operating performance and financial condition which, as they knew, reflected the above-described fraudulent adjustments to WorldCom's expenses and revenue, and (b) failed to disclose that they had caused others to manipulate artificially WorldCom's expenses and revenue in an effort to meet analysts' expectations.

35. Following the close of each reporting period from the third quarter of 2000 through the first quarter of 2002, BERNARD J. EBBERS, Scott D. Sullivan, and their co-conspirators made statements to the investing public, including on conference calls held with analysts and investors. In these statements, EBBERS and Sullivan made materially false statements concerning WorldCom's financial results and operating performance and omitted to state facts necessary to make the statements that were made complete, accurate, and not misleading. Among the materially false statements and misleading omissions made by EBBERS and Sullivan were the following:

a. On or about October 26, 2000, during a conference call with analysts, EBBERS made the following statement, which he knew was false:

> We are pleased with our industry-leading incremental revenue growth of $1.1 billion this quarter. Commercial services revenues of $6.4 billion is up 19% year-over-year. And while we continued to hit bumps in the road in the dial-up Internet business, we did produce good results in dedicated Internet and our consumer services businesses. All in all, this was a solid quarter for WorldCom.

b. On or about October 26, 2000, during a conference call with analysts, Sullivan made the following statement, which he knew was false:

> This was another solid quarter for WorldCom. Cash earnings per share increased 21% to $0.57 per share. Earnings per share increased 27% to $0.47 per share.

c. On or about February 8, 2001, during a conference call with analysts, EBBERS made the following statement, which he knew was false:

> On the WorldCom side of the business, we are sticking with our 12% to 15% revenue growth guidance for 2001. Let me restate that. On the WorldCom side of the business we are sticking with our 12% to 15% revenue guidance for 2001. That's the range of the average that we will achieve throughout the year, and we will be increasing that revenue growth rate between the first quarter and the end of the year.

d. On or about April 26, 2001, during a conference call with analysts, EBBERS made the following statement, which he knew was false:

> WorldCom is certainly not immune to the effects of the economy. We are being impacted like everyone else. But, with the visibility we have in our significant growth engines, we continue to have confidence in our ability to achieve our 12 to 15% 2001 growth target on the WorldCom tracker. And I guess the thing that always frustrates me when I hear people talk about visibility as it's kind of like landing a plane — how much visibility do you really have? And so I thought I would just compare it to a weather forecast and say that if we look out for the remainder of 2001, we do not see any storms on the horizon at this time.

e. On or about October 25, 2001, during a conference call with analysts, Sullivan made the following statement, which he knew was false:

> Let me reiterate the main points Bernie [EBBERS] made. First, we reported a solid quarter of double-digit revenue growth in a challenging economic climate . . . . WorldCom Group posted 12% revenue growth in the third quarter, with Data & Internet growing at a combined rate of 22% this quarter. Data revenues were $2.3 billion and grew 18% in the third quarter.

f. On or about February 7, 2002, during a television interview on a CNBC program, EBBERS made the following statement, which he knew was false:

> The new day is that we're going, we have, finally this morning had a chance to put to rest all the rumors that have been circulating about us. None of which have been true. We have been a very sound financial company. We've been very conservative on our accounting practices and we wanted an opportunity for the last couple of weeks when we've seen this tremendous loss of market capitalization in our stock to be able to address the issues.

As EBBERS and Sullivan knew, these statements were materially false and misleading when they were made, because WorldCom's true financial condition and operating performance, including its revenue growth rate and EPS, were not as represented.

THE CONSPIRACY

36. From in or about September 2000 through in or about June 2002, in the Southern District of New York and elsewhere, BERNARD J. EBBERS, the defendant, and others known and unknown, unlawfully, willfully, and knowingly did combine, conspire, confederate, and agree together and with each other to commit offenses against the United States, namely (a) to commit fraud in connection with the purchase and sale of securities issued by WorldCom, in violation of Title 15, United States Code, Sections 78j(b) and 78ff, and Title 17, Code of Federal Regulations, Section 240.10b-5; (b) to make and cause to be made false and misleading statements of material fact in applications, reports, and documents required to be filed under the Securities Exchange Act of 1934 and the rules and regulations thereunder, in violation of Title 15, United States Code, Sections 78m(a) and 78ff; and (c) to falsify books, records, and accounts of WorldCom, in violation of Title 15, United States Code, Sections 78m(b)(2)(A), 78m(b)(5) and 78ff, and Title 17, Code of Federal Regulations, Section 240.13b2-1.

<u>Objects Of The Conspiracy</u>

<u>Fraud In Connection With The</u>
<u>Purchase And Sale Of Securities</u>

37. It was a part and an object of the conspiracy that BERNARD J. EBBERS, the defendant, and others known and unknown, unlawfully, willfully, and knowingly, directly and indirectly, by use of the means and instrumentalities of interstate commerce, the mails, and the facilities of national securities exchanges, would and did use and employ manipulative and deceptive devices and contrivances in connection with the purchase and sale of securities issued by WorldCom, in violation of Title 17, Code of Federal Regulations, Section 240.10b-5, by (a) employing devices, schemes, and artifices to defraud; (b) making and causing WorldCom to make untrue statements of material facts and omitting to state material facts necessary in order to make the statements made, in the light of the circumstances under which they were made, not misleading; and (c) engaging in acts, practices, and courses of business which operated and would operate as a fraud and deceit upon the purchasers and sellers of WorldCom securities, in violation of Title 15, United States Code, Sections 78j(b) and 78ff.

<u>False Statements In</u>
<u>Annual And Quarterly SEC Reports</u>

38. It was further a part and an object of the conspiracy that BERNARD J. EBBERS, the defendant, and others known and unknown, unlawfully, willfully, and knowingly, in applications, reports, and documents required to be filed under the Securities Exchange Act of 1934 and the rules and regulations thereunder, would and did make and cause to be made statements that were false and misleading with respect to material facts, in violation of Title 15, United States Code, Sections 78m(a) and 78ff.

False Books And Records

39. It was further a part and an object of the conspiracy that
BERNARD J. EBBERS, the defendant, and others known and
unknown, unlawfully, willfully, and knowingly would and did,
directly and indirectly, falsify and cause to be falsified books,
records, and accounts subject to Section 13(b)(2) of the Securities
Exchange Act of 1934, namely books, records, and accounts of
WorldCom, an issuer with a class of securities registered pursuant to
the Securities Exchange Act of 1934, which WorldCom was required
to make and keep, accurately and fairly reflecting, in reasonable
detail, the transactions and dispositions of the assets of WorldCom,
in violation of Title 15, United States Code, Sections 78m(b)(2)(A),
78m(b)(5) and 78ff, and Title 17, Code of Federal Regulations,
Section 240.13b2-1.

Means And Methods Of The Conspiracy

40. Among the means and methods by which BERNARD J.
EBBERS, and his co-conspirators would and did carry out the
conspiracy were the following:

a. EBBERS and Sullivan directed members of WorldCom's
Revenue Accounting Department to book entries that increased
revenue, solely in an effort to satisfy analysts' expectations, thereby
causing, among other things, figures for WorldCom's publicly
reported EPS, EBITDA, revenue growth rate, and net income to be
false and materially misleading.

b. With EBBERS's knowledge and approval, Sullivan
directed members of WorldCom's General Accounting Department
to book entries that reduced liability and reserve accounts without
supporting documentation or proper business rationale, thereby
falsely inflating, among other things, figures for WorldCom's
publicly reported EPS, EBITDA and net income.

c. With EBBERS's knowledge and approval, Sullivan
directed members of WorldCom's General Accounting Department
to transfer expenses from line cost accounts to capital expenditure
accounts without business justification or supporting documentation,

thereby falsely inflating, among other things, figures for WorldCom's publicly reported EPS, EBITDA, net income, and current assets.

    d. EBBERS, Sullivan, and their co-conspirators caused WorldCom to file publicly with the SEC quarterly and annual reports that materially misstated, among other things, figures for WorldCom's EPS, EBITDA, net income, assets, and liabilities.

    e. EBBERS, Sullivan, and their co-conspirators provided false and misleading financial information to the investing public and analysts.

Overt Acts

    41.   In furtherance of the conspiracy and to effect its illegal objects, BERNARD J. EBBERS and his co-conspirators committed the following overt acts, among others, in the Southern District of New York and elsewhere:

    a. In or about October 2000, EBBERS and Sullivan discussed WorldCom's deteriorating financial health and poor operating performance, and the improper adjustments required to meet analysts' expectations.

    b. On or about October 26, 2000, EBBERS and Sullivan provided false and misleading financial information to securities analysts and the investing public.

    c. In or about March 2001, EBBERS and Sullivan discussed WorldCom's deteriorating financial health and poor operating performance, and agreed to capitalize line costs solely in an effort to satisfy analysts' expectations for WorldCom's EPS, EBITDA, and net income.

    d. In or about April 2001, with EBBERS's knowledge and approval, Sullivan directed members of WorldCom's General Accounting Department to transfer approximately $771 million in line cost expenses to capital accounts in WorldCom's general ledger.

    e. On or about April 26, 2001, EBBERS and Sullivan provided false and misleading financial information to securities analysts and the investing public.

    f. On or about June 19, 2001, Sullivan left a voicemail message for EBBERS which stated, in part:

This MonRev just keeps getting worse and worse. The copy, the latest copy that you and I have already has accounting fluff in it . . . all one time stuff or junk that's already in the numbers. With the numbers being, you know, off as far as they were, I didn't think that this stuff was already in there. . . .

g. In or about July 2001, with EBBERS's knowledge and approval, Sullivan directed members of the General Accounting Department to transfer approximately $560 million in line cost expenses to capital accounts in WorldCom's general ledger.

h. On or about July 10, 2001, EBBERS sent a memorandum to a senior WorldCom officer requesting information concerning "those one time events that had to happen in order for us to have a chance to make our numbers."

i. In or about October 2001, with EBBERS's knowledge and approval, Sullivan directed members of WorldCom's General Accounting Department to transfer approximately $743 million in line cost expenses to capital accounts in WorldCom's general ledger.

j. On or about October 25, 2001, EBBERS and Sullivan provided false and misleading financial information to securities analysts and the investing public.

k. In or about February 2002, with EBBERS's knowledge and approval, Sullivan directed members of WorldCom's General Accounting Department to transfer approximately $941 million in line cost expenses to capital accounts in WorldCom's general ledger.

l. On or about February 7, 2002, EBBERS and Sullivan provided false and misleading financial information to securities analysts and the investing public.

m. On or about March 13, 2002, EBBERS and Sullivan signed WorldCom's Annual Report on Form 10-K for the Year Ending December 31, 2001.

n. On or about March 13, 2002, EBBERS and Sullivan caused WorldCom's Annual Report on Form 10-K for the Year Ending December 31, 2001 to be filed with the SEC from New York, New York.

o. In or about April 2002, with EBBERS's knowledge and approval, Sullivan directed members of WorldCom's General

Accounting Department to transfer approximately $818 million in line cost expenses to capital accounts in WorldCom's general ledger.

     p. On or about April 25, 2002, EBBERS and Sullivan provided false and misleading financial information to securities analysts and the investing public.

(Title 18, United States Code, Section 371.)

COUNT TWO
(Securities Fraud)

     The Grand Jury further charges:

     42. The allegations contained in paragraphs 1 through 35 and paragraphs 40 and 41 of this Indictment are repeated and realleged as if fully set forth herein.

     43. From in or about September 2000 up to and including in or about June 2002, in the Southern District of New York and elsewhere, BERNARD J. EBBERS, the defendant, unlawfully, willfully and knowingly, directly and indirectly, by the use of the means and instrumentalities of interstate commerce, and of the mails, and of facilities of national securities exchanges, in connection with the purchase and sale of securities, used and employed manipulative and deceptive devices and contrivances in violation of Title 17, Code of Federal Regulations, Section 240.10b-5 by (a) employing devices, schemes and artifices to defraud; (b) making untrue statements of material fact and omitting to state material facts necessary in order to make the statements made, in the light of the circumstances under which they were made, not misleading; and (c) engaging in acts, practices and courses of business which operated and would operate as a fraud and deceit upon purchasers and sellers of WorldCom securities.

(Title 15, United States Code, Sections 78j(b) and 78ff;
Title 17, Code of Federal Regulations, Section 240.10b-5;
Title 18, United States Code, Section 2.)

COUNTS THREE THROUGH NINE
(False Filing With The SEC)

The Grand Jury further charges:

44. The allegations contained in paragraphs 1 through 35 and paragraphs 40 and 41 of this Indictment are repeated and realleged as if fully set forth herein.

45. On or about the dates listed below, in the Southern District of New York and elsewhere, BERNARD J. EBBERS, the defendant, unlawfully, willfully, and knowingly, made and caused to be made statements in reports and documents required to be filed with the SEC under the Act and the rules and regulations promulgated thereunder, which statements were false and misleading with respect to material facts, to wit, EBBERS caused others to submit in New York, New York, the filings listed below to the United States Securities and Exchange Commission:

COUNT	FILING	APPROXIMATE DATE OF FILING
THREE	Form 10-Q for WorldCom, Inc., for the Third Quarter of 2000	11/14/00
FOUR	Form 10-K for WorldCom, Inc., for the year ending December 31, 2000	3/30/01
FIVE	Form 10-Q for WorldCom, Inc., for the First Quarter of 2001	5/15/01
SIX	Form 10-Q for WorldCom, Inc., for the Second Quarter of 2001	8/14/01
SEVEN	Form 10-Q for WorldCom, Inc., for the Third Quarter of 2001	11/14/01
EIGHT	Form 10-K for WorldCom, Inc., for the Year Ending December 31, 2001	3/13/02
NINE	Form 10-Q for WorldCom, Inc., for the First Quarter of 2002	5/15/02

(Title 15, United States Code, Sections 78m(a) and 78ff;
Title 17, Code of Federal Regulations, Section 240.13a-1;

and Title 18, United States Code, Section 2.)

_____   _____
FOREPERSON   DAVID N. KELLEY
                                             United States Attorney

Plea Agreements

ENRON

IN THE UNITED STATES DISTRICT COURT
FOR THE SOUTHERN DISTRICT OF TEXAS
HOUSTON DIVISION

UNITES STATES OF AMERICA,	)
	)
Plaintiff,	)
	)
v.	) No. CR-H-04-25(S-2)
	)
RICHARD A. CAUSEY,	)
	)
Defendant.	)
	)

PLEA AGREEMENT

Pursuant to Rule 11(c)(1)(C) of the Federal Rules of Criminal Procedure, the United States Department of Justice by the Enron Task Force ("the Department") and Richard A. Causey ("Defendant") agree to the following:

1. Defendant will plead guilty to Count 19 of the Superseding Indictment, charging him with securities fraud, in violation of Title

17, Code of Federal Regulations, Section 240.10b-5, Title 15 United States Code, 78j(b) and 78ff. Defendant agrees that he is pleading guilty because he is guilty, and that the facts contained in Exhibit A (attached and incorporated herein) are true and supply a factual basis for his plea. At the time the offenses were committed by the Defendant, the offense of securities fraud carried the following statutory penalty:

Count 19 — Securities Fraud

a. Maximum term of imprisonment: 10 years
    (17 C.F.R. § 240.10b-5, Title 15 U.S.C. 78j(b) and 78ff)
b. Minimum term of imprisonment: 0 years
    (17 C.F.R. § 240.10b-5, Title 15 U.S.C. 78j(b) and 78ff)
c. Maximum supervised release term: 3 years, to follow any term of imprisonment; if a condition of release is violated, Defendant may be sentenced to up to two years without credit for pre-release imprisonment or time previously served on post-release supervision (18 U.S.C. §§ 3583 (b) & (e))
d. Maximum fine: $1,000,000 or twice the gain/loss (18 U.S.C. § 3571(b)(3))
e. Restitution: As determined by the Court pursuant to statute. (18 U.S.C. §§ 3663 and 3663A)
f. Special Assessment: $100 (18 U.S.C. § 3013)

Sentencing Guidelines

2. The defendant understands that, in imposing the sentence, the Court will be guided by the United States Sentencing Guidelines (the "Guidelines"). The defendant understands that the Guidelines are advisory, not mandatory, but that the Court must consider the Guidelines in determining a reasonable sentence. The Department and the Defendant agree that the applicable Sentencing Guideline range exceeds 84 months.

3. Pursuant to Rule 11(c)(1)(C) of the Federal Rules of Criminal Procedure, the Defendant and the Department agree to ask the Court to impose an agreed-upon sentence of 84 months incarceration and to order forfeiture in the amount of $1,250,000.00. The Defendant

and the Department agree that if the Court refuses to accept the plea agreement with this agreed-upon sentence, the agreement will be null and void. The Defendant agrees that he will not seek a sentence below 84 months incarceration, and Defendant understands that except under the circumstances described in paragraph 4 below, the Court will be required to impose a sentence of 84 months and to order the agreed-upon forfeiture amount, or the plea agreement will be null and void.

4. If the Defendant provides truthful, complete, and accurate information to the Department, then the Department in its sole and exclusive discretion may move the Court, pursuant to Sentencing Guideline Section 5K1.1 and 18 U.S.C. § 3553(e), to depart downward from the 84-month agreed-upon sentence set forth in paragraph 3. Defendant understands and agrees that under the terms of this Agreement and Rule 11(c)(1)(C) and regardless of any such motion that the Department may make, Defendant cannot and will not be sentenced to a period of incarceration of less than 60 months. Defendant further agrees that he will not move for a downward departure on any grounds and that no such grounds are applicable.

5. The parties further agree that the Defendant's forfeiture of $1,250,000.00 in criminal proceeds and his agreement to relinquish any claim he may have to deferred compensation, as described in paragraphs 11 and 12 below, fully satisfies the forfeiture, fine, and restitution provisions of the sentencing laws and Guidelines.

Waiver of Rights

6. If the Court accepts the plea agreement pursuant to Rule 11(c)(1)(C) and sentences Defendant to the agreed-upon sentence as set forth in paragraphs 3, 4, and 5, Defendant will not file an appeal or collaterally attack his conviction, guilty plea, or sentence.

7. Defendant waives all defenses based on venue (but reserves the right to request a change of venue if his plea is vacated or plea withdrawn), speedy trial under the Constitution and Speedy Trial Act, and the statute of limitations with respect to any prosecution that is not time-barred on the date that this Agreement is signed, in the event that (a) Defendant's conviction is later vacated for any reason, (b)

Defendant violates any provision of this Agreement, or (c) Defendant's plea is later withdrawn.

8. Defendant understands that by pleading guilty he is waiving important rights including: (a) the right to persist in his previously entered plea of not guilty; (b) the right to a jury trial with respect to guilt or sentencing; (c) the right to be represented by counsel — and if necessary to have the court appoint counsel to represent him — at trial and at every other stage of the proceedings; (d) the right at trial to confront and cross-examine adverse witnesses, to be protected from compelled self-incrimination, to testify and present evidence, and to compel the attendance of witnesses; and (e) the right to additional discovery and disclosures from the Department. Defendant waives any right to additional disclosure from the Department in connection with his guilty plea.

Defendant's Obligations

9. Defendant agrees not to accept remuneration or compensation of any sort, directly or indirectly, for the dissemination through books, articles, speeches, interviews, or any other means, of information on regarding his work at Enron or the investigation or prosecution of any civil or criminal cases against him.

Forfeiture and Monetary Penalties

10. Defendant agrees to pay the special assessment of $100.00 by check payable to the Clerk of the Court at or before sentencing. 18 U.S.C. § 3013(a)(2)(A); U.S.S.G. § 5E1.3.

11. Defendant agrees to forfeit to the government $1,250,000.00, to be satisfied from funds located within Wachovia Securities Account 2005-0471, which contains sufficient funds for this purpose and which constitutes proceeds of the offense to which Defendant will plead guilty pursuant to this Agreement. Defendant warrants that he and his wife, Elizabeth A. Causey, are the sole owners of all property listed above, and they agree to hold the United States, its agents and employees harmless from any claims whatsoever in connection with the seizure or forfeiture of property covered by this

agreement. Defendant further agrees to waive all interest in the amount listed above for forfeiture in any administrative or judicial forfeiture proceeding, whether criminal or civil, state or federal. Defendant's wife, Elizabeth A. Causey, also agrees to waive her right, title, and interest in the Wachovia Securities Account 2005-0471 up to and including the forfeiture amount, and her execution of the attached Stipulation and Waiver is a condition precedent of this Agreement. Defendant agrees to consent to the entry of orders of forfeiture for such property and waives the requirements of Federal Rules of Criminal Procedure 32.2 and 43(a) regarding notice of forfeiture in the charging instrument, announcement of the forfeiture at sentencing, and incorporation of the forfeiture in the judgment. Defendant acknowledges that he understands that the forfeiture of assets is part of the sentence that may be imposed in this case and waives any failure by the court to advise him of this, pursuant to Rule 11(b)(1)(J), at the time his guilty plea is accepted. Defendant further agrees to waive all constitutional and statutory challenges in any manner (including direct appeal, habeas corpus, or any other means) to any forfeiture carried out in accordance with this agreement on any grounds, including that the forfeiture constitutes an excessive fine or punishment. Defendant agrees to take all steps as requested by the United States to pass clear title to the forfeitable assets to the United States, and to testify truthfully in any related judicial proceeding. Defendant agrees not to seek a refund from the United States Treasury of the amount that he paid in taxes in connection with the receipt of $1,250,000.00 in proceeds from the offense to which he will plead guilty, and waives his right, title, and interest to the taxes paid on that amount.

12. Defendant further agrees to relinquish any claim he may have to deferred compensation, severance, or any other form of payment related to his employment by Enron or any related entity.

The Department's Obligations

13. The Department agrees that, except as provided for in this Agreement, no further criminal charges will be brought against Defendant for any act or offense in which he engaged in his capacity

as an officer and/or employee of Enron Corporation, or arising out of such employment, and the Department will move after sentencing to dismiss the remaining counts of the Superseding Indictment against him with prejudice.

14. The Department further agrees that no statements made by Defendant during any debriefing meetings with the Department will be used against him in any criminal proceedings instituted by the Department, except as provided in paragraphs 1, 3, 4, and 5.

Hyde Amendment Waiver

15. Defendant agrees that with respect to all charges contained in the Superseding Indictment in the above-captioned action, he is not a "prevailing party" within the meaning of the "Hyde Amendment," Section 617, PL 105-119 (Nov. 26, 1997), and will not file any claim under that law.

Scope

16. This Agreement does not bind any federal, state, or local prosecuting authority other than the Department, and does not prohibit the Department or any other department, agency, or commission of the United States from initiating or prosecuting any civil, administrative, or tax proceedings directly or indirectly involving Defendant.

Complete Agreement

17. No promises, agreements or conditions have been entered into by the parties other than those set forth in this Agreement and none will be entered into unless memorialized in writing and signed by all parties. This Agreement supersedes any prior promises, agreements, or conditions between the parties, including any written proffer agreements. To become effective, this Agreement must be signed by all signatories listed below and in the addenda.

Dated: Houston, Texas
December 28, 2005

                                 SEAN BERKOWITZ
                                 Director, Enron Task Force

By: _____
      Kathryn Ruemmler
      Deputy Director, Enron Task Force

ADDENDUM FOR DEFENDANT CAUSEY

I have consulted with my attorneys and fully understand all my rights with respect to the Superseding Indictment filed by the United States Department of Justice. I have consulted with my attorneys and fully understand all my rights with respect to the provisions of the U.S. Sentencing Commission's Guidelines Manual which, although not binding on the Court, may apply in my case. I have read this Agreement and carefully reviewed every part of it with my attorneys. No promises have been made to me by the Department except as set forth in this Agreement. I understand this Agreement and I voluntarily agree to it.

12-28-05
_____   _____
Richard A. Causey   Date
Defendant

ADDENDUM FOR DEFENSE COUNSEL

I have fully explained to Defendant Richard A. Causey his rights with respect to the Superseding Indictment, Cr. No. H-04-25 (S-2). I have reviewed the provisions of the U.S. Sentencing Commission's Guidelines Manual and I have fully explained to Defendant the provisions of those Guidelines which, although not binding on the Court, may apply in this case. I have carefully reviewed every part of this Agreement with Defendant. To my knowledge, Defendant's decision to enter into this Agreement is an informed and voluntary one.

_____	12-28-05 _____
Reid Weingarten, Esq.	Date
Attorney for Defendant Causey	

_____	12-28-05 _____
Mark Hulkower, Esq.	Date
Attorney for Defendant Causey	

UNITED STATES DISTRICT COURT
SOUTHERN DISTRICT OF TEXAS
HOUSTON DIVISION

UNITED STATES OF AMERICA	§	
	§	
v.	§	Cr. No. H-04-25 (S-2)
	§	(Lake, J.)
RICHARD A. CAUSEY,	§	
	§	
Defendant.	§	
	§	

Exhibit A to Plea Agreement

The following factual statement made by defendant Richard A. Causey is submitted to provide a factual basis for my plea of guilty to Count Nineteen (securities fraud) of the above captioned Superseding Indictment, charging me with securities fraud, in violation of Title 15, United States Code, Sections 78j(b) and 78ff.

1. I was the Chief Accounting Officer ("CAO") of Enron Corporation ("Enron") from 1998 through Enron's bankruptcy in December 2001. While CAO, I and other members of Enron's senior management fraudulently misled investors and others about the true financial position of Enron in order to inflate artificially the price of Enron's stock.

2. More specifically, I conspired with members of Enron's senior management to make false and misleading statements, in Enron's filings with the Securities and Exchange Commission ("SEC") and in analyst calls, about the financial condition of Enron, which did not fairly and accurately reflect Enron's actual financial condition and performance as I knew it.

3. Certain of the conduct, for which I accept responsibility, is detailed below.

False and Misleading Statements in SEC Filings

4. Along with others in senior management, I was responsible for the preparation and drafting of the financial statements that were included in Enron's annual reports filed with the SEC on Form 10-K and its quarterly reports on Form 10-Q. I, along with others in senior management, were responsible for ensuring that the financial statements contained in Enron's public filings fairly presented Enron's true financial condition. The financial statements were required to include a section entitled Management, Discussion and Analysis ("MD&A"), which required, among other things, that management disclose information necessary to an understanding of Enron's financial condition and results of operations. I reviewed drafts of Enron's quarterly and annual reports, and I signed these reports attesting to their accuracy. As set forth below, I participated along with others in Enron's senior management in efforts to use Enron's public filings and public statements to mislead the investing public about the true nature of Enron's financial performance by making false and misleading statements, and omitting facts necessary to make certain statements not misleading.

5. For example, in the first quarter of 2000, Enron recorded $85 million in earnings from a partnership interest it held in a vehicle named JEDI, which held Enron stock. I and others reported these earnings as recurring earnings from operations when, as I and others knew, the earnings in fact came from a dramatic increase in Enron's stock price resulting from positive investor reaction to Enron's January 20, 2000 analyst conference. I and others understood that it would have been material information to investors and analysts that a significant portion of Enron's reported earnings from its Assets and Investments business came solely from an increase in its own stock price. I and others misled investors by describing the earnings as coming from the strong performance of Enron's portfolio of energy related and other investments. I and others intentionally failed to disclose the true nature of the earnings and the fact that Enron management was taking large positions in Enron stock.

6. Another example concerns disclosures in 2001 relating to Enron's retail business, Enron Energy Services ("EES"). During the

first quarter of 2001, I became aware that EES had incurred hundreds of millions of dollars in losses resulting from California regulatory actions and the identification of significant valuation errors in EES contracts. These losses were in excess of EES's targeted earnings for the entire year of 2001. I understood that EES had been promoted by Enron management as a growth segment of the company that was a major contributor to Enron's stock price. I and others in senior management believed that had these losses been disclosed to Enron's shareholders and the analyst community, the reaction would have been severely negative and the stock price would have declined.

7. I and others in senior management made a decision to move the risk management function of EES into another business unit, Enron Wholesale Services ("EWS"). This reorganization allowed us to avoid reporting the losses in EES's results so that I and others in senior management could continue to tout EES as a growing and successful business. I and others in management intentionally failed to disclose to the investing public any reference to EES's losses, which we knew was material information.

8. On April 17, 2001, Enron issued its earnings release for its first quarter 2001 results, a copy of which I reviewed. I and others reported to Enron's shareholders and the investing public that EES had earned $40 million in recurring IBIT for the first quarter of 2001. We did not disclose that EES had in fact incurred hundreds of millions of dollars in losses during the first quarter of 2001 that through an accounting change we had concealed in EWS. By failing to disclose the true performance of EES, I and others intentionally misled Enron's shareholders and the investing public.

10-Q for the First Quarter 2001

9. On or about May 15, 2001, Enron filed its Form 10-Q, which I reviewed and signed. While the 10-Q disclosed the transfer of risk management functions, the 10-Q did not disclose the losses that EES would otherwise have incurred, which was required in order to fairly present to Enron's shareholders and the investing public Enron's true financial condition. This information was material and would have been important to a reasonable investor. I and others in senior

management failed to include this information in Enron's 10-Q because we were concerned that disclosing such information would have a negative effect on Enron's stock price.

10. On or about May 15, 2001, within the Southern District of Texas, Enron filed via electronic transmission its Form 10-Q for the first quarter 2001, with the Securities and Exchange Commission. As set forth above, in connection with Enron's Form 10-Q for the first quarter 2001, a copy of which I signed, I and others in Enron senior management did willfully and unlawfully use and employ manipulative and deceptive devices and contrivances and directly and indirectly (i) employ devices, schemes and artifices to defraud; (ii) make untrue statements of material facts and omit to state facts necessary in order to make the statements made, in light of the circumstances under which they were made, not misleading; and (iii) engage in acts, practices, and courses of conduct which would and did operate as a fraud and deceit upon members of the investing public, in connection with purchases and sales of Enron securities.

11. I understood that my conduct and the conduct of those with whom I conspired would have a material effect on Enron's financial statements which Enron shareholders and potential shareholders relied upon in making investment decisions. Enron's stock was traded on the New York Stock Exchange. I also understood that interstate wire transmissions, including fax transmissions, email and telephone calls, would be used and were used in furtherance of the scheme. Specifically, I knew that Enron's annual and quarterly reports were filed with the SEC via interstate wire transmissions.

12. The preceding is a summary of facts that make me guilty, which I make for the purpose of providing the Court with a factual basis for my guilty plea to Count 19 of the Superseding Indictment. It does not include all of the facts known to me concerning criminal activity in which I and other members of Enron senior management engaged. I make this statement knowingly and voluntarily because I am in fact guilty of the crime charged.

_____

Richard A. Causey   December 28, 2005
Defendant

IN THE UNITED STATES DISTRICT COURT
FOR THE SOUTHERN DISTRICT OF TEXAS
HOUSTON DIVISION

UNITED STATES OF AMERICA,)
)
                    Plaintiff,   )
)
          v.   ) No. CR-H-04-25(S-2)
)
RICHARD A. CAUSEY,   )
)
                    Defendant.   )
_____)

STIPULATION AND WAIVER

1. I, Elizabeth A. Causey, hereby agree to waive all right, title, and interest I have in $1,250,000 of the assets in Wachovia Securities Account 2005-0471 ("Forfeited Assets") which is held in the name of Richard and Elizabeth Causey.

2. I warrant that I and/or my husband, Richard A. Causey, are the sole owners of all of the Forfeited Assets, and agree to hold the United States, its agents and employees harmless from any claims whatsoever in connection with the seizure or forfeiture of the Forfeited Assets.

3. I acknowledge that, pursuant to paragraphs 5 and 11 of the plea agreement in United States v. Causey, Cr.-H-04-25 (S-2), Richard Causey has acknowledged that the criminal activities to which he is pleading guilty resulted in $1.25 million in criminal proceeds, which are located within the Wachovia account referenced above. The Wachovia account contains money in excess of $1,250,000, and I understand that only $1,250,000 will be forfeited. I agree to relinquish any and all right, title, and interest I may have in the Forfeited Assets, and agree that such right, title and interest can be forfeited to the United States, without further notice to me. I also agree to execute and record any and all documents necessary to

transfer the Forfeited Assets to the United States as part of a forfeiture judgment.

4. In addition, I agree to waive all right, title and interest I may have in any claim that my husband, Richard Causey, may have for deferred compensation, severance, or any other form of payment related to his employment at Enron or any related entity. In understand that Richard Causey has waived any interest in such a claim as well pursuant to paragraph 12 of his Plea Agreement.

5. I make this stipulation and waiver knowingly and voluntarily.

AGREED AND CONSENTED TO:

_____

Elizabeth A. Causey   Dated: December 28, 2005

IN THE UNITED STATES DISTRICT COURT
FOR THE SOUTHERN DISTRICT OF TEXAS
HOUSTON DIVISION

UNITED STATES OF AMERICA,	)
	)
Plaintiff,	)
	)
v.	) Cr. No. H-02-0665
	)
ANDREW S. FASTOW,	)
	)
Defendant.	)
	)

PLEA AGREEMENT

Pursuant to Rule 11 of the Federal Rules of Criminal Procedure, the United States Department of Justice by the Enron Task Force ("the Department") and Andrew S. Fastow ("Defendant") agree to the following (the "Agreement"):

1. Defendant will plead guilty to count two of the above-captioned Superseding Indictment, charging a violation of 18 U.S.C. § 371, conspiracy to commit wire fraud. Defendant also will plead guilty to count five of the above-captioned Superseding Indictment, charging a violation of 18 U.S.C. § 371, conspiracy to commit wire and securities fraud. Defendant agrees that he is pleading guilty because he is guilty, and that the facts contained in Exhibit A (attached and incorporated herein) are true and supply a factual basis for his pleas. Counts two and five each carry the following statutory penalties, which Defendant understands will be imposed consecutively:

    a.   Maximum term of imprisonment: 5 years
         (18 U.S.C. § 371)
    b.   Minimum term of imprisonment: 0 years
         (18 U.S.C. § 371)

c. Maximum term of supervised release: 3 years, to follow any term of imprisonment; if a condition of release is violated, Defendant may be sentenced to up to two years without credit for pre-release imprisonment or time previously served on post-release supervision (18 U.S.C. §§ 3583 (b) & (e))

d. Maximum fine: $250,000 or twice the gain/loss (18 U.S.C. § 3571(b)(3))

e. Restitution: As determined by the Court pursuant to statute (18 U.S.C. §§ 3663 and 3663A)

f. Special Assessment: $100 (18 U.S.C. § 3013)

Sentencing Guidelines

2. Defendant's sentence is governed by the United States Sentencing Guidelines, in effect on October 24, 2001. Defendant understands that his sentence is within the discretion of the sentencing judge. The parties agree that Defendant's sentence under the Sentencing Guidelines shall include 120 months in the custody of the Bureau of Prisons. Defendant agrees that he will not move for a downward departure from the offense level or guideline range calculated by the Court and that no grounds for a downward departure exist.

3. The Department will advise the Court and the Probation Office of all information relevant to sentencing, including criminal activity engaged in by Defendant, and all such information may be used by the Court in determining Defendant's sentence.

Waiver of Rights

4. Defendant will not appeal or collaterally attack his convictions or guilty pleas. Defendant will not appeal or collaterally attack his sentence unless the Court imposes a term of imprisonment greater than 120 months.

5. Defendant waives all defenses based on venue (but reserves the right to request a change of venue), speedy trial under the Constitution or Speedy Trial Act, or the statute of limitations with respect to any prosecution that is not time-barred on the date that this

Agreement is signed in the event that (a) Defendant's conviction is later vacated for any reason, (b) Defendant violates any provision of this Agreement, or (c) Defendant's plea is later withdrawn.

6. Defendant understands that by pleading guilty he is waiving important rights including: (a) the right to persist in his previously entered plea of not guilty; (b) the right to a jury trial; (c) the right to be represented by counsel — and if necessary to have the court appoint counsel to represent him — at trial and at every other stage of the proceedings; (d) the right at trial to confront and cross-examine adverse witnesses, to be protected from compelled self-incrimination, to testify and present evidence, and to compel the attendance of witnesses; and (e) the right to additional discovery and disclosures from the Department. The Defendant waives any right to additional disclosure from the government in connection with the guilty plea.

Defendant's Obligations

7. Defendant will provide truthful, complete, and accurate information to and will cooperate fully with the Department, both before and after he is sentenced. This cooperation will include, but is not limited to, the following:

a. Defendant agrees to make himself available at all meetings with the Department and to respond truthfully and completely to any and all questions put to him, whether in interviews, before a grand jury, or at any trial or other proceeding.

b. Defendant waives all claims of attorney-client privilege, whether in his personal or official capacity, as to communications with any attorney or law firm that represented Enron, LJM Cayman, LJM2, or any related entity, where such communications concerned or related to Enron, LJM Cayman, LJM2, or any related entity. Defendant agrees to provide all documents and other material that may be relevant to the investigation and that are in his possession or control.

c. Defendant agrees not to reveal any information derived from his cooperation to any third party without prior consent of the Department, and to instruct his attorneys to do the same. Defendant agrees to inform the Department of any attempt by any third party to interview, depose, or communicate in any way with him regarding this case, his cooperation, or any other information related to Enron or transactions involving Enron.

d. Defendant agrees to testify truthfully at any grand jury, court, or other proceeding as directed by the Department.

e. Defendant consents to adjournments of his sentencing hearing as requested by the Department and agrees that his obligations under this Agreement continue until the Department informs him in writing that his cooperation is concluded.

8. The Department and Defendant further agree that Defendant's counsel may be present at any meetings or debriefings between Defendant and the Department, and the Department will endeavor to provide reasonable notice of such meetings or debriefings, but counsel's presence is not required and Defendant agrees to be present and cooperate notwithstanding his counsel's unavailability.

9. Defendant agrees not to accept remuneration or compensation of any sort, directly or indirectly, for the dissemination through books, articles, speeches, interviews, or any other means, of information regarding his work at Enron Corporation, the transactions alleged in the above-captioned Superseding Indictment, or the investigation or prosecution of any civil or criminal cases against him.

10.   Defendant will voluntarily surrender to the institution designated by the United States Bureau of Prisons following the release from custody of Lea W. Fastow.

The Department's Obligations

11. The Department agrees that, except as provided in paragraphs 1, 5, and 24, no further criminal charges will be brought against Defendant for any act or offense in which he engaged in his capacity as an officer and/or employee of Enron, LJM, or related entities, or arising out of such employment.

12. The Department further agrees that no statements made by Defendant during the course of his cooperation will be used against him in any criminal proceedings instituted by the Department, except as provided in paragraphs 1, 3, 5, and 24.

13. The Department is not obligated to and will not at any time in the future file any motion for a reduction in Defendant's sentence under U.S.S.G. § 5K1.1, 18 U.S.C. § 3553, or Fed. R. Crim. P. 35, based on information provided by Defendant related directly or indirectly to Enron, any entity related to Enron, or any transaction involving Enron or any entity related to Enron.

14. If and when, in its sole and exclusive judgment, the Department determines that Defendant has cooperated fully and truthfully, and otherwise complied with all the terms of this Agreement, and in consideration of Defendant's cooperation, it will move to dismiss the remaining counts of the Superseding Indictment and the underlying indictment with prejudice. Defendant hereby waives all defenses based on the speedy trial clause of the Constitution and the Speedy Trial Act with respect to such charges, which may be tried in accordance with this Agreement.

15. The Department agrees that, provided Defendant fulfills the financial obligations imposed by this Agreement and any obligations required under any agreement with the Securities and Exchange Commission, it will recommend that no additional fine, forfeiture or restitution be ordered by the Court against Defendant at the time Defendant is sentenced. The Department agrees that this amount is appropriate and fully satisfies the fine, forfeiture, and restitution provisions of the law. Defendant understands that the Department's recommendation is not binding on the Court, and the Court may order Defendant to pay an additional fine, forfeiture or restitution notwithstanding the Department's recommendation. Should the Court order Defendant to pay additional forfeiture sums, restitution or a fine, he will not be permitted on that basis to withdraw his guilty plea.

Forfeiture and Monetary Penalties

16. Defendant agrees to pay the special assessment of $200 by check payable to the Clerk of the Court at or before sentencing. 18 U.S.C. § 3013(a)(2)(A); U.S.S.G. § 5E1.3.

17. Defendant agrees to forfeit the following specific assets which have an approximate value of $23,800,000 and constitute proceeds of the offenses to which he will plead guilty:

a. The following bonds, worth approximately $13,049,809.10 (as of June 30, 2003), contained in Fidelity Brokerage Services Account number Z11-068497, in the name of Lea W. Fastow and Andrew S. Fastow:

Number	Name of Bond	Date Purchased	Quantity
1	City of Austin Imp	10/13/00	1,000,000
2	Texas A&M Univ Revs Financing	08/06/01	300,000
3	Katy Independent School District Tex Perm Sch Fund	08/07/01	500,000
4	San Antonio Independent School District	08/30/01	1,050,000
5	Irving Independent School District	09/13/01	1,000,000
6	Hays County Tax Genl Purpose Fund	09/18/01	500,000
7	Comal Independent School District	09/24/01	1,000,000
8	University of Texas Univ Rev Financing Sys	10/02/01	500,000
9	University of Texas Univ Rev Financing Sys	10/02/01	500,000
10	University of Texas Univ Rev Financing Sys	10/02/01	500,000
11	Carrolton Farmers Branch Independent School District	11/01/01	1,110,000
12	Port of Houston Auth Tex Harris County Port	11/29/01	500,000

Number	Name of Bond	Date Purchased	Quantity
13	Port of Houston Auth Tex Harris County Port	11/29/01	1,000,000
14	Port of Houston Auth Tex Harris County Port	11/29/01	500,000
15	City of Austin Tex Wtr & Water Sys Revs Ref	12/20/01	1,000,000
16	Waxahachie	08/24/01	1,000,000
17	Round Rock	08/27/01	800,000
18	Texas Public Finance	08/16/01	605,000

b. The contents of JP Morgan Chase account number Q65183-00-8, in the name of the Fastow Family Foundation, which contained approximately $4,121,362.00 at the time of restraint;

c. The contents of JP Morgan Chase account number 054-05023866, in the name of Lea W. Fastow and Andrew S. Fastow, which contained approximately $1,000.89 at the time of restraint;

d. The contents of JP Morgan Chase account number Q62603-00-8, in the name of Andrew S. and Lea W. Fastow, TIC, which contained approximately $2,079,805.62 at the time of restraint;

e. The contents of JP Morgan Chase account number 340160, in the name of Lea W. Fastow and Andrew S. Fastow, which contained approximately $780,029.80 at the time of restraint;

f. Currency on deposit with the United States Marshal in the amount of $3,341,694.50, which represents the net sales proceeds of real property known as 3005 Del Monte Dr.;

g. All of defendant's right, title, and interest in real property known as 3216 Musket Lane, Galveston, Texas;

h. All of defendant's right, title, and interest in real property known as 208 Happy Hill Road, Norwich, Vermont.

18. Defendant warrants that he and his wife, Lea W. Fastow,[1] are the sole owners of all of the property listed above, with the exception of the property listed in paragraph 17(b), and agrees to hold the United States, its agents and employees harmless from any claims whatsoever in connection with the seizure or forfeiture of property covered by this Agreement. Defendant's wife, Lea W. Fastow, also agrees to waive her right, title, and interest in the property forfeited under this Agreement; the execution of this waiver is a condition of this Agreement.

19. Defendant agrees that he will not contest forfeiture of the properties identified above in connection with the related civil forfeiture actions in Civ. No. H-02-3974, United States v. Contents of Charles Schwab account no. 1104-2180 and Civ. No. H-02-3844, United States v. Real Property Known as 3005 Del Monte Dr. Defendant agrees to enter into stipulations of settlement regarding forfeiture (attached hereto as Exhibit B) and to fully assist the government in effectuating the surrender of the forfeited assets. Defendant's wife, Lea W. Fastow, also agrees to sign stipulations of settlement, waiving any right, title, and interest she may have in the properties. Her entering into the stipulations of settlement is a condition of this Agreement.

20. Defendant further agrees to waive all interest in any asset listed above for forfeiture in any administrative or judicial forfeiture proceeding, whether criminal or civil, state or federal. Defendant agrees to consent to the entry of orders of forfeiture for such property and waives the requirements of Federal Rules of Criminal Procedure 32.2 and 43(a) regarding notice of the forfeiture in the charging instrument, announcement of the forfeiture at sentencing, and incorporation of the forfeiture in the judgment. Defendant acknowledges that he understands that the forfeiture of assets is part of the sentence that may be imposed in this case and waives any

---

[1]Lea W. Fastow is entering into a separate agreement with the Department pursuant to which she agrees to enter into the forfeiture provisions noted in this Agreement. This Agreement refers to her obligations thereunder because her entering into such obligations is a condition of this Agreement with Andrew S. Fastow.

failure by the court to advise him of this, pursuant to Rule 11(b)(1)(J), at the time his guilty plea is accepted.

21. Defendant knowingly and voluntarily agrees to waive his right to a jury trial on the forfeitability of the assets identified for forfeiture, and to waive all constitutional and statutory challenges of an kind (including direct appeal, habeas corpus, or any other means) to any forfeiture carried out in accordance with this Agreement on any grounds, including that the forfeiture constitutes an excessive fine or punishment or that it violates the Ex Post Facto Clause of the Constitution.

22. Defendant agrees to take all steps as requested by the United States to pass clear title to the forfeitable assets to the United States, and to testify truthfully in any judicial forfeiture proceeding. Defendant agrees not to seek a refund from the United States Treasury of the amount of any taxes paid in connection with the receipt of any proceeds from Enron, LJM Cayman, LJM2, or any related entity from 1997 to the present, or with respect to any offense to which he will plead guilty, and waives his right, title, and interest to the taxes paid on such amount.

Bankruptcy Waiver

23. Defendant agrees not to avoid or attempt to avoid paying any forfeiture, fine, or restitution imposed by the Court in this proceeding through any proceeding pursuant to the United States Bankruptcy Code. Defendant waives all rights, if any, to obtain discharge or to delay payment of any fine or restitution obligation arising from this proceeding or alter the time for payment by filing a petition pursuant to the Bankruptcy Code. Defendant stipulates that enforcement of any fine or restitution obligation arising from this proceeding by the Department is not barred or affected by the automatic stay provisions of the United States Bankruptcy Code and that enforcement of any forfeiture, fine, or restitution obligation arising from this proceeding by the Department is a valid exercise of its police or regulatory power within the meaning of Title 11, United States Code, Section 362(b). Defendant stipulates and agrees not to institute or participate in any proceeding to interfere with, alter, or bar enforcement of any

forfeiture, fine, or restitution obligation arising from this proceeding pursuant to the automatic stay or other provision of the Bankruptcy Code in any case filed by Defendant or his creditors. Upon request of the Department, Defendant will execute a stipulation granting the Department relief from the automatic stay or other Bankruptcy Code provisions in order to enforce any forfeiture, fine, or restitution obligation arising from this proceeding. Defendant stipulates that any forfeiture, fine, or restitution obligation imposed by the Court in this proceeding is not dischargeable pursuant to Title 11, United States Code, Section 523 in any case commenced by Defendant or his creditors pursuant to the Bankruptcy Code. Defendant stipulates that the Forfeiture Amount that is contained in the accounts identified in this Agreement is not exempt under any state or federal exemption, whether arising under 11 U.S.C. § 524(b)(1)-(2), or under any applicable state law. Nothing in this Agreement shall constitute a modification or waiver of Defendant's state or federal exemptions with respect to property other than the Forfeiture Amount. Defendant's waivers, stipulations, and agreements set forth in this paragraph are made in exchange for the Department's entering into this Agreement.

Breach of Agreement

24. Defendant must at all times give complete, truthful, and accurate information and testimony, and must not commit, or attempt to commit, any further crimes, including but not limited to perjury and obstruction of justice. Should it be determined by the Department, in its sole and exclusive discretion, that Defendant has violated any provision of this Agreement, Defendant will not be released from his guilty pleas but the Department will be released from all its obligations under this Agreement, including its promise not to prosecute Defendant for any offenses charged in the Superseding Indictment and the underlying indictment, and other offenses arising from his employment at Enron or any related entity. Defendant agrees that, in any such prosecution, all statements and other information that he has provided at any time, including all statements he has made and all evidence he has produced during

proffers, interviews, testimony, and otherwise, may be used against him, regardless of any constitutional provision, statute, rule, prior agreement, or other term of this Agreement to the contrary.

25. This Agreement is conditioned upon the following: the defendant Lea W. Fastow (the "covered defendant") entering a guilty plea to Count 6 of the Indictment in the case of <u>United States v. Lea Fastow</u>, H-03-150. If the covered defendant does not satisfy this condition, or violates any provision of her agreement with the United States, the Department will be released from all its obligations under this Agreement, including its promise not to prosecute Defendant for any offenses charged in the Superseding Indictment and the underlying indictment, and other offenses arising from his employment at Enron or any related entity, and its promise not to use any statements made during his cooperation against him. In addition, if Defendant breaches this Agreement the Department, in its sole and exclusive discretion, may void its agreement with the covered defendant and proceed to trial.

Hyde Amendment Waiver

26. Defendant agrees that with respect to all charges contained in the indictments returned by the grand jury in the above-captioned action, he is not a "prevailing party" within the meaning of the "Hyde Amendment," Section 617, PL 105-119 (Nov. 26, 1997), and will not file any claim under that law.

Scope

27. This Agreement does not bind any federal, state, or local prosecuting authority other than the Department, and does not prohibit the Department or any other department, agency, or commission of the United States from initiating or prosecuting any civil or administrative proceedings directly or indirectly involving Defendant.

Complete Agreement

28. Apart from the written proffer agreement originally, dated December 18, 2003, no promises, agreements or conditions have been entered into by the parties other than those set forth in this Agreement and none will be entered into unless memorialized in writing and signed by all parties. This Agreement supersedes all prior promises, agreements, or conditions between the parties, including the written proffer agreement. To become effective, this Agreement must be signed by all signatories listed below and in the addenda.

Dated: Houston, Texas
      January 14, 2004   LESLIE R. CALDWELL
                          Director, Enron Task Force

                          ANDREW WEISSMANN
                          Deputy Director, Enron Task Force

     By: _____

                          JOHN H. HEMANN
                          LINDA A. LACEWELL
                          MATTHEW FRIEDRICH
                          Assistant United States Attorneys

                          LAUREL LOOMIS
                          Senior Trial Attorney

ADDENDUM FOR DEFENDANT FASTOW

I have consulted with my attorneys and fully understand all my rights with respect to the Superseding Indictment and the underlying indictment. I have consulted with my attorneys and fully understand all my rights with respect to the provisions of the U.S. Sentencing Commission's Guidelines Manual which may apply in my case. I have read this Agreement and carefully reviewed every part of it with my attorneys. I understand this Agreement and I voluntarily agree to it.

_____   1-14-04
Andrew S. Fastow   Date
Defendant

ADDENDUM FOR DEFENSE COUNSEL

    I have fully explained to Defendant Fastow his rights with respect to the pending Superseding Indictment and underlying indictment. I have reviewed the provisions of the U.S. Sentencing Commission's Guidelines Manual and I have fully explained to Defendant the provisions of those Guidelines which may apply in this case. I have carefully reviewed every part of this Agreement with Defendant. To my knowledge, Defendant's decision to enter into this Agreement is an informed and voluntary one.

_____   Jan. 14, 04
David Gerger, Esq.   Date
Gerger & Associates
Attorney for Defendant Fastow

_____   Jan. 14, 2004
Jan Nielsen Little   Date
Keker & Van Nest
Attorney for Defendant Fastow

IN THE UNITED STATES DISTRICT COURT
FOR THE SOUTHERN DISTRICT OF TEXAS
HOUSTON DIVISION

UNITED STATES OF AMERICA,	)
	)
Plaintiff,	)
	)
v.	) Cr. No. H-O2-665
	)
ANDREW S. FASTOW,	)
	)
Defendant.	)
_____	)

SENTENCE DATA SHEET

DEFENDANT: ANDREW S. FASTOW

CRIMINAL NO: H-02-665

GUILTY PLEA: Count Two (Conspiracy to Commit Wire Fraud); Count Five (Conspiracy to Commit Wire and Securities Fraud)

SUBSTANCE OF
AGREEMENT: Pursuant to Fed. R. Crim. P. 11(c)(1)(B), Defendant will plead guilty to counts two and five of the Superseding Indictment (conspiracy to commit wire and securities fraud). The parties agree that the sentence should be the statutory maximum for those charges, a total of ten years.

COUNT TWO: Conspiracy (18 U.S.C. § 371)

COUNT FIVE: Conspiracy (18 U.S.C. § 371)

ELEMENTS: 1) An agreement between two or more persons,
2) to commit a crime against the United States, and
3) an overt act committed by one of the conspirators in furtherance of the agreement.

PENALTY: On each count: Imprisonment not to exceed 5
                    years and a fine not to exceed $250,000 or twice
                    gain/loss. 18 U.S.C. §§ 371 and 3571(b)(3).
                    Supervised release after imprisonment of not
                    more than 3 years. 18 U.S.C. §§ 3559(a)(4) and
                    3583(b)(2).

SENTENCING
GUIDELINES: Applicable.
SPECIAL
ASSESSMENT: $200. 18 U.S.C. § 3013(a)(2)(A) ($100 per each
                    count).
ATTACHMENT: Plea Agreement
DEFENDANT
WAIVED HIS
RIGHT TO
APPEAL: Yes

IN THE UNITED STATES DISTRICT COURT
FOR THE SOUTHERN DISTRICT OF TEXAS
HOUSTON DIVISION

UNITED STATES OF AMERICA,	)
	)
Plaintiff,	)
	)
v.	) Cr. No. H-02-0665
	)
ANDREW S. FASTOW,	)
	)
Defendant.	)

<u>Exhibit A to Plea Agreement</u>

This statement by defendant Andrew S. Fastow is submitted to provide a factual basis for my plea of guilty to Counts 2 and 5.

1. I was the Chief Financial Officer ("CFO") of Enron Corporation ("Enron") from March 1998 until October 24, 2001. While CFO, I and other members of Enron's senior management fraudulently manipulated Enron' s publicly reported financial results. Our purpose was to mislead investors and others about the true financial position of Enron and, consequently, to inflate artificially the price of Enron's stock and maintain fraudulently Enron's credit rating.

2. I also engaged in schemes to enrich myself and others at the expense of Enron's shareholders and in violation of my duty of honest services to those shareholders.

3. Certain of these fraudulent transactions and schemes, for which I accept responsibi1ity, are detailed below.

<u>Manipulation of Financial Statements — Count Five:</u>

4. I conspired with others at Enron to manipulate the company's financial statements by, among other things, causing Enron and the LJM entities under my control, including LJM Cayman and

LJM2 (collectively "LJM") to enter into improper transactions. The purpose of certain of these transactions was to improve the appearance of Enron's financial statements by (1) generating improper earnings and funds flow; (2) enabling Enron to set inflated "market" prices for assets; and (3) improperly protecting Enron's balance sheet from poorly performing and volatile assets. Certain LJM transactions lacked economic substance and were improper for accounting purposes, in part because I and others secretly agreed that LJM would not lose money through participation in the transactions.

5. Among the improper Enron-LJM transactions were four special purpose entities ("SPEs") known as the "Raptors." The Raptors purported to be independent, unconsolidated entities with which Enron would hedge the value of certain assets I and others knew that the Raptors were not sufficiently independent from Enron and should not have been deconsolidated. As a result, Enron overstated its earnings. I and other members of Enron's senior management knew the impact of the Raptors on Enron's financial statements.

6. The first Raptor vehicle, Talon, was created in April 2000 to protect Enron's balance sheet from decreases in the value of certain investments. Talon was capitalized mainly by Enron through a promissory note and Enron's own stock. The remainder of Talon's capitalization came from LJM2's payment of $30 million. The purpose of this $30 million payment was to provide Talon the "outside equity at risk," required for accounting purposes, to qualify Talon as an independent third party entity. The structure of Talon was used as the model for two of the remaining three Raptor entities.

7. I and others at Enron, including Enron's Chief Accounting Officer, had an unwritten agreement that LJM2 would be paid the return of its investment, plus a profit, prior to Talon engaging in any hedging, in exchange for my agreement to allow Enron to flexibly determine what assets would be hedged by Talon and the values at which they were hedged.

8. To fulfill this agreement, I and others arranged for Enron to pay $41 million to LJM2 before Talon, the first Raptor, would engage

in the hedging transactions for which it was created. The $41 million payment was accomplished by Enron and Talon entering into a "put" agreement, that is, a transaction that purportedly served to hedge Enron against a decline in its own stock value. In September 2000 Enron paid LJM2 the $41 million[2] and, thereafter, dictated the assets that would be hedged by Talon and their values. The put was designed as an ostensible reason to make a distribution of $41 million to LJM2, economically providing a return both of and on capital.

9. Following the payment of the $41 million, Enron exercised control over Talon and used it fraudulently to meet Wall Street expectations regarding Enron's financial performance. I, on Talon's behalf, allowed Enron to place numerous problematic assets in Talon, without regard to the present or future value of the assets or to their potential effect on Talon's financial viability. I understood Talon was set up as a way to conceal the poor performance of certain Enron assets, and that the hedging of these assets at values set by Enron misled investors by fraudulently improving the appearance of Enron's financial statements.

10. One example of how the Raptors were improperly used by me and others involved a "hedge" of an investment Enron made in a fledgling technology company known as AVICI ("the AVICI hedge"). I and others, including Enron's Chief Accounting Officer, agreed to date the AVICI hedge August 3, 2000, in order to lock in the value of AVICI (a volatile stock) at its all-time high and not incur the known and quantifiable loss from the AVICI stock having declined after August 3, 2000. Although this agreement provided no economic benefit to LJM2, it took place because LJM2 already had received its money and guaranteed profit from Enron in the form of the $41 million payment.

---

[2]Approximately $6 million was placed back into Talon pursuant to an unwritten agreement I had with Enron's Chief Accounting Officer.

Self-Dealing Transactions — Count Two:

11. I also conspired with others to and did engage in transactions designed to enrich myself and others in violation of my duties to Enron's shareholders.

12. One of these transactions involved an SPE called LJM Swap Sub, LP ("Swap Sub"). The general partner of Swap Sub was LJM Cayman, which I controlled, and the limited partners were affiliates of National Westminster Bank ("NatWest") and Credit Suisse First Boston ("CSFB"). As explained below, in March 2000, in my capacity as general partner of Swab Sub, I misled Enron so that Swap Sub would improperly obtain approximately $19 million. I knew that the money was to be distributed to individuals and entities who were not entitled to receive it, including employees of Enron and LJM.

13. In June 1999, LJM Cayman and Swap Sub entered into a series of derivative transactions with Enron concerning a company that Enron invested in called RhythmsNetconnections, Inc. ("RhythmsNet"). The purpose of these derivatives was to afford Enron price protection in the event that the share price of RhythmsNet declined. In exchange for these derivatives, Swab Sub received approximately 3.1 million shares of Enron stock and approximately $3.75 million.

14. Due to a dramatic increase in the market price of Enron stock, the value of Swap Sub (whose primary asset was Enron stock) had also increased dramatically. I was, however, barred from profiting from any increase in the value of Enron stock held by Swap Sub. In approximately February 2000, I and others, including three bankers employed by NatWest, participated in a scheme to extract this increased value by defrauding Enron and NatWest.

15. Enron paid $30 million for the Swap Sub buyout. That price was based on my misleading representation to Enron that the limited partners of Swap Sub had agreed to sell their interests in Swap Sub for $20 million and $10 million, respectively. In fact, NatWest had agreed to sell its interest in Swab Sub for only $1 million, not $20 million. I knew that the NatWest bankers

induced NatWest to sell its interest in Swap Sub for $1 million at a time that they knew the interest was worth significantly more.

16. As a result of their participation in the scheme, the three NatWest bankers together received approximately $7.3 million in proceeds. The balance of the remaining proceeds went to individuals and entities who were selected as "investors" in an entity called Southampton Place LP ("Southampton"). The Southampton "investors" were (1) a foundation in the name of my family, which contributed $25,000 and received approximately $4.5 million; (2) Enron employee Michael Kopper, who contributed $25,000 and caused another entity under our control to loan an additional $750,000, and received approximately $4.5 minion; and (3) five Enron and LJM employees agreed upon by Kopper and met who contributed a total of less than $20,000 and received a total of approximately $3.3 million. I caused the foundation, called the Fastow Family Foundation, to be created for the purpose of receiving funds from the sale of Swap Sub. I intended to use and did use the foundation to make charitable contributions that I might otherwise have made from my own assets for the purpose of enhancing my position and stature in the community. In addition, by allowing the LJM employees to "invest", I personally benefitted as I did not have to pay these employees year-end bonuses out of money that would otherwise have gone to me as general partner.

* * * * *

17. I understood that these schemes would have a material effect on Enron's financial statements (which Enron shareholders and potential shareholders relied upon in making investment decisions) or would have an otherwise deleterious impact on the company. Enron's stock was traded on the New York Stock Exchange. I also understood that interstate wire transmissions would be and were used in furtherance of each scheme. Specifically, I knew that the payment of proceeds to me and others, and filings by Enron with regulators of misleading financial statements, would be sent and received by means of interstate wires.

18. The preceding statement is a summary, made for purpose of providing the Court with a factual basis for my guilty pleas to Counts 2 and 5 of the Superseding Indictment. It does not include all of the facts known to me concerning criminal activity in which I and other members of Enron's senior management engaged. I make this statement knowingly and voluntarily and because I am in fact guilty of the crimes charged.

_____   1-14-04
Andrew S. Fastow   Date

Proposed Legislation

ATTORNEY-CLIENT PRIVILEGE PROTECTION ACT OF 2007

109TH CONGRESS   **S.   30**
2D SESSION

To provide appropriate protection to attorney-client privileged communications and attorney work product.

IN THE SENATE OF THE UNITED STATES

December 8, 2006

Mr. Specter introduced the following bill; which was read twice and referred to the Committee on the Judiciary

---

A BILL

To provide appropriate protection to attorney-client privileged communications and attorney work product.

Be it enacted by the Senate and House of Representatives of the United States of America in Congress assembled,

SECTION 1. SHORT TITLE.

This Act may be cited as the "Attorney-Client Privilege Protection Act of 2006 ".

SEC. 2. FINDINGS AND PURPOSE.

(a) FINDINGS.— Congress finds the following:

(1) Justice is served when all parties to litigation are represented by experienced diligent counsel.

(2) Protecting attorney-client privileged communications from compelled disclosure fosters voluntary compliance with the law.

(3) To serve the purpose of the attorney-client privilege, attorneys and clients must have a degree of confidence that they will not be required to disclose privileged communications.

(4) The ability of an organization to have effective compliance programs and to conduct comprehensive internal investigations is enhanced when there is clarity and consistency regarding the attorney-client privilege.

(5) Prosecutors, investigators, enforcement officials, and other officers or employees of Government agencies have been able to, and can continue to, conduct their work while respecting attorney-client and work product protections and the rights of individuals, including seeking and discovering facts crucial to the investigation and prosecution of organizations.

(6) Despite the existence of these legitimate tools, the Department of Justice and other agencies have increasingly employed tactics that undermine the adversarial system of justice, such as encouraging organizations to waive attorney-client privilege and work product protections to avoid indictment or other sanctions.

(7) An indictment can have devastating consequences on an organization, potentially eliminating the ability of the organization to survive post-indictment or dispute the charges against it at trial.

(8) Waiver demands and other tactics of Government agencies are encroaching on the constitutional rights and other legal protections of employees.

(9) The attorney-client privilege, work product doctrine, and payment of counsel fees shall not be used as devices to conceal wrongdoing or to cloak advice on evading the law.

(b) PURPOSE. — It is the purpose of this Act to place on each agency clear and practical limits designed to preserve the attorney-client privilege and work product protections available to an organization and preserve the constitutional rights and other legal protections available to employees of such an organization.

SEC. 3. DISCLOSURE OF ATTORNEY-CLIENT PRIVILEGE OR ADVANCEMENT OF COUNSEL FEES AS ELEMENTS OF COOPERATION.

(a) IN GENERAL. — Chapter 201 of title 18, United States Code, is amended by inserting after section 3013 he following:

"§ 3014. Preservation of fundamental legal protections and rights in the context of investigations and enforcement matters regarding organizations

"(a) DEFINITIONS. — In this section:

"(1) ATTORNEY-CLIENT PRIVILEGE. — The term 'attorney-client privilege' means the attorney-client privilege as governed by the principles of the common law, as they may be interpreted by the courts of the United States in the light of reason and experience, and the principles of article V of the Federal Rules of Evidence.

"(2) ATTORNEY WORK PRODUCT. — The term 'attorney work product' means materials prepared by or at the direction of an attorney in anticipation of litigation, particularly any such materials that contain a mental impression, conclusion, opinion, or legal theory of that attorney.

"(b) IN GENERAL. — In any Federal investigation or criminal or civil enforcement matter, an agent or attorney of the United States shall not —

"(1) demand, request, or condition treatment on the disclosure by an organization, or person affiliated with that organization, of any communication protected by the attorney-client privilege or any attorney work product;

"(2) condition a civil or criminal charging decision relating to a organization, or person affiliated with that organization, on, or use as a factor in determining whether an organization, or person affiliated with that organization, is cooperating with the Government —

"(A) any valid assertion of the attorney-client privilege or privilege for attorney work product;

"(B) the provision of counsel to, or contribution to the legal defense fees or expenses of, an employee of that organization;

"(C) the entry into a joint defense, information sharing, or common interest agreement with an employee of that organization if the organization determines it has a common interest in defending against the investigation or enforcement matter;

"(D) the sharing of information relevant to the investigation or enforcement matter with an employee of that organization; or

"(E) a failure to terminate the employment of or otherwise sanction any employee of that organization because of the decision by that employee to exercise the constitutional rights or other legal protections of that employee in response to a Government request; or

"(3) demand or request that an organization, or person affiliated with that organization, not take any action described in paragraph (2).

"(c) INAPPLICABILITY. — Nothing in this Act shall prohibit an agent or attorney of the United States from requesting or seeking any communication or material that such agent or attorney reasonably believes is not entitled to protection under the attorney-client privilege or attorney work product doctrine.

"(d) VOLUNTARY DISCLOSURES. — Nothing in this Act is intended to prohibit an organization from making, or an agent or attorney of the United States from accepting, a voluntary and unsolicited offer to share the internal investigation materials of such organization."

(b) CONFORMING AMENDMENT. — The table of sections for chapter 201 of title 18, United States Code, is amended by adding at the end the following:

"3014. Preservation of fundamental legal protections and rights in the cotext of investigations and enforcement matters regarding organizations."

Sentencing Transcript

IMCLONE

UNITED STATES DISTRICT COURT
SOUTHERN DISTRICT OF NEW YORK
- -x

UNITED STATES OF AMERICA

    v.   03 Cr. 717 (MGC)

MARTHA STEWART   Sentence

    Defendant.
- -x

                                     New York, N.Y.
                                       July 16, 2004
                                       10:00 a.m.

Before:

    HON. MIRIAM GOLDMAN CEDARBAUM

                            District Judge

APPEARANCES

DAVID N. KELLEY
United States Attorney for the
Southern District of New York
    One St. Andrew's Plaza
    New York, N.Y. 10007
KAREN PATTON SEYMOUR
MICHAEL S. SCHACHTER
WILLIAM A. BURCK
    Assistant United States Attorneys

MORVILLO, ABRAMOWITZ, GRAND, IASON &
SILBERBERG, P.C.
Attorneys for Defendant Stewart
    565 Fifth Avenue
    New York, New York 10017
    (212) 856-9600
BY: ROBERT G. MORVILLO, ESQ.
        JOHN J. TIGUE, JR., ESQ.
        BARRY A. BOHRER, ESQ.
        REBECCA A. MONCK, ESQ.

EMERY CELLI CUTI BRINCKERHOFF & ABADY, P. C.
Attorneys for Defendant Stewart
    545 Madison Avenue
    New York, New York 10022
    (212) 763-5000
BY: JOHN CUTI, ESQ.

WALTER E. DELLINGER, III, ESQ.
Attorney for Defendant
    Duke University School of Law
    Durham, North Carolina

(Case called)

THE COURT: Good morning. Please be seated.

Martha Stewart, have you read the pre-sentence report?

THE DEFENDANT: I have, your Honor.

THE COURT: And have you discussed it with your lawyer?

THE DEFENDANT: I have indeed.

THE COURT: I have carefully read the written objections which I received to the pre-sentence report yesterday afternoon, and I make the following rulings.

The probation department is directed to delete the word "arrest" from paragraphs 69 and 93.

The probation department is directed to strike the words "based upon that information" from the last sentence of paragraph 27. Since I heard the evidence at the trial, I do not rely in any event on any of the description or the information about the crimes contained in the pre-sentence report in setting my sentence.

Now I will hear anything you would like to tell me, Ms. Stewart, and anything your lawyer would like to tell me in connection with sentence.

MR. MORVILLO: May I proceed, your Honor?

THE COURT: You may.

MR. MORVILLO: Would it be more comfortable if I speak from over there?

THE COURT: It is entirely up to you. I didn't realize that this was set up here. Was this your choice?

MR. MORVILLO: No.

THE COURT: The last time I saw it, it was in the back.

MR. MORVILLO: I can speak from anywhere. If it is easier to hear me from there, I am happy to do it.

THE COURT: Whatever is your preference is fine with me.

MR. MORVILLO: I don't know whether this microphone works.

THE COURT: I think perhaps you should move it back. Maybe it was for the benefit of the court reporter that it was moved over.

MR. MORVILLO: Your Honor, we live, fortunately, in a nation that puts a premium on the concept of freedom. It is the belief of the overwhelming majority of the American population that only the most serious conduct should lead to a deprivation of freedom. In this context I submit to your Honor that the false statements found by the jury did not seriously impede the government's investigation. Indeed, Ms. Stewart was acquitted on the most significant alleged false statement with respect to the $60 target price.

I understand that the government is entitled to the truth when they conduct an investigation. But in evaluating whether to deprive Martha Stewart of freedom, the significance of the effect of the false statements is relevant. Is the denial of misconduct in an unsworn interview so serious that it warrants society's severest penalty, the deprivation of freedom? I do not believe that it does.

Also, your Honor, something that is relevant to this sentence and to all sentences is another notion firmly embedded in our value system, and that is that the punishment should fit the crime. Here, unlike so many other white collar cases, no one has lost any money. No fraud is involved. No big damage has occurred. And no underlying crime was concealed.

In fitting the punishment to the crime, one should, I think, take into consideration the punishment that Martha Stewart has already endured by being the subject of the investigation and the prosecution in this case. She has been scorned, ridiculed, and become the butt of all forms of derogatory humor. The publicity has been unrelenting, universal, and virtually all negative.

Your Honor, it is hurtful. It is hurtful to any human being to get up almost every morning of your life and face ridicule, scorn, and accusation heaped upon accusation, many of which are personal, many of which are vicious, many of which are false. And that is what has happened in this case, not through any fault of anyone's other than the fact that Martha Stewart is a celebrity and well known to the American populous and the media.

Her assets have been substantially depleted. She is still the subject of numerous civil lawsuits arising from the filing of this case. She has been forced to step down as an officer and director of the company she founded, she built, and she loves with all her soul. Indeed, if this conviction is upheld, she faces a lifetime bar from playing that role in the future with regard to that company which she holds so dear to her.

The company, of course, remains of grave concern to Martha Stewart. You have seen in our memo and the company's letter to the Court the dramatic effect that this case has had on the company and its employees. There is no question that a sentence of incarceration will make things worse. In my view, my personal view, the company's ability to survive hinges on this sentence.

There is little doubt that Martha Stewart, free to devote herself to the rejuvenation of the company, will be important to its recovery. There is little doubt that if the company does not recover, hundreds, perhaps thousands, of innocent people will suffer needlessly. Many have already suffered by having lost their job because of the cutbacks in the company.

Finally, there is little doubt about the uniqueness of this situation and the Court's power under Milikowsky to protect those innocent people. I understand the Milikowsky fact situation. I understand the government's argument that it can be distinguished on its facts. But Milikowsky stands for a broader principle, your Honor. It stands for the principle that the Court has the power to protect innocent third parties by downwardly departing, and it is an important concept embedded in the harsh realities of the sentencing guidelines.

Finally, in fashioning a fair sentence, I think the Court needs to see through the sensationalistic coverage that has depicted Martha Stewart as cold, uncaring, abusive, shrill, untrustworthy.

Your Honor, I have been doing this a long time, perhaps too long, because I can remember when 318 was the central calendar part.

THE COURT: As can I, Mr. Morvillo.

MR. MORVILLO: I have never seen a case in which so many people have taken time out of their lives to submit to the Court so many thoughtful and heart-wrenching letters telling the Court the impact that Martha Stewart has had on them and telling the Court what they think about Martha Stewart personally.

Those letters come from a cross-section of the country. They come from far-away places, they come from near places. They come from people who only know Martha Stewart as a public figure. They come from people who know Martha Stewart as a television personality. But they also come from people who have touched Martha Stewart, people who know Martha Stewart, people who have worked with Martha Stewart, people who have been helped by Martha Stewart.

Nobody can read those letters, your Honor, I think, without coming to the conclusion that Martha Stewart has a number of very, very nice characteristics. She is warm, she is gracious, she is generous, she is caring. She is attentive to the needs of others in an extraordinary way. She is giving, she is kind.

She leads by demonstrating her dedication to hard work. I have never seen anyone in all my life experience work harder than Martha Stewart works. There are days, many days, your Honor, when my phone rings at 6 o'clock in the morning and on the other end of that phone is Martha Stewart who is already at work.

She constantly tries to improve and better educate herself for the benefit of others. She gets joy out of teaching the simplest chore or the most complex plan of home improvement. She strives to offer the best, the absolute best, of everything that she does. And she gets ridiculed for it because of the feeling that she is presenting an image of being perfect. She knows she is not perfect. But she also knows that one should strive, if one is to give products, give service, give advice to the public, to make that as good as possible, to make that as perfect as possible.

That is the true Martha Stewart. That is the Martha Stewart that comes through in the more than 500 letters that were sent to the Court by people who were moved to doing something which they ordinarily don't do, writing to courts with regard to a public sentencing.

I think through the role of sentencing and the role of the judge and I ask: How does anyone measure a life in determining an appropriate punishment for a transgression? The guidelines have been criticized for failing to do this. They really don't measure the life. They sort of treat all defendants within a range similarly, and they have been criticized for that because they have taken outside in some ways of the sentencing process those individual characteristics that are so important in making judgments about how to measure a person's life.

Some people have in fact led more positive lives than others. Some people have made greater contributions to society than others. Some people have had to overcome more substantial disadvantages than others. These factors I submit to your Honor need to be weighed by courts in fashioning a justly individual sentence.

One way to measure a life, obviously — not the only way, but one normal way to do it — is to reflect on achievement. Martha Stewart's achievements have been prodigious. She is unique. She is a role model for women who are entrepreneurial and career-oriented, having built an enormously successful company with other women from scratch in an environment hostile to women in the marketplace and restricted by the glass ceiling. She has helped to implement pride in the performance of home making tasks by a variety of teachings and brought satisfaction to women who could not or did not pursue a career outside of the home.

She has brought a measure of beauty to our everyday world with refined color schemes, floral arrangements, and culinary delights. She has stood for the values of quality and making products as perfect as possible. She has educated and inspired millions with a plethora of ideas, facts, and suggestions.

In short, she has contributed significantly to our culture, our country, and its populace more than can ultimately be defined by me in words. She is and has been a phenomenon.

Your Honor, let me read briefly from just two of the many, many letters which capture the essence of what I am trying to say. From a woman in the Bronx is penned the thought:

"Martha Stewart did a great service to millions of women. She took a part of our lives that was pure drudgery and elevated it to an art form. She changed our attitudes and therefore brought a feeling of well-being to our lives. I even think of her when I am ironing pillowcases. Such good therapy she gave."

A similar thought: "Martha Stewart has done more for domestic America than any one person in our country's history. Her influence has helped our economy in countless ways. Her contribution to our culture is profound. Her success story itself is an inspiration.

"Martha Stewart has been the most notable female contributor to entrepreneurial business in America. The beauty of that statement is in the fact that she accomplished this through hard work, perseverance, and a natural will to succeed. She didn't accomplish this goal by stealing or cheating people, but by her pure love for what she does and the desire to let others share that love.

"Martha Stewart is an inspiration to millions of people and a role model for most of them. Her supporters are flooding her website with stories of how she has touched their lives and in some cases profoundly affected their lives. This is a woman who lives to help others. Her success directly reflects the magnitude of her life's work. She has brought welcome goodness into millions of people's lives regardless of gender, age, race, religion, or political affiliation.

"Regardless of whether or not I know Martha Stewart personally, I know that she has contributed much to my life. She has inspired me in everyday existence to take a little bit more pride in the things I do, to make even the most mundane tasks a little bit more meaningful. Her magazine is truly a work of art. Her television program is a wonderful breath of fresh air in today's typically violent or nonsensical programming."

Your Honor knows that I could go on for hours and hours and read similar thoughts expressed by the hundreds and hundreds of people who have taken the time to write to you. I only iterate these thoughts in the context of describing the achievements of Martha Stewart because it is one measure of her life.

In having achieved all of these things, Martha Stewart has never asked for anything and asks today only that your Honor fashion a just and fair sentence and one borne with compassion.

Your Honor, the world understands this case and looks to the Court could conclude it justly. We ask the Court for a sentence of probation and an opportunity for Martha Stewart to serve the community and to continue to serve the community by working with economically disadvantaged women who themselves are seeking to improve their lives. She can benefit them and, in doing that, add one more facet to the many, many facets of having helped this society.

Thank you for your patience, your Honor. I have concluded my remarks.

THE COURT: Thank you.

Ms. Stewart, is there anything you would like to tell me in connection with sentence?

THE DEFENDANT: Judge Cedarbaum, the letter I sent to you yesterday afternoon privately addressed my feelings and concerns about today's sentencing, yet I would like to say a few words, if I may.

Today is a shameful day. It is shameful for me, for my family, and for my beloved company and all of its employees and partners. What was a small personal matter became over the last two and a half years an almost fatal circus event of unprecedented proportions spreading like oil over a vast landscape, even around the world.

I have been choked and almost suffocated to death during that time. And while I am more concerned about the well-being of others than for myself, more hurt for them and for their losses than for my own, more worried for their futures than for the future of Martha Stewart the person, you are faced with a conundrum, a problem of monumental, to me, proportions.

What to do? I ask that, in judging me, you remember all the good that I have done, all the contributions I have made through the company I founded, as well as personally over the past decades of my life that have been devoted almost entirely to productive, creative, and useful activities. I ask, too, that you consider all the intense suffering that I and so many dear others have endured every single moment of the past two and a half years.

I seek the opportunity to continue serving my country and my community in the same positive manner I always have. I seek the opportunity to repair the damage wrought by the situation, to get on with what I have always thought was a good, worthwhile, and exemplary life.

My heart goes out to you and to everyone in this courtroom, and my prayers are with you. My hopes that my life will not be completely destroyed lie entirely in your competent and experienced and merciful hands. Thank you and peace be with you.

THE COURT: Does the government have a statement?

MS. SEYMOUR: Very briefly, your Honor.

Your Honor, in fashioning the sentence today, Ms. Stewart is asking for leniency far beyond that which ordinary people who are convicted of these crimes would receive under the sentencing guidelines. I won't belabor the arguments, the guidelines arguments, for departure that we set forth in our brief. I simply ask the Court to, in fashioning the appropriate sentence here, remember the seriousness of the offense.

Contrary to what Mr. Morvillo said, this is a serious offense, and it has broad implications for administration of justice in this country, your Honor. Citizens like Ms. Stewart who willingly take the steps to lie to officials when they are under investigation about their own conduct, those citizens should not expect the leniency that Ms. Stewart seeks.

The sentence should also reflect the evenhandedness of our criminal justice system. It is a fundamental importance. It does not matter whether Ms. Stewart is a powerful, wealthy woman coming before the Court or whether she is a destitute who is unknown when the Court is evaluating her crimes. We just ask that the Court consider not only all of the factors that Mr. Morvillo and Mrs. Stewart have stated about her, but also the seriousness and the implications of this sentence for other cases and for what it means for justice in our country, your Honor. Thank you.

THE COURT: Thank you.

I adopt the guideline calculation of the probation department. The applicable offense level is 12. Your request, Ms. Stewart for a two-level deduction for minimal role is denied. The evidence does not support such an adjustment. Also, this case does not fall outside the heartland. I find that there does not exist a mitigating circumstance of a kind or to a degree not adequately taken into consideration by the sentencing commission in formulating the guidelines.

The facts of Milikowsky and Somerstein are entirely distinguishable. Therefore, I cannot conscientiously grant your motion for a downward departure from the offense level prescribed by the applicable sentencing guidelines. But I have set sentence at the bottom of the guideline range.

If you and your lawyer would like to rise, I will now sentence you.

I sentence you to 5 months in prison, to be followed by 2 years of supervised release with the special condition of 5 months of home confinement, to run concurrently on Counts One, Three, Four, and Eight.

In addition, there is a $30,000 fine and a special assessment of $400. Both shall be paid immediately.

I grant you the privilege of voluntary surrender to the correctional facility designated by the Bureau of Prisons.

During home confinement, you will remain at a single place of residence except for employment and other activities approved by your probation officer. Can you now choose the residence, the single residence for home confinement?

THE DEFENDANT: Yes.

THE COURT: What is that?

THE DEFENDANT: Bedford, New York.

THE COURT: Very well. Employment and all other activities, including medical appointments, religious services, and shopping for household necessities, shall not exceed 48 hours per week. One day per week during which you may not leave your residence is mandatory.

You will maintain a telephone at your place of residence without call forwarding or a modem or caller ID or call waiting or portable cordless telephones for the period of home confinement.

You shall wear an electronic monitoring device and follow electronic monitoring procedures specified by your probation officer.

Home confinement shall commence on the date to be determined by the probation officer. You shall pay the costs of home confinement as directed by the probation officer.

The standard conditions of supervised release and this special condition shall apply. The special condition of drug testing is waived.

You may be seated now.

The sentence I have just imposed is, in my opinion, the minimum permitted under current law. In imposing a minimum sentence, I have not lost sight of the seriousness of the offenses of which you have been convicted. Lying to government agencies during the course of an investigation is a very serious matter regardless of the outcome of the investigation. Our regulatory agencies cannot function if fabrication and dishonesty are tolerated, excused, or ignored, even if no other criminal conduct is ultimately uncovered. Thus, in my view, a term of imprisonment is justified and appropriate in this case.

My reasons for imposing a minimum sentence are as follows:

1. You have no record of prior criminal conduct.

2. I have received more than 1500 letters relative to sentencing and have carefully read them all. It is apparent that you have helped many people outside of your own family and that you have a supportive family and hundreds of admirers.

3. The public interest objective of this prosecution has been achieved by the jury verdict. Finally, I believe that you have suffered and will continue to suffer enough.

The rules require that I advise you that you have a right to appeal both my sentence and your conviction and that your notice of appeal must be filed within 10 days of today.

Yes?

MR. MORVILLO: Your Honor, I have a number of applications in the context of your Honor's sentence, if it is OK.

THE COURT: Yes.

MR. MORVILLO: First of all, I would ask your Honor to designate or direct that the sentence be served not in a penitentiary but in a halfway house. Given the unique circumstances of the relationship of Ms. Stewart to her company it would assist the company substantially if they could have more access to her. I believe your Honor has the power to designate that the sentence be served in a halfway house.

THE COURT: That is a matter of controversy at the moment.

MR. MORVILLO: I know it is, but many judges in this district —

THE COURT: I am happy to recommend the prison camp that you request. I will not recommend a halfway house. That is really the purpose of home confinement.

MR. MORVILLO: In the context of that, we would ask your Honor to recommend to the Bureau of Prisons that she serve her sentence in Danbury.

THE COURT: I will make that recommendation. As you know, that is up to the Bureau of Prisons, but I will recommend that.

MR. MORVILLO: Your Honor, it is my view that somebody of Ms. Stewart's background does not need to go through the process of supervised release. I would ask your Honor to reconsider that portion of the sentence dealing with the 2 years of supervised release. I don't think it is mandatory.

THE COURT: It is mandatory.

MR. MORVILLO: Finally, your Honor, it is my understanding that there are two ways to monitor home confinement. One is by virtue of the bracelet that your Honor has designated, and the other is simply the telephone system which is installed in the home and there are random calls made to verify that the person is at home. I would ask your Honor to eliminate the bracelet and simply to have the monitoring be done by the electronic telephone system, which will assure that she is in the house when she is supposed to be in the house by the random calls.

THE COURT: I am advised by the probation department that this is the usual way in which they monitor.

MR. MORVILLO: There are two ways.

THE COURT: There may have been a time when they followed your procedure. They tell me that this is the way that they recommend. But I will look into it.

MR. MORVILLO: Thank you, your Honor.

Your Honor, the last application I have, it is my understanding that the government does not object to the continuation of bail pending appeal. It is our intention to file a notice of appeal and to process an appeal in this case. Therefore, I ask your Honor to continue bail pending appeal.

THE COURT: That application I grant. In view of the turmoil resulting from the Supreme Court's decision in Blakely v. Washington, as evidenced by the Second Circuit's certification of questions to the Supreme Court regarding the validity of the federal sentencing guidelines, I grant your application for a stay of sentence pending appeal.

MR. MORVILLO: Thank you, your Honor.

MS. SEYMOUR: Your Honor, on the supervised release, looking at the statute 3583(b), it does use the word "may" about supervised release.

THE COURT: Thank you. In any event, since home confinement must be used as a condition of supervised release in this case, I think it is appropriate.

MS. SEYMOUR: Your Honor, the only remaining application that we would make is to dismiss the counts in the underlying indictment. This was a superseding indictment. So we would move to dismiss the open counts.

THE COURT: That motion is granted.

Is there anything further?

MS. SEYMOUR: No, your Honor.

MR. MORVILLO: Nothing, your Honor.

THE COURT: Then this matter is adjourned.

(Adjourned)